# POETICAL PEN-PICTURES

OF

# THE WAR:

## SELECTED FROM OUR UNION POETS.

By J. HENRY HAYWARD.

Published for the purpose of founding a BUILDING FUND for the "Union Home and School," established for the Education and Maintenance of our VOLUNTEERS' CHILDREN who may be left unprovided for. Organized May, 1861. Chartered by Act of Legislature, April, 1862.

And Christ said —"Whosoever shall give unto these Little Ones, shall in no wise lose his reward."—Matt. x. 42.

NEW YORK:
PUBLISHED BY THE EDITOR.
13 PARK ROW.
1863.

ENTERED ACCORDING TO ACT OF CONGRESS, IN THE YEAR 1863,

By J. HENRY HAYWARD,

IN THE CLERK'S OFFICE OF THE DISTRICT COURT OF THE UNITED STATES, FOR THE SOUTHERN DISTRICT OF NEW YORK.

T. R. DAWLEY,
ELECTROTYPER AND PRINTER
13 PARK ROW, N. Y.

## Editor's Preface.

In presenting this collection of Poems to the American Public it is not the intention of the Editor to claim for them the highest literary excellence, or offer them as the finished productions of the highest standard of poetical ability of the country, as a glance at the signatures affixed to each will at once show; for although we have selected as much as possible from our best writers, we have not confined ourself exclusively to that class, from the fact, that had we done so, our field would have been very limited, our collection very incomplete, and many productions of decided merit, would, in consequence, have been excluded; therefore, we do not offer them as the *Ne Plus Ultra* of literary excellence, but simply as a series of Pen-Pictures of the War, such as have from time to time welled up from the great heart of the Nation, when deeply moved by some great national, or individual event; and, as such, we think we here offer all that could be desired even by the most fastidious.

Every Nation, civilized and savage, have their war-songs, war-hymns, war-anthems, and war-ballads,—and why not America? Even in the face of the assertion, made by the learned Editor of the "National Hymns," to the effect, that there was not a Poet in the land, who possessed sufficient ability to give one to the people, —an assertion which is refuted every hour of the day by the untutored voice of childhood along our streets, the bass of the mechanic in the workshop, as well as cultivated vocal strains, which proceed from the perfumed parlors of the higher circles of society! The great mistake of our contemporary, laid in the fact, that he was looking for a grand National Epic, one calculated to suit the refined ear, and exalted taste of the critic, instead of some sublime metrical harmony which would sweep like an angel's fingers over the sensitive spirit-string of the human heart, and produce those sympathetic strains which linger on the ear—which dwell in the memory and reverberate through the land, until at length a whole nation takes up the theme, and hymn it before the Nation's Altar! It is just such metrical harmonies as this that we have sought for, and found, and here present to the reader—we care not for the critic—feeling satisfied that the great voice of the people will, in the future, render a verdict in our favor.

In making this collection, it is but proper here to state, that we have gathered together no less than four thousand poems, all posessed of more or less merit, yet, as a matter of course, unfit for our purpose, which was to secure a series of Pen Pictures, descriptive, —not of the most important events of the War, for that would be simply metrical history,—but of those events which have relation to the individual, that each and every particular poem might come home to some heart, and there find its abiding place through all time; in so doing, one fact, above all others, has occurred to us as most singular, it is this:—that as most of England's war-ballads are of a Naval, just to the same extent are those of America of a Military character, exclusively, as not more than ten or twelve Naval poems have been written during the entire war, which fact, when taken in connection with the very large share which our Navy has taken in the struggle, is, to say the least, remarkable, and can only be accounted for by the fact, that our war is internecine, instead of international; and yet, this of itself is hardly sufficient to satisfy us upon this mooted point, of which we here make passing mention, to account for the almost entire absence of all naval poems in this collection.

In regard to the design of the work, it was at first the intention of the Editor, to make it an exact chronological history of all the principal events of the war, by affixing the date, and *locale* of each event to some particular poem, which might be found best adapted to each and all; but this purpose had soon to be set aside as entirely impracticable from the fact, that those events soon became so numerous that our space would not permit a record of even one-half which had occurred, so we have simply confined the work to those only of the greatest importance.

With these few necessary introductory remarks, we will without further hesitation submit the work to the reader, trusting that it will meet all reasonable expectations, and serve, eventually, to lighten the sufferings of those little ones, who are left homeless and destitute in our midst, by the sad casualities of this great National struggle

NEW YORK, *October 7th*, 1863.

TO

THE ORPHAN CHILDREN

OF

OUR HEROIC VOLUNTEERS

WHO HAVE FALLEN

IN THE DEFENCE OF THE UNION,

**This Work,**

AND THE AID WHICH MAY BE SECURED THEREBY,

IS HUMBLY DEDICATED.

## WEEP WITH US.

### THE VOLUNTEERS' ORPHANS' APPEAL

### WRITTEN FOR THE CHILDREN OF THE UNION HOME AND SCHOOL.

PITY us, friends, we poor Volunteers' children,
Whose homes are deserted where joy was of yore—
Where once beam'd the smile of peace and contentment
But now hangs the dark mantle of death and of war.
Our fathers, who left us to fight for the Union—
Our brothers, who rushed forth to battle for right—
Are still firm defending our loved Constitution,
Or on the field lay, their bones mold'ring and white.

We ask but your pity, kind friends of humanity—
We ask but a tear of sympathy shed
O'er the graves of our fathers, and beloved brothers,
A sigh for the heroes who sleep with the dead.
We children assembled beneath our loved banner,
Pray for the return of each absent brave,
And ask you to follow where valor hath fallen—
To kneel with us, weep with us, over each grave.

J. HENRY HAYWARD.

## CONTENTS.

——:o:——

MISCELLANEOUS.

## Managers' and Advisory Committees' Notice.

THE Institution for which this Volume is published has now been in active operation over two years, having been organized by a number of prominent ladies, (upon the occasion of a visit of Gen. Anderson at the Institution of the Young Deaf Mutes of this city,) among whom were the following:—Mrs. Little, Mrs. Rev. Hardenburg, Miss H. Sherman, Mrs. J. Thompson, Miss F. M. Hoyt, Mrs. S. P. Mather, Mrs. Olive M. Devoe, and Mrs. David Hoyt. This Organization was perfected May 20, 1861, and after having been in actual operation for one year, the State Legislature, in consideration of the benevolent purpose for which it was organized, and the great public and private good wrought by its operations, granted it a Charter, April 22d, 1862; since which time it has given such unmistakable evidence of its efficiency, that we can without the slightest hesitation, come before the public in this, or any other guise, which may promise to forward the good work before us—viz., that of educating and maintaining the little orphans entrusted to our care, by those noble Volunteers, who have fallen, or yet may fall in the defence of the Union; and to forward this object, this Volume—which it is but proper here to remark is the gift of Mr. HAYWARD to the "Union Home and School,"—is now issued exclusively for the benefit of said Institution so long as it shall remain in existence, with the ultimate design of founding by this means a Building Fund, with which to erect a suitable edifice wherein the little orphans of our heroes may be properly cared for until they have reached their maturity.

The purpose for which the volume is issued, is certainly the most exalted and beneficial that can actuate us, and is well worthy of all the care and trouble we can bestow upon it; and in consequence, if properly aided and sustained in our endeavor, we feel confident of entire success, and a great work of benevolence and patriotism will thereby be accomplished. Respectfully submitted:—

### *OFFICERS.*

| | |
|---|---|
| HON. PRES.—MRS. GEN. R. ANDERSON, | TREAS. MRS. OLIVE M. DEVOE, |
| ACT. PRES. MRS. DRAKE MILLS, | REC. SEC. MRS. DR. WINSLOW, |
| VICE PRES, MRS. A. V. STOUT, | COR. SEC, MRS. JOHN S. VOORHIS |

### *MANAGERS.*

| | | |
|---|---|---|
| Mrs. J. S. Voorhis. | Miss E. R. Pitcher, | Mrs. H. G. Adams, |
| Mrs. W. Kidder, | Miss H. Sherman, | Mrs. J. Thompson, |
| Mrs. S. P. Mather, | Miss A. Barry, | Mrs. Dr. Hind, |
| Mrs. Howell, | Miss F M. Hoyt, | Mrs. J. S. Williams, |
| Mrs. David Hoyt, | Mrs. H. Wells, | Mrs. C. S. Hayward. |

### *ADVISORY COMMITTEE.*

| | | |
|---|---|---|
| Gen. Rob't Anderson, | Rev. J. C. Smith, | George Denison, |
| Prosper M. Wetmore, | Rev. A. D. Gillette, | Judge Bell, |
| Cyrus W. Field, | G. P. B. Hoyt, | S. M. Ostrander. |

*PHYSICIAN*—Dr. E. D. WINSLOW.

# INTRODUCTORY.

---

# BEFORE THE REBELLION.

# BEFORE THE REBELLION.

## AN ALLEGORY.

A SORT OF MYTHOLOGICAL EXPLANATION OF THE CAUSE AND ORIGIN OF THE WAR, WHEREIN THE AUTHOR TAKES A FEW NECESSARY LIBERTIES WITH THE GODS OF THE PAST AND THE PRESENT AGE, IN ORDER TO SET FORTH CERTAIN HISTORICAL PROBABILITIES IN AN ALLEGORICAL MANNER, THEREBY ELEVATING THE SUBJECT, AND NICELY AVOIDING THE POSSIBILITY OF GIVING OFFENCE TO THE READER, NO MATTER WHAT PARTICULAR POLITICAL OR GEOGRAPHICAL POSITION HE MAY CHANCE TO OCCUPY.

ONCE Mars and Peace together met,
Resolved to have a friendly word,
I listened well, therefore I am
Prepared to tell all I then heard;
Where this took place I need not pause
With much precision here to state;
Nor for my purpose need I halt,
Here to set down the exact date.

Suffice to know, that such a thing,
Upon this sphere of strife and sin,
By the mere course of strange events,
Once might, could, would, or should have been.
Old Mars with bombast was quite full,
While Peace was very meek and mild,
He really seem'd the god of war,
And she, but Intellect's bright child.

"Well, Peace," said Mars, "I trust that you
Enjoy, as yet, the best of health;
What think you now of this great world,
With all its splendor, fame and wealth?
I'm sure you must be pleased with all,
Which differs much from days of yore,
When you contended that you could
For mankind do, more than could war."

"Nay, Mars," said Peace, "I don't agree
With all that you are pleased to say;
The world is better'd, I admit,
But not by you—don't frown, I pray,
For I contention much despise,
And do but wish by argument
To prove that you have claimed too much,
And what I say is all well meant."

"Hey-day:—Miss Peace, I think that you
Are getting rather pert of late,
You seem to hope to smile me down
And controvert thus all I state:
A pretty pass has come indeed,
When you presume thus to deny
That I have made the world by *war*,
And raised the human standard high!"

"You may be right," said Peace; "yet stay,
If we could now the matter test,
You'd find yourself quite in the wrong—
That all such good is *my* conquest;
You'd find that man, though valiant yet,
And loves to have his own way still,
Would rather lay aside the sword,
And win his triumphs with a quill!"

"Tut!—tut!—you know not what you say,
Or if you do you know you boast,
I do not wish to kill you, Peace,
But still, *I'd like to see your ghost!*
Why, child, I have now in this world,
A tribe of men both strong and brave,
Who any hour would leave a feast,
That they might fill a hero's grave!"

"Indeed!" said Peace;—"If this be true
Then all my labor is in vain:
I hope 'tis not!"—she clasp'd her hands,
And dropp'd her eyes, and sighed with pain:
Then starting from her musing mood,
She even Mars seemed to defy,
And said:—"Where are those braves you name,
Who thus for fame so wish to die?"

"What ho! ye gods,—just hear her words,
She even doubts me, as I live!"
Said Mars, as with a fierce, grim smile,
He bade her then attention give;
"'Tis situate' in the far west,
Between two oceans wide and deep,
North bounded by a chain of lakes,
While its South shores a gulf doth sweep."

"Indeed, you much mistaken are,
Or I mistaken much must be!"
Said Peace, "for in that land abides
My fairest child—*sweet Liberty:*
The tribe of whom you speak, dear sir,
To warlike things are not inclined;
They deal in cotton, grain and gold,
And are at peace with all mankind!"

"Hold there, Miss Peace," said frowning Mars,
"Do you pretend to say that I
Am fool enough to misjudge men,
Or sneak enough to tell a lie?
Oh! swords and pistols, blood and strife,
But things have reached a pretty pass,
When deeds of arms are set at naught,
And Mars sent like a calf to grass!"

"Oh! sir, pray do not anger'd be,
  Your majesty I'd not offend;
Be kind enough to stay your rage,
  And hear me out, e'en to the end:
You say this tribe is brave and strong,
  Which I'd not willingly deny;
But still they love me far to well,
  To seek for fame, and for it die!"

"Oh! thunder, wake!—where is thy roar?
  Oh! light'ning, where is now thy flash?
That ye lie silent and concealed,
  While Peace presumes to talk such trash?
By all the blood that's wet the ground
  Since valiant Cain his brother slew,
I'll make it now my aim to prove
  Your statement false, and my words true!"

"Nay—nay," said Peace; "be not so fast,
  For you must know I've power too;
I've built my temple there so strong,
  That 'twill resist all you can do!
Commercial interest is the hinge,—
  Financial trust, the lock and key,—
Which bolts the door of social good,
  Where dwells my child, sweet Liberty!"

"It matters not, your bolts and bars
  Against my strength will not avail,
For I will send no forign foe
  This time your stronghold to assail;
But in your house, so firmly built,
  I'll cast a shell of discontent,—
I'll wield the sword of fierce discord,
  Till ev'ry social tie is rent!"

"With gold I'll batter down the walls
Of public good, and social right;
I'll sap the base of moral law,
And blast the bonds of legal might.
In human form I'll devils send,
Who shall invade both Church and State,
Who shall firm grasp the pen—your pow'r—
And with it write in blood your fate!"

"What you supposed to be your strength,
I'll prove to be your weakness yet,
Your men of peace, I'll force to war,
Till they all human love forget;
The house where dwells sweet Liberty,
Shall totter with my vengeful breath,
Till I have proved that valiant men
Will seek for honor, e'en to death!"

"Nay—nay, in mercy hold your hand,
In mercy seek not to o'erthrow
The quiet of my peaceful house,
Nor lay it level with a blow;
I know the weakness of mankind,
I know how quick they fall from state,
When once the demon, Discontent,
Awakens in their bosoms hate!"

"What!—think you that I am so weak,
As to gainsay what I have said?"
Cried Mars, as with a ghastly smile,
He clenched his hands, all grim and red,
"A pretty pass, it were indeed,
To give myself the downright lie;
I've said it, Peace!—it shall be so,
E'en if, by it, all mankind die!"

Now all this time the God of gods,
Was gazing on this scene below,
He knew how weak was man's vile heart—
How soon the blood of war would flow,—
If they were left now to themselves,
Without his power to defend,
And said :—" Weep not, oh ! gentle Peace,
For I, myself, will shape the end !"

Mars heard the voice, and trembling stood,
As if deprived of all his might,
Then with his sword hid 'neath his wings,
At once took to ignoble flight:
But Peace remained with upraised hands,
And beaming face so bright and fair,
Then o'er the busy world knelt down,
And raised her voice in holy prayer!

To work fierce Mars in due time went,
To bring about his purpose fell,
To Pandemonium he sped,
To ask aid of the King of Hell;
He found him there just as he wished—
For he had heard of Mars' design—
With goblets filled with liquid fire,
Which he drank off as men do wine.

On tables spread in his best style,
With iron plates all quite red hot,
While on a fire watched by small imps
Hung spit, and boiler, pan, and pot,
All filled with fiendish broils and stews,
Such as we oft' have in this world,
But which here made such rich smell that,
The chief cook's nose with pleasure curl'd.

A red hot throne he sat upon,
  And to another pointed Mars,
Who humbly begged to be excused,
  As hell-like thrones left ugly scars;
Old Satan smiled, an awful smile,
  Indeed he seem'd quite full of fun,
And said—"That few men paused to think
  What kind of throne they sat upon!"

The god of war in a few words,
  The purpose of his visit told,
Old Pluto's eyes looked deadly hate,
  But smiled when he did all unfold,
And said:—"I take you at your word,
  Will give you all the help I can,
For such an end, I'd pour hot hell,
  And all its demons out on man!

"For long I've watch'd with jealous eye,
  The work of Peace, in that fair land,
To bid defiance to my will,
  And make impotent e'en my hand:
But hell I need not empty out
  To help you, and your pleasure share,
For I long back have been at work,
  And have a host of imps now there.

"This you, perchance, may deem quite strange,
  Not thinking that I knew your will,—
That you would to me come, and ask
  My help, your bloody maw to fill;
Yet so it is, and I've arranged
  All things complete, to meet that end;
So listen, now, and I'll relate
  What I have done—and what intend!

"My imps have donn'd the human shape
  With intellect to fit them for
All stations in the hated world,
  Or any chance that may occur;
E'en now they crowd the Halls of State,
  The Chair of *Justice*, too, they fill,
The social board they also grace,
  All waiting but to do my will.

"This is a cunning way I have
  Of making man mankind betray,
I send them fiends in human shape,
  Who give advice, and they obey;
If man knew what he was about,
  While passing through life's busy mart,
He'd often look to see who walks
  Beside him, to corrupt his heart.

"You know I had some old imps here,
  Who almost set my will at naught,—
Who raised such thunder 'round my throne
  That oft' I've had to spoil their sport;
Well those I've sent out in the world
  To sway the Spirit of the Press,
According to my wish and will,
  And well they 've done it, I confess.

"Then, in the Halls of State I've placed
  A man—this I could not avoid,
For he, though old, and weak, and dull,
  The people's confidence enjoyed!
He in the highest Seat I've placed,
  To be employed as I think best,
While I have hedged the dotard in,
  By imps in ev'ry honor drest.

"Among them all a Chief I have,—
I almost envy him his fate,—
He's doomed to have such hellish fun,
And raise on earth such fiendish hate,
E'en now by his own cunning he
Has gained a place of mortal fame,
First in what they the Cab'net call;
He I now need not pause to name.

"So 'tween them all, I think I'll reach
The end for which I long have toiled,
I would have done it long ago,
Had Peace—the jade—my game not spoiled;
I long have waited for you, Mars,
You failed me when I last did try,
But then you know that jade, 'sweet Peace,'
Did not, as now, your pow'r defy!

"Therefore, I'm sure, you ready are
To give me all the help you can,
We need but here devise the way—
The work will all be done by man;
They are such fools they know not how
To prize the bliss they once enjoy,
Therefore we'll find it not so hard,
The wisest of them to decoy!

"There was a time when I despair'd
Of ever reaching such an end;
But that is pass'd—no power now
That nation's welfare can defend!"
So come, Mars, with me take a sip
Of nectar, which I only make,
'Tis very pleasant to the taste,
But serves not much the thirst to slake."

Again Mars begged to be excused,
  As he then thought he'd rather not;
For tho' he fancied much warm blood,
  He didn't take it *quite* so hot!
Again old Pluto smiled and said,
  "'Twas strange that Mars should hesitate,
For he had known him to drink blood,
  When it was boiling hot with hate!"

However, he excused him then,
  And drank his nectar all alone,
As he in regal majesty
  Sat on his smoking red-hot throne,
The imps flew 'round in gleeful trim,
  And stirr'd each kettle, pot and pan,
In which old Pluto had prepared
  Such broils and stews for fallen man.

And so the matter stood between,
  The fiendish twain—both satisfied
That each would do all that he could,
  The happy Union to divide—
Where dwelt in peace, the worthy sons
  Of patriot sires—all joined as one,
Whom God had blest with every good,
  That could be found beneath the sun!

But He whose gaze pervades e'en hell,
  Had seen and heard all that there passed;
And said—"Though you may triumph now,
  Good shall prevail with man at last!"
Old Pluto heard the mighty voice,
  Which shook all hell, e'en to its base;
And as Mars fled to shun the *wrath*,
  The Devil fell and hid his face!

Thus years rolled by—old Pluto worked,
Now quite recovered from his fright,
And Mars—his hand just to keep in—
Had now and then a *gentle* fight;
While Peace, all watchful for man's good,
Marked sadly the dread work of War,
And by her counsels to the wise,
Kept carnage from sweet Freedom's door.

This was what Pluto most desired,
For thus he hoped to lull to sleep
The power, which had so faithful prov'd,
And thus such sleepless guard could keep;
In this he was not far from right,
For Peace, though faithful to her trust,
Now found her sons began to think,
The sword too long had hung in rust.

This she by every means did strive
To banish from their hearts and ken,
Bv pleading, and by counsel wise
Through the great minds of worthy men;
But all in vain—old Pluto, he,
With imps, a host, were still at work,
They made all eloquence as gall,
And turned the pen into a dirk!

With which they dealt such fatal blows,
Directed by old Pluto's hand,
Through the wild passions of the heart,
Deep in the vitals of the land!
That 'mong men wild discussion rose,
Then discord from discussion came,
'Till soon a throe of anguish deep
Swept thro' the land—a hell-like flame.

Peace held aloft her pleading hand,
  And called on man to stay his rage,
And told how fierce would be the storm,
  If they in strife should e'er engage;
But all in vain, old Pluto, he,
  Had proved too cunning and too wise,
The imps they too—meant all they did,
  And with vile hate obscured man's eyes.

The Press it team'd with wrath and gall,
  And scatter'd o'er the happy land,
Such thoughts as only come from hell,
  Such words as issue from the damn'd!
The Church perverted then became,
  And men in robes cleric arrayed,
Held forth on politics, and thus
  The souls of their meek flocks betray'd!

The Ministers of Justice, too,
  Forgot the culprit to descend
Upon the floor, that they might thus,
  Some point in politics defend!
Till soon mankind with one accord,
  Led on by Press, by Church, by State,
Plunged in the flood of strife and woe,
  And dared the wrath of God, and fate!

The Halls of State reel'd 'neath the shock,
  Which wrathful swept from shore to shore,
The Temple where sweet Freedom dwelt
  Was rent in twain!—could hell do more?
Do more? Alas! the end's not yet!
  And who can now the cause defend?
None else than God, who hath declared,
  *That He himself will shape the end!"*

J. Henry Hayward.

# POETICAL PEN-PICTURES

# OF THE WAR.

## THE FALL OF OUR FLAG.

### AT THE SURRENDER OF FORT SUMTER, APRIL 13TH, '61.

UNFURL our banner, upon the ramparts high!
  Where Columbia's foes may descry it;
The " Stars and the Stripes" we now swear to defend,
  Though they in perfidy defy it:
The shouts of the rebels may fall on our ears,
  The cannon their thunder may rattle,
But, while God is with us, its stars still shall shine,
  In triumph throughout every battle!

Its bright folds shall be, o'er land and o'er sea,
  By us e'er sustained and defended;
The balls of the rebels must pierce our true hearts,
  E re the Flag of Fort Sumter is rended!

Unfurl our banner, upon the ramparts high!
  Though hunger and thirst may torment us;
The vile foe may threaten, but we still shall hope,
  That relief will e'er long be sent us:
We ask not the comforts, nor pleasures of home,
  Our lives to our country we tender,
So long as we have but the strength to contend,
  Our Flag we will never surrender!

Its bright folds shall be, o'er land and o'er sea,
  By us e'er sustained and defended;
The balls of the rebels must pierce our true hearts,
  E re the Flag of Fort Sumter is rended!

Unfurl our Banner, upon the ramparts high!
The base traitors' guns thunder 'round us,
The balls crush our wall—the shells burst in air—
And with fierce destruction surround us!
See!—see! in our midst, 'mid the terrors of strife,
New horrors of war gleam before us,
The Fort is on fire;—the magazine explodes!—
Still our Flag in triumph waves o'er us.

Its bright folds shall be o'er land and o'er sea,
By us e'er sustained and defended;
The balls of the rebels must pierce our true hearts,
E re the Flag of Fort Sumter is rended!

Unfurl our Banner, upon the ramparts high;
We swear that no hand e'er shall humble
The Flag of our Country, by hauling it down,
Though Sumter in ruins may crumble!
Oh! see, comrades, see, our oath is made good,
God speaks—tho' our sad hearts are grieving,—
A chance ball has stricken our Flag to the earth,
Secure it!—we will take it on leaving!

Its bright folds shall be o'er land and o'er sea,
By us e'er sustained and defended;
The balls of the Rebels must pierce our true hearts,
E re the Flag of Fort Sumter is rended!

J. HENRY HAYWARD.

## TO ARMS! TO ARMS!

**FIRST CALL FOR SEVENTY-FIVE THOUSAND VOLUNTEERS.**

APRIL 15TH, '61.

"To ARMS!—to arms!"—the call resounds,
In startling tones throughout the land,
In grief, sweet Peace lays down the scythe,
To grasp again War's bloody hand!
Where once our Flag in glory waved,
Dark battle-clouds bedim the sky;
Oh! ye, who would have freedom live,
For her, must now prepare to die!
"To arms!—to arms!"—the sound prolong,
'Till it resounds from shore to shore;
Haste all, who would have freedom live,
And grasp the sword, till strife is o'er!

"To arms!—to arms!"—oh! gentle Peace,
Shall we no more thy pleasures know,
When still'd shall be all sounds of strife,
And brothers' blood no longer flow?
No! not till we the rebels crush,
And, "Union as it was," restore,
Shall we invoke thy smile sweet Peace,
Or lay aside the blade of war!
"To arms!—to arms!"—the sound prolong,
'Till it resounds from shore to shore;
Haste all, who would have freedom live,
And grasp the sword, till strife is o'er!

J. HENRY HAYWARD.

## THE REVEILLE.

THE MARCH OF THE 1ST REGIMENT FOR WASHINGTON, APRIL 17TH, '61.

Hark! I hear the tramp of thousands,
And of armed men the hum—
Lo! a nation's hosts have gather'd
'Round the quick alarming drum,
Saying, "Come,
Freemen, come,
Ere your heritage be wasted!"
Said the quick alarming drum.

"Let me of my heart take counsel—
War is not of life the sum;
Who shall stay and reap the harvest
When the autumn days shall come?'
But the drum
Echoed, "Come!
Death shall reap the braver harvest!"
Said the solemn sounding drum.

"But when won the coming battle,
What of profit springs therefrom?
What if conquest, subjugation,
Even greater ills become?"
But the drum
Answered, "Come!
You must do the sum to prove it!"
Said the Union answering drum.

"What if 'mid the cannons' thunder,
 Whistling shot and bursting bomb,
When my brothers fall around me,
 Should my heart grow cold and numb?"
  But the drum
  Answered, "Come!
Better there in death united,
 Than in life a recreant! Come!"

Thus they answered—hoping, fearing—
 Some in faith, and doubting some—
'Till a trumpet voice, proclaiming,
 Said, "My chosen people, come!"
  Then the drum,
  Lo! was dumb,
For the great heart of the nation,
 Throbbing answered, "Lord, we come!"

T. B, HART.

## THE ARSENAL.

THE DESTRUCTION OF THE WORK AT HARPER'S FERRY, APRIL 19th, '61.

This is the Arsenal. From floor to ceiling,
 Like a huge organ, rise the burnished arms:
But from their silent pipes no anthem pealing
 Startles the villagers with strange alarms.

Ah! what a sound will rise, how wild and dreary,
  When the death-angel touches these swift keys!
What loud lament and dismal Miserere
  Will mingle with their awful symphonies!

I hear e'en now the infinite fierce chorus,
  The cries of agony, the endless groan,
Which through the ages that have gone before us,
  In loud reverberations reach our own.

The tumult of each sacked and burning village;
  The shout that every prayer for mercy drowns;
The soldiers' revel in the midst of pillage;
  The wail of famine in beleaguered towns;

The bursting shell, the gateway wrenched asunder,
  The rattling musketry, the clashing blade;
And ever and anon, in tones of thunder,
  The diapason of the cannonade.

Were half the power that fills the earth with terror,
  Were half the wealth bestow'd on camps and courts,
Giv'n to redeem the human mind from error,
  There were no need ot arsenals or forts.

The warrior's name would be a name abhorred!
  And every nation that should lift again
Its hand against a brother, on its forehead
  Would wear forevermore the curse of Cain.

Down the dark future, through long generations,
  The echoing sounds grow fainter, and then cease;
And like a bell, with solemn, sweet vibrations,
  I hear once more the voice of Christ say "Peace!"

Peace! and no longer from its brazen portals
  The blast of war's great organ shakes the skies!
But beautiful as songs of the immortals,
  The holy melodies of love arise.

H. W. LONGFELLOW.

## VAINLY I WAIT FOR THEE.

CAPTURE OF THE STAR OF THE WEST.

APRIL 16TH, '61.

I AM waiting, sadly waiting,
  'Neath the trysting tree—
Waiting for thy welcome footsteps,
  And thy smile of love for me.
Evening shadows fast are falling,
  Night comes on apace,
Vainly through the dusk I'm peering.
  Thy dear form to trace.

Never more shall I behold thee,
  Low in death thou'rt lain,
On the battle-field so gory,
  For thy country slain.
From mine eyes the tears are falling—
  Bitter tears of grief and pain,
But methinks thy sweet voice whispers,
  "Cheer thee, love, we'll meet again."

HELENE OSGOOD.

## THE MARTYRED THREE.

### THE MARCH TO THE CAPITOL.

Our mother, Massachusetts,
Hath sons of valiant mould—
Bright-eyed and gentle-featured,
Strong-limbed and stalwart-souled!
Within her lap she holds them—
Her lap of fruitful soil;
And, bosomed on her fragrant hills,
They drink the milk of toil.

And so they wax to manliness,
By bread of freedom nurs'd;
And so they love all lands above,
Old Massachusetts first!
One day, through all the nation—
From blue Potomac's stream
To woods of far Aroostook,
There flash'd a lightning gleam:

In scrolls of fire electric
The battle-word went forth—
Like burning brand from hand to hand,
Through all the loyal North:
"The Capitol's in danger!—
So every soul rehears'd,
And pass'd the brand from hand to hand—
Old Massachusetts first!

Then out from all the hill-paths,
  And up from every wold,
The sturdy yeomen muster'd
  Like minute-men of old:
From all the marts of merchants,
  And all the fields of toil;
And left the iron at the forge,
  The ploughshare in the soil!

And down to save the Capitol,
  In gallant haste they burst—
From hill and glen, like minute-men,
  And Massachusetts first!
From old Ticonderoga,
  And Mohawk's storied gorge—
From Bunker Hill and Monmouth,
  And ice-bound Valley Forge;

As bread and wine to strengthen souls,
  Ye draw from sacred pyx,
So draw we from our battle-fields,
  The strength of 'Seventy-six!
And then, to save the Capitol,
  From treason's power accurst,
With war-like throes the States arose—
  Old Massachusetts first!

The Nineteenth Day of April!
  O day remember well!
The greybeards and the schoolboys
  Its hallow'd legends tell;
How four-score years and six have gone,
  Since Freedom's snow white bud,
New blossoming then from heroes' hearts,
  Grew red with priceless blood:

At Lexington and Concord—
  When Freedom's flower out-burst,
With fragrance bland to fill the land—
  Old Massachusetts first!
The Nineteenth Day of April!
  How thrilled our loyal land,
When marched the Union soldiers
  O'er Susquehanna's strand:

When Treason's steel was lifted,
  By dark Patapsco's flood.
And Maryland's Magnolia white
  Grew red with martyr's blood!
The old, old strife of freedom
  With freedom's foes reversed
Alike the day, alike the fray—
  Old Massachusetts first!

All silently, all manfully,
  Beside the road we form'd:
Around us gathering, wolf-like,
  The howling traitors swarm'd:
To left and right still mustering,
  With swift and fierce attacks,
They taunted us, and spat on us,
  And smote us at our backs!

But on we march'd, unfaltering,
  Nor answer'd, while they curs'd,
With yells of hate, each loyal State—
  Old Massachusetts first!
Before us, o'er the pavements,
  They trailed the Union flag,
And flaunted in our faces
  Secession's hateful rag.

Oh, Heaven! to brook *that* insult,
  Our blood grew hot, like flame—
And one brave man, with daring hand,
  Struck down the thing of shame!
And then we grasp'd our rifles
  And dared them to their worst—
And so we bore through Baltimore—
  Old Massachusetts first!

From gateways and from house-tops
  Their iron rain they cast;
With coward shots from casements,
  They pierced us as we pass'd;
Then sank our youngest comrade—
  All torn with cruel scars—
And raised aloft his bleeding hands,
  And hailed the Union stars!

"All hail! the Stars and Stripes!" he cried;
  And thus his bold heart burst;
And thus we gave our soldiers brave—
  Old Massachusetts first!
Our Mother, Massachusetts!
  She bears no craven sons:
Through heroes and through martyrs
  Her life-blood freely runs!

And when, from dark Patapsco,
  The death-news swiftly sped,
"Bring back," she said, "my loyal ones—
  Bear tenderly my dead!"
And then, with shrouded flags and drums,
  And soldiers' arms revers'd,
To glory's bed we bore the dead—
  Old Massachussetts first!

On headlands of New England,
  The strong Atlantic breaks;
And swiftly stride the whirlwinds
  O'er stormy Northern lakes;
And grandly roll the rivers
  Through Western vales and hills;
But stronger—swifter—grander far,
  Is FREEDOM—when she WILLS!

And wheresoe'er her trumpet
  Shall sound, with lofty burst,
You'll find in camp, with loyal tramp,
  Old MASSACHUSETTS first!

A. J. H. DUGANNE.

## NOT YET.

DESTRUCTION OF THE GOSPORT NAVY YARD,

APRIL 20TH, '61.

O COUNTRY, marvel of the earth!
  O realm to sudden greatness grown!
The age that gloried in thy birth,
  Shall it behold thee overthrown?
Shall traitors lay that greatness low?
No, Land of Hope and Blessing, No!

And we who wear thy glorious name,
  Shall we, like cravens, stand apart,
When those whom thou hast trusted aim
  The death-blow at thy generous heart?
Forth goes the battle-cry, and lo!
Hosts rise in harness, shouting, No!

And they who founded in our land
  The power, that rules from sea to sea,
Bled they in vain, or vainly planned
  To leave their country great and free?
Their sleeping ashes, from below,
Send up the thrilling murmur, No!

Knit they the gentle ties which long
  These sister States were proud to wear,
And forged the kindly links so strong,
  For idle hands in sport to tear—
For scornful hands aside to throw?
No, by our fathers' memory, No!

Our humming marts, our iron ways,
  Our wind-tossed woods on mountain crest,
The hoarse Atlantic, with his bays,
  The calm, broad Ocean of the West.
And Mississippi's torrent flow,
And loud Niagara, answer, No!

Not yet the hour is nigh, when they
  Who deep in Eld's dim twilight sit,
Earth's ancient kings, shall rise and say:
  "Proud country, welcome to the pit!
So soon art thou, like us, brought low?"
No, sullen group of shadows, No!

For now, behold, the arm that gave,
  The vict'ry in our fathers' day,
Strong, as of old, to guard and save—
  That mighty arm which none can stay—
On clouds above and fields below,
Writes, in men's sight, the answer, No!

WM. CULLEN BRYANT.

## "UNION" AND "DISUNION."

DECLARATION OF WAR BY THE CONFEDERATE STATES
MAY 4TH, '61.

HAIL, chivalric brothers of the South,
And ye of each Northern State give ear;
List to the voice from Reason's mouth—
The day of your destiny draws near!
Aye, it draws near, 'mid discord and din—
The offspring base, of all human sin!

Ah! where in the world has fled your love
Of Freedom and Truth, that formed the tie
Which long has held you above the sway
Of base Political Insanity?
Corruption's pow'r in Church, and in State.
Oh! my loved country—what is thy fate?

Say, where is the hope of sire and son,
As wounded to death, they laid them down,
While fighting for cause so nobly won,
On which you, their sons, presume to frown;
Presume to frown on, when you declare
"Freedom all sham!" and "the Union air!"

Where, now, is the cry of babe and wife
Mother, and sister, in heart-felt grief,
Mourning the work of musket and knife
And calling on God to give relief?
To give relief, which you now deride,
Ye senseless sons of folly and pride!

Where, now, is the tramp of Despot's heel,
  That once left its imprint on your sod?
Are you ready, now, to smirk and kneel
  To some Potentate, instead of God?
Instead of God, for such is the fate
Of those whose laws are discord and hate.

Ah! where is the hallow'd memory
  Of Washington's worth, and Henry's zeal?
Has it, with them, sped to eternity,
  And left you now blind to woe or weal?
To woe or weal—to honor and fame;
Ah! brothers now pause, Where is your shame?

Say—where is that SCROLL, held in such awe,
  Your forefathers' gift—bearing their seal?
Is it still sacred as it was of yore?
  Or press'd, like dead leaves, 'neath your base heel.
Press'd, like dead leaves, when summer has fled,
And laid all its joys on the graves of the dead!

And where are the words of truth and light
  Left by our grand-sires to guide the way
To the goal of peace, of glory, and might,
  Thro' darkness and storm, to calm and day?
The calm and day, such as Freemen know,
When brotherly love thro' their *systems* flow.

Ah! where is the scorn that flushed each brow,
  When statesmen and sage first breathed the tho't
That you would prove faithless to the vow
  Of Union and Freedom, so dearly bought?
Too dearly bought—which heaven forefend,
When strife is its Alpha, and woe its End!

And where is the fire that lit each eye
  As star after star rose to your gaze,
In that cluster bright, spread out in the sky,
  And dazzled all earth with its mighty blaze?
Has it vanished, as does the light'ning's flash,
To be felt, anon, in the bolt's sharp crash?

For such is the end, if you but dare
  To draw the first stone from the Arch of State,
'Twill crumble and fall—a thing of air—
  *Precedent*, too oft, shapes human fate.
Shall history's page your dishonor tell?
And woe fill the land, as sin fills hell?

Do you know that the eye of God is bent,
  As that of the world, on this spot of dust,
Watching each movement with gaze intent,
  To pronounce and hear the verdict just?
Say, will you prove true to God and State?
Oh! my loved country—what is thy fate?

J. HENRY HAYWARD.

## "ALL'S WELL."

### FIRST UNION OFFENSIVE OPERATION AT SEWELL'S POINT.

### MAY 18TH, '61.

MIDNIGHT upon the placid stream,
  All nature seems at rest;
The silver moonbeams lightly beam
  Upon the harbor's breast.
But hark, from yonder ship a sound
Disturbs the silence reigning 'round;
It is the frigate's midnight bell,
And watch proclaiming "All's well!"
    "All's well!"—the lonely watchman's cry
      Succeeds the stroke of midnight bell;
    The ship is safe—no foe is nigh!
      The hour is peaceful—"All's well!"

"All's well!" Then rest in peace, brave crew,
  In port now safe at last;
The fearful scenes you've battled thro'
  Are naught, for danger's past!
The noble ship secure doth ride
Upon the harbor's mirror'd tide,
Far from old ocean's restless swell.
Sleep on, brave crew, for "All's well!"
    "All's well,"—the lonely watchman's cry
      Succeeds the stroke of midnight bell;
    The ship is safe—no foe is nigh!
      The hour is peaceful—"All's well!"

"God of our Fathers," speed the day
  When the fierce storm shall cease,
And bring our Ship of State, we pray,
  Safe to the Bay of Peace.
Soon may we hear the watchman's voice
Proclaiming to the world, "Rejoice!"
Wide let the welcome tidings swell—
Freedom hath triumphed—"All's well!"

"All's well!"—the lonely watchman's cry
  Succeeds the stroke of midnight bell;
The ship is safe— no foe is nigh!
  The hour is peaceful—"All's well!"

J. GORDON EMMONS.

## "ONLY ONE."

UNION ADVANCE INTO ALEXANDRIA.

MAY 24TH, '61.

THE dark night is ended, the skirmish is done,
Of wounded there is none, our dead, only one,
Lies out 'neath the stars in mute grandeur alone,
    Where the moonlight falls 'round him,
And the rustling leaves, like a spirit's low tone,
    Are his requiem sounding.

No songs 'round the fire, no laughing word said;
There's a hush in the camp, the sentry's firm tread
Falls softened and low as it passes the dead,
    In calm slumber lying,
With pure, holy light streaming o'er his young head,
    Death's shadows defying.

That head, which so proudly was lifted this morn
At the signal of danger—the note of alarm,
Now broken and bow'd 'neath the weight of the storm
That was over it sweeping.
The battle is ended—the foe are all gone,
This memorial leaving.

"Only one on our side," a loss counted slight;
But I think, as I gaze on this pale brow to-night,
What kisses have pressed these lips, now so white,
What hearts wild and breaking,
Would give years of life to stand by my side,
This farewell taking.

I think *somewhere* 'neath those same starlit skies
There's a home that is dark for the light in these eyes;
And some sigh, mayhap, breath'd for him, while he lies
Here, so peacefully sleeping;
Never dreaming of home, or of love's tender ties,
For no glory wreath seeking.

Beyond tears, and prayers, and love's winning tone,
A deep voice has called him—he heard, and is gone,
Past sentries and guards, to that glorious Throne,
Far "over the river,"
Where the voices of battle and war are unknown,
And peace reigns forever.

His low grave is made, and the muffled drums beat;
We will bear him forth now, with slow, mournful feet,
To the place of his rest, and then leave him to sleep
With the sod for his pillow—
It is only one grave, but, alas! it is deep,
And some life-path 'twill shadow.

FLETTA.

## THE SQUADRON IS FORMING.

### SKIRMISH AT FAIRFAX COURT HOUSE, MAY 31ST, '61.

THE Squadron is forming, the war-bugles play,
To saddle brave comrades, stout hearts for a fray!
Our captain is mounted—strike spurs, and away!

No breeze shakes the blossoms, or tosses the grain;
But the wind of our speed floats the galloper's mane,
As he feels the bold rider's firm hand on the rein.

Lo! dim in the starlight their white tents appear!
Ride softly! ride slowly! the onset is near!
More slowly! more softly! the sentry may hear!

Now fall on the rebel—a tempest of flame!
Strike down the false banner whose triumph is shame!
Strike, strike for the true flag, for freedom and fame!

Hurrah! sheath your swords! the carnage is done,
All red with our valor, we welcome the sun,
Up, up with the stars! we have won! we have won!

But still on the field our brave comrade lies,
All wounded and bleeding—see now he dies!
While still for the "Union forever" he cries!

Take him up gently—for his work is done,
The debt he has paid let none of us shun!
For he hath both freedom and victory won!

ANONYMOUS.

## "THE CROSS BEGINS TO BEND."

FIGHT OF THE HARRIET LANE AT PIG POINT BATTERY.

JUNE 6TH, '61.

"MIDNIGHT is past—the Cross begins to bend!"
So sings the sailor on the Southern seas,
Longing for darkness and the night to end,
And letting such old signs his fancy please!

The night-watch, that began in storm and gloom,
Wearied his soul—its dull hours dragging by—
He smiles in seeing black clouds lift—make room,
For this sweet writing of the stars, on high!

And so I think, as through all our ranks to-day,
Look answers look, and friend speaks quick to friend
Soldier to soldier, brother to brother, say,
"Midnight is past—the Cross begins to bend!"

Ay, ringing bells, throughout this summer air,
With all their happy tide of music, blend,
The voice and blessing—of *our dead*, who share
With us this joy—"*The Cross begins to bend!*"

ANONYMOUS.

## MY HERO.

### AT THE BATTLE OF BIG BETHEL, JUNE 10TH, '61.

THE hand of fate has written out
  Strange things upon my map of time,
And many are the eyes that read
  Its lines of mingled woe and crime.
Sometimes I draw the veil aside
  That shuts me from the buried past,
And wander o'er its barren fields
    At last, at last!

One picture has a ten-fold power—
  'Tis graven with a mighty pen:
A plume torn from an eagle's wing,
  Dipped in the warmest blood of men!
A battle field with reeking sod,
  With stars and stripes and bugle's blast,
And brave men fleeing from a foe,
    At last, at last.

The meadow grass was low and green,
  The primrose drooped upon its stem;
The sky was calm, the ground was strewn
  With sweet wild stars of Bethlehem.
And on that soil my hero fell.
  Amid the carnage raging fast,
Those withered blossoms drank his blood,
    At last, at last.

They told me this, they said in death
  His pale lips breathed a loved one's name,
And blessed the cause for which he died,
  The cause he never brought to shame.
The words came sweeping o'er my soul
  Like some mad river rushing past,
Only to drown my living dreams,
    At last, at last.

They told me this at eventide,
  But morning never dawned for me:
Can sunlight dance upon my brow,
  And even wake one smile, when he
Is lying 'neath a starry sky,
  With battle sods above him cast?
A hero in a nameless grave,
    At last, at last

I whisper low when fevered winds
  Beat mockingly around my cheek;
*My* hero! who in all the world
  Will know the name I dare not speak?
None, none! the veil swings slowly back,
  And shuts me from the gloomy past;
I turn away and weep alone,
    At last, at last,

EMMA EGGLESON.

## NOW FOR THE UNION.

### THE ENGAGEMENT AT ROMNEY, VA.

JUNE 12TH, '61.

A CHEER now for the Union,
The shrine of liberty—
The birthplace of dear freedom,
Where all may equal be,
We'll gather 'round the altar,
Rear'd by a nation's hand,
And swear to pause nor falter, till—
Nor falter, till
We save our native land.

A *blow* now for the Union,
No traitor shall divide;
For it we'll crush the rebels
And all the world beside.
In the fight for its salvation
Fierce death our fathers braved:
Can we do less than conquer, that—
Than conquer, that
The Union may be saved.

A *prayer* now for the Union,
From wives and sisters dear—
From children and from mothers,
Which God above may hear—
A prayer while we do battle
For those who fighting fall—
A prayer now for the Union, and—
The Union, and
For freedom and for all.

J. HENRY HAYWARD.

## DO THEY MISS ME?

### THE RAIL ROAD ENGAGEMENT AT VIENNA, VA., JUNE 17TH, '61.

Do THEY miss me at home, do they miss me to-night,
When parlors are lighted and faces are bright;
While treacherous winds, ever ready for ill,
Make raids on the flowers that grow on the hill?

Do they think of the absent, while pattering rain
Beats the startling long-roll on the tall window-pane;
While the gunboats of nature are shelling the air,
Do *they* wish that dear Willie was home from the war?

There's Frankie, and Katie, and Belle in their glee,
Playing "puss in the corner," do *they* think of me?
Do they wish that big brother could lay down his gun,
And not be a soldier-boy, "only for fun?"

Then there's sister Carrie, with dark waving hair;
With laughing blue eyes, and with features so fair;
She is old enough now, and—gracious! who knows
But what she's already a dozen of beaux?
As she sits by the window, so pensive and still,
And thinks of her lovers, does *she* think of "poor Will?"

And there is my mother in the old rocking-chair.
Those eyes are yet sparkling, that face is still fair;
Though her hair has been frosted for many a day,
The youth of her heart has not faded away;

As she watches the little ones, full of their joy,
Does *she* think of Willie—her "brave soldier-boy?"
There, too, is my father; his summer has fled,
And the snow-flakes of winter have silvered his head;
Full many a furrow on his cheek may be seen,
Where the rude hand of sickness and sorrow has been.
To-night, ere they slumber, when all bend the knee,
And he prays for God's blessing, will *he* think of me?

DEMPS' SEAWELL.

## UP AND AT THEM.

AT THE ENGAGEMENT AT BOONVILLE, MO.,

JUNE 18TH, 1861.

Up and at them once again!
Freemen, up! the way is plain,
At the traitors once again!
Let no brief reverses daunt us;
Let no craven fears assail;
Treason's banner now may taunt us
In the fierce but fleeting gale:
But the time again will come,
When again that flag shall cower;
And the boasting voice be dumb,
Shouting now its little hour!
Up and at them, Freemen, then, the way is plain;
At the traitors once again!

Up and at them once again!
Madmen! fierce though ye drain
War's red chalice, it is vain!
Never shall ye rend asunder
Freedom's flag of stripes and stars;—
Freedom guards it with her thunder;
Down will smite your thing of bars;
Down your wretched counterfeit!
In her roused and sacred rage
She will tear and trample it!
Holy is the war we wage!
Up and at them, Freemen, then, the way is plain;
At the traitors once again!

Up and at them once again,
Though our blood be shed like rain,
At the traitors once again!
By our Nation's ancient story,
By the deeds of other days,
By our hope of future glory,
By the deep disdain or praise
That our action now awaits,
As we yield or dare the strife;
Let us, through all adverse fates,
Swear to guard the Nation's life!
Up and at them, Freemen, then, the way is plain;
At the traitors once again!

ALFRED STREET.

## THE NOBLE DEAD.

SKIRMISH AT COLE, MO.

JUNE 18TH, '61.

Weep, mortals, weep;
With sadly sorrowing hearts bow low the head,
The solemn dirge sounds for the noble dead,
A hero's spirit, pure unstained, has fled;
He slumbers deep,
But angels o'er his form their white wings spread
And bright watch keep.

Unsullied, brave,
The soul of truth, for truth he nobly fought,
Nor lived to see that revolution wrought,
That on his country's name dishonor brought;
He strove to save,
And nobly dying with his life's blood bought,
A hero's grave.

O sacred spot,
Where mouldering lies a patriot's earthly frame,
Who justly lived, and dying leaves no shame
To soil the brightness of a noble name
Not soon forgot.
But graven on the spotless roll of fame,
Without a blot.

ANONYMOUS.

## THE REBEL'S DOOM.

SKIRMISH AT EDWARD'S FERRY, VA.,
JUNE 18TH, '61.

As the cohorts of Pharaoh, o'erwhelmed by the wave,
All uncoffined were hurled to a fathomless grave,
So the red tide of vengeance terrific shall flow,
'Till the ranks of the Southron lie pallid below!
Tho' their warriors are marshalled with fire in each eye,
Not a stone in the future shall point where they lie,
For their bones shall ne'er know the repose of a tomb;
That they were will be known by the page of their doom
Which all dreadful shall frown in the blackness of wrath
As a warning to those who'd pursue the same path,
For 'twill tell how the children of Judas were born,
And grew up in the brightness of Liberty's morn;
But, as Satan once walked in the gardens of light,
And did homage to God, in the pure garments of white;
And bursting from power raised the standard of Hell,
And a prison of fire yawned beneath as he fell:—
So these demons of earth, whose insatiate lust,
Made them false to their God, and earth's holiest trust.

BUYLER.

## 'TIS GROWING VERY DARK, MOTHER.

SKIRMISH AT PATTERSON'S CREEK, VA.,

JUNE 26TH, '61.

'Tis growing very dark, mother,
I cannot see the light,
The sun behind the purple hills
Has sunk too soon to-night.
The gathering gloom falls like a veil,
I cannot see the stars,
I cannot see our floating flag,
With its white and crimson bars.

'Tis growing very dark, mother,
I cannot see your face,
Yet I know that you are kneeling
In your old familiar place;
And the low tones of your voice, mother,
Come through the dark'ning air,
As you bow beside my vacant bed,
And pray your evening prayer.

'Tis growing very dark, mother,
The night comes cold and still,
I cannot see the watch-fires gleam
On yonder tent-crown'd hill;
A mist is on the river's marge,
A haze comes o'er my sight,
I wait in vain for day to dawn,
And bless me with its light.

'Tis growing very dark, mother,
  Would God that you were here,
For by the chill which o'er me steals
  I know that death is near.
Yet darker, darker falls the gloom,
  But there is peace within,
But e're the morn yon pearly gates
  Will ope' and let me in.

'Tis growing very light, mother,
  I see the angel's wings;
No more the startling cry, "To Arms!"
  Out on the still air rings;
But music from immortal lips
  Is softly floating down,
And One whose head a halo wears,
  Holds forth a victor's crown.

M. B. S.

## SEND THEM HOME TENDERLY.

ENGAGEMENT AT MATHIAS' POINT, VA
JUNE 27TH. '61.

Send them home tenderly,
  The sleepers at rest,
With hands meekly folded
  On each silent breast;
Let them come back to slumber
  Beneath northern skies,
Where true hearts may weep o'er them,
  And prayer-incense rise,

Send them home tenderly,
  The noble and true,
Scarce gone from their hearthstones,
  Scarce whispered "ADIEU,"
Gone forth for their country,
  Its rights to sustain,
But, all bleeding and lifeless,
  Returning again.

Send them home tenderly,
  Our martyred and brave,
With the stripes and stars ,round them,
  All robed for the grave,
Bereaved mothers shall clasp them
  In pride to their breast,
And the good of our nation
  Shall weep where they rest.

Send them home tenderly,
  Each wound gaping wide
Shall send myriads of voices
  From the dark purple tide;
And strong hands shall be grasping
  The bright, unsheathed sword,
With fresh fervor to battle
  For right and the Lord.

## "HOME THOUGHTS."

SKIRMISH AT FALL'S CHURCH, VA.,
JUNE 28TH, '61.

Alone upon the battle-field,
  The weary soldier stands,
And mournfully surveys the scene,
  Where fought the patriot bands.
Around upon the dreary plain,
  Lies many a mangled form,
Whose heart that morn beat wild with joy,
  And hope so bright and warm.

The evening stole with trembling steps,
  The sun's last pleasant ray,
And gloomy shadows grim and cold,
  Shot through the twilight gray;
Imagination conjured up
  Many a glowing scene,
And joys of by-gone happy days,
  Kept by memory green.

Of loving friends left far behind,
  Their prayers and smiles so dear,
The sunshine of his happy home,
  Affections silent tear.
How soon the bravest heart's o'ercome
  By hopes and memories wild,
For thoughts like these so good and pure,
  Oft make the man a child.

FRANCIS B. MURTHA.

## THE SOLDIER'S BETROTHED.

ENGAGEMENT AT HAYNESVILLE, VA.,
JULY 1st, '61,

Oh! pale, pale face! Oh, helpless hands!
Sweet eyes by fruitless watching wronged,
Yet, turning ever towards the lands
Where war's red hosts are thronged.

She shudders when they tell the tale
Of some great battle lost and won,
Her sweet child-face grows old and pale,
Her heart falls like a stone!

She sees no conquering flag unfurled,
She hears no victory's brazen roar,
But—a dear face which was her world—
Perchance she'll kiss no more!

Even there comes between her sight
And the glory that they rave about;
A pale, dead brow, and eyes whose light
Of splendor hath gone out!

The midnight glory of his hair,
Where, late, her fingers like a flood
Of moonlight wandered—lingereing there
Is stiff and dark—with blood!

She must not shriek—she must not moan—
  She must not ring her quivering hands;
But sitting dumb and white, alone,
  Be bound with veinless bands!

Because her suffering life enfolds
  Another dearer, feebler life;
In death-strong grasp her heart she holds,
  And stills its torturing strife.

Last eve, they say, a field was won—
  Her eyes ask tidings of the fight!
But tell her of the dead, alone,
  Who lay out in the night!

In mercy tell her that his name
  Is not upon that fatal list;
That not among the heaps of slain,
  Lie low the lips she's kissed!

EDWARD GLYNDON.

## I AM STILL ALIVE AND WELL

AFTER THE FIGHT AT BUCKHANNON VA.

JULY 1ST, '61.

THOU'RT living still, though blood-stained war
  Is strewing our land with dead,
And fiercely and wildly alarum afar,
The roaring cannon and the rattling car,
  Is filling stout hearts with dread.

Thou'rt living still the hope of the brave,
  Thy great burning thoughts, yet true,
And nerving the arms our country shall save,
Tho' their bodies shall rest in the patriot's grave,
  They die for the red, white and blue!

Thou'rt living still, for how canst thou die
  While Liberty bides in our land?
You lived with her, fought for her, bearing on high
Her banner when treason's foul legions were nigh,
  When the strife came had e'en to hand!

Thou'rt living still, the thousands who fall,
  In the battle for right, shall live
In the memory urn of their country, whose call
Bade them leave friends, home, and their all,
  To die that freedom might life.

Live on, then, ye heroes! ye triumph in right!
  Stout hearts of oak in your day!
Your names in our annals shall ever be bright,
And when freedom again shall need us to fight,
  Be your brave virtues our stay!

ANONYMOUS

## WAS MY BROTHER IN THE BATTLE.

BATTLE AT WILLIAMSPORT, VA.
JULY 2D, '61.

Tell me, tell me, weary soldier,
  From the rude and stirring wars
Was my brother in the battle
  Where you gained those noble scars?
He was ever brave and valiant,
  And I know he never fled;
Was his name among the wounded.
  Or was numbered with the dead?
Was my brother in the battle,
  When the tide of war raged high?
You would know him 'mong a thousand
  By his dark and flashing eye.

Was my brother in the battle,
  When the noble Highland host
Were so wrongfully outnumbered
  On the Carolina coast?
Did he struggle for the Union,
  'Mid the thunder and the rain,
Till he fell among the fallen
  On a bleak Virginia plain?
Oh, I'm sure that he was dauntless,
  And his courage ne'er would lag,
While contending for the honor
  Of our dear and cherished flag.

Was my brother in the battle
  When the flag of Freedom came
To the rescue of the Union,
  And protection of our fame?
While the Fleet from off the waters
  Poured out terror and dismay;
Till the bold and erring foemen.
  Fell like leaves in autumn day.
When the bugle called to battle,
  And the cannon deeply roared,
Oh, I wish I could have seen him
  Draw his sharp and glittering sword.

C. S. FOSTER.

## THE STRUGGLE.

### SKIRMISH AT FARMINGTON, VA.

JULY 2D, '61.

Say not, the struggle nought availeth
  The labor and the wounds are vain,
The enemy faints not, nor faileth,
  And as things have been they remain.

If hopes were dupes, fears may be liars;
  It may be, in yon smoke concealed,
Your comrades chase e'en now the fliers,
  And, but for you, possess the field.

And not by eastern windows only,
  When daylight comes, comes in the light.
In front, the sun climbs slow, how slowly,
  But Westward, look the land is bright.

ARTHUR HUGH CLOUGH.

## A NATION'S PRAYER.

FIRST NATIONAL CELEBRATION DURING THE WAR.

JULY 4TH, '61.

GOD of our fathers, now extend
  Thy ever gracious hand,
And grasp from destruction's pow'r
  Our poor, distracted land—
The land so blessed by Thee with all
  A nation could desire,
Where like a beacon for the world
  Has burned dear Freedom's fire.

God of our fathers, still the storm
  That sweeps across our shore,
And into every throbbing heart
  The sweets of concord pour;
Bid Thou the winds of passion stay,
  The waves of anger keep—
No longer let the fearful gale
  'Round Freedom's cradle sweep.

God of our fathers, give us light,
  Turn darkness into day,
Let wisdom in our councils sit,
  'Mid those who would betray.
Oh! yield them light, that they may see
  How fearful is the blow
That gives a nation to despair,
  And Freedom up to woe!

God of our fathers, He who hears
  The soul's last whisper'd prayer,
Now listen to our people's voice,
  And take them 'neath thy care.
Thy hand is mighty to protect,
  Thy voice the dead may wake—
Stretch forth thy hand—oh! speak the word,
  For our dear country's sake!

J. HENRY HAYWARD,

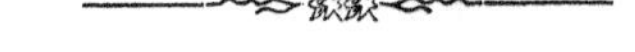

## OH WEEP NOT MOTHER.

BEFORE THE BATTLE OF CARTHAGE, MO.

JULY 5TH, '61.

O! weep not mother—weep not now,
  Though I'm going away;
Our country is in danger, mother—
  Her summons I obey.
Remember that 'tis duty calls—
  There's glory to be won;
And fortune waits impatiently
  To crown with fame your son.

You surely would not hold me back,
  To prove a coward knave,
And see our country rent in twain,
  While I've an arm to save.
No! mother, no! that starry flag
  Must never be disgraced;
Our swords shall have no peace or rest
  'Till ev'ry stain's effaced.

The Union must be saved, mother,
  Cost us what it will—
The North, and South, and East, and West
  Shall be united still.
Those traitors will be curs'd, mother,
  Aye, e'en beneath the sod;
For traitors to their country
  Are traitors to their God.

Then weep not, mother—weep not now,
  Though I now go away;
Our country is in danger, mother—
  Her summons I obey.
Remember that 'tis duty calls—
  There's glory to be won;
And fortune waits impatiently
  To crown with fame your son.

FRANCIS B. MURTHA.

## THE SOLDIER'S MOTHER'S THOUGHTS.

SKIRMISH AT BIRD'S POINT, MO.

JULY 8TH, '61.

HE is twenty, I know; and boys younger than he,
In the ranks going by every day we can see;
And those stronger and prouder, by far, I have met,
But I never have seen a young soldier yet
With so gallant a mein or so lofty a brow—
How the sun and the wind must have darkened it now!
How he will be chang'd when he comes from the South.
His beard shutting out the sweet smiles of his mouth!
And the tremulous beauty, the womanly grace,
Will be bronzed from the delicate lines of his face,
Where of late only childhood's soft beauty I saw,
For he seemed like a child till he went to the war!

JOHN BOYD.

## DIED, ON THE BATTLE-FIELD,

SECOND ENGAGEMENT AT BUCKHANNON, VA.
JULY 10TH, '61.

FAR from his native home he died;
The clash of arms on every side,
The roar of cannon, and the tide
Of red blood flowing.
Slowly the spark of life went out,
As rang the gallant victors' shout,
Telling the foe were put to rout
By his brave comrades.

No gentle mother softly laid
On his hot brow her hand, or prayed
As his soul heavenward strayed—
Heavenward ascended.
But as the glorious field was won,
While rushed the conquering army on,
As blood-red sank the setting sun,
Gloriously he perished,

Around his green and hallowed grave
Fond friends shall sadly mourn the brave,
Saying, "He gladly died to save
His land from ruin."
Over this lowly mound of his
All that he asked or wished for is
Graved on his narrow headstone this—
"DIED FOR HIS COUNTRY!"

ANONYMOUS.

## THE HEROE'S LAST DREAM.

AFTER THE BATTLE AT RICH MOUNTAIN, VA.

JULY 11TH, '61.

THE pale moon looked down where the hero lay dying,
Thro' the thin, shad'y clouds that were ling'ring by
She alone save the wind o'er the dreary plain sighing
Could hear the last prayer, could see the brave die;
The conflict was past, and the vict'ry was ended,
And his fond dreams of glory had vanish'd away,
His brow was all pale and with gore his locks blended,
On the battle-field where his wound'd form lay!

He thought of his home, of the scenes of his childhood,
Far down in the vale where the bright waters flow—
Of blissful hours spent in the deep tangled wildwood,
Ere his young heart was fired with ambition's glow;
He thought of a voice—of a soft, flowing cadence,
And "Mother," the name from his quivering lips fell,
As in fancy he gazed on her tear-drops at parting,
Or felt her last kiss as she breathed a farewell,

He tho't of a bower, with the green woodbine clinging,
A type of the love which his proud heart had won,
And dark woodland path with cheerful strains ringing
And soft voice combin'd with the lute's melting tone
But vain the delusion—those fairy-like fingers
Will playfully twine his dark ringlets no more,
Nor that voice shall he hear, tho' its music still ling'rs,
And greets his lone ear on a far distant shore.

The vict'ry was won, but his life's blood was ebbing—
  A crimson stream flow'ed o'er the once flow'ry plain;
His spirit once more the bright haunts seem'd treading
  The homestead his dim eyes could see ne'er again,
His country was free—but life's taper was waning,
  And Death's turbid waters beat loud on his ear,
In the first flush of manhood life's fount was draining,
  Alone, all alone, with no kindred form near.

Night's shadows were gone, the clear rosy morning
  Stooped over the battle-field, crimson with gore,
Where the heart warm'd with glory's bright dawning
  Was cold in the bosom to throb never more,
The young hero lay, but the warm sun was gleaming
  Upon the rude spot where his pallid cheek laid,
No more that heart of Fame's proud laurels dreaming,
  For his dark eye was glazed, and the hero was dead!

LOUISE SMITH.

## AFTER THE BATTLE.

### THE VICTORY OF BEVERLY, VA.

### JULY 12TH, '61.

HIGH up from the plain curled the wreathing smoke;
The cannon's loud roar and the sabre stroke
Were hushed for awhile; and the midnight air
Was filled with the groans of the dying there.
The daylight had fled, and the battle plain
Ran deep with the blood of the noble slain ;
Above, in the sky, in her sheeny light
The silv'ry moon rode as queen of the night.

The glimmering rays of the stars shone forth,
Far over the plain from the south to the north,
Where fierce struggling armies had fought in pride,
And tents glistened while on the green hillside.
The wounded now murmured in tones of despair,
And kneeling beside the fond mother's chair,
And the plain blushed red in the moon's bright glare;
And bodies were heaped on the verdant sod,
Their souls taken flight to the realms of God.

The Jackal's loud howl, and the wolf's long bay,
Were silenced and stilled by the dawn of the day,
Camp-fires were smould'ring, the watches were done,
And the hill-side was gleaming in light of the sun.
Away from this scene in the noisy town,
As the orient beams of the sun stream down,
All active with life, and all busy with care;
Not all was of joy, for stern grief had a share.

A mother is wailing a dear son's doom,
And sisters are groping in gath'ring gloom,
While hearts for loved ones are mourning the slain
Now lying so cold on the still battle plain.
Young children are weeping in hopeless despair,
And kneeling beside the fond mother's chair,
While on bended knee, in low solemn tone,
A prayer ascends unto God's great throne.

"O, help us, our Father, to suffer this blow!
O, strengthen our hearts by this pitiless woe;
For death has descended like flames blasting blight,
Our day star of hope is enshrouded in night,"
In a silence like death, in their hearts inmost fane.
A strength from their weakness, joy from their pain
Their hearts 'neath the death blow rose calmly and bold
And fresh for new labor in life's dreary world,

ANONYMOUS.

## THE MINIATURE.

### AT THE BATTLE OF ST. GEORGE, VA.

JULY 13TH, '61.

THE moon through the rack of the driving clouds,
  Like a frightened creature swept,
As if nerved with despair from crag to crag
  Of the driving scud she lept ;
And the pale stars peered through the murky gloom
  At the flight of their queen so fair ;
While some in their terror dropped through the void,
  Like red burning bombs in the air.

And stern Mars shone forth with his bloodshot eye,
  Through the night's black driving bars,
Presaging to earth and her countless hosts
  Wild tumults and crimson wars,
And the wind with its trembling fingers smote
  The leaves from the forest trees,
While it struck the strings of its viewless harp
  To wild and weird melodies.

But there were sights and sounds more drear by far
  Than clouds or piping blast,
For through that field of life, from dawn till dusk,
  The grim reaper Death had passed !
His arm might be stiff and his sickle dull,
  From his crop of human grain,
For the streams ran red and the meadow groaned
  With its weight of ghastly slain !

The rifle, mortar, and parrot gun
  Had belched like the fires of hell,
And the sickle of Death mowed its living swath
  With grape and the bursting shell;
And the charging squadrons thundering dashed
  Till they shook the moaning earth,
And heaven in pity veiled her fair face,
  While hell shrieked wildly with mirth!

Thus from gray-eyed dawn till the dusky eve
  The battling hosts contended,
Till night, o'er the scene of carnage and woe,
  In dewy tears descended;
When the seried hosts of friend and of foe
  Retired from the field of strife,
Leaving at eve ten thousand mangled dead
  Who at dawn were full of life.

The while thousands of wounded groaning lay
  In their pain and dark despair,
And the wounded coursers plunged 'mid the dead,
  While their screams disturbed the air;
"Water, cool water, O give me to drink,
  My blood is scorching like fire,
Give me to drink from my own father's well—
  Drink—drink—O, God, I expire!"

"Alone! alone! on the red field of fame,
  Dear maid, I perish afar,
But still as in life, thou ever hast been,
  In death thou art my lone star!
Dear Ella, this picture you gave ere we marched,
  'Tis dyed with life's crimson gore,
Ella, I kiss thee, 'mid darkness of death——"
  He ceased—the brave was no more.

W. A. DEVON.

## "LIST OF THE KILLED."

FIGHT AT BUNKER HILL, VA.,
JULY 15TH, '61.

MOTHERS who sit in dumb terror and dread,
  Holding that terrible list,
Fearing to look lest you see 'mid the dead,
  The name of the boy you have kissed—
Kissed e'en as those who in anguish and pain,
  Kiss precious faces of clay,
E'en as you would had you shuddering lain,
  That dear one in grave-robes away—

I pity you, sitting with faces so white,
  Striving to parry the blow;
I know how that name will torture your sight,
  Can fathom the depth of your woe.
By the pang that has rent my desolate heart,
  By this crushing weight of despair,
I know how you too will shudder and start,
  Reading that dear-loved name there.

I know you'll hush that passionate wail,
  Thinking of him as he lies,
With beautiful face upturned to the sky,
  Death veiling the glorious eyes.
Mothers' love triumphs. Men call women weak—
  Ah, well, perhaps it is so!
I know there are tears e'en now on my cheek
  For the boy that's laying so low.

ANONYMOUS.

## OUR UNKNOWN HEROES.

ENGAGEMENT AT BLACKBURN FORD, VA.,
JULY 18TH, '61.

In the din and crash of battle,
'Mid its rush and deafening roar,
There have fell ten thousand heroes—
There will fall ten thousand more;
And the true and loyal hearted,
Whose brave feet the path have trod
That leads down to death's dark river,
And whose souls have gone to God,
Lie in myriad numbers, countless,
And the winds their vigils keep,
O'er the places sad and lonely,
Where our unknown heroes sleep.

Men who, scorning name or station,
With a purpose strong and pure,
Battle for the *Right*, and deemed it
Fame and honor to endure
For their country perils deadly,
Danger dire, by field and flood;
Who poured out their dearest treasures—
Life itself—their heart's best blood,
Thinking, caring not, for glory—
Seeking not the world's applause—
Well content to do their duty,
Mindful only of the *Cause.*

Thick the yellow mounds are lying,
  Nameless, stoneless, and forgot;
With no hand to plant the willow,
  Weeping lowly o'er the spot;
Where the murky waters flowing,
  Clear beneath a Southern sky,
And the bosom of calm Blackburn,
  With blood stains doth quiet lie.
The sweet Land of Peace they've entered
  On its fair and sinless coasts
They have joined the immortal armies,
  Marshaled by the Lord of Hosts.

Hail! oh brave and noble patriots,
  With your purpose pure and high,
In the hearts of a glad nation,
  Your great deeds shall never die,
But glad millions in the future,
  Shall thy sacred memories keep,
Of the dear though unknown places,
  Where our bravest heroes sleep.
And when peace shall dawn upon us,
  When this carnage fierce is done,
When the last wild strife is ended,
  And the final victory won,

And when brothers' hand shall be stained,
  In brothers' blood no more,
And the awful tide of battle,
  Shall roll back from our fair shore,
Then in history's burning pages,
  Which we to the world will give,
There in never dying letters,
  Shall our unknown heroes live!

## THE NEWS OF A DAY.

### FIRST BATTLE OF BULL RUN, VA.

JULY 21ST, '61.

" GREAT battle ! Great Battle ! " the news-boy cried,
But it scarcely rippled the living tide
That ebbed and flowed in the noisy street,
With its throbbing heart and busy feet,
Again through the hum of the city thrilled,
"Great battle ! Great battle ! Ten thousand killed !"
And the little carrier hurried away
With the sorrowful news of that summer day.

To a dreary room in an attic high
Trembled the words of that small, sharp cry;
And a lonely widow bowed her head,
And murmured " Willie, my Willie, is dead.
O I feared it was not an idle dream
That led me last night to that dark, deep stream,
Where the ground was wet with a crimson rain,
And strewn all over with ghastly slain.
The stars were dim, for the night was wild,
But I threaded the gloom till I found my child.

The cold rain fell on his upturned face,
And the swift destroyer had left no trace
Of the sudden blow, and the quick, sharp pain,
But a little wound and a purple stain.
I tried to speak, but my voice was gone,
And my soul stood there in that cool, gray dawn,
Till they rifled his body with ruthless hand,
And covered him up with the reeking sand.

"Willie, O Willie! it seems but a day
Since thy baby head on my bosom lay;
Since I heard thy prattle, so soft and sweet,
And guided the steps of thy tottering feet,
And thou wert the fairest and last of three
That the Father in Heaven had given to me;
And the life of my heart, love, hope and joy,
Was treasured in thee, my strong, brave boy;
And the last faint words that thy father said,
Were, 'Willie will mind thee when I am dead.'
But they tore the flag from thy death-cold hand,
And covered thee up in the damp reeking sand.

She read the names of the missing and slain;
But one she read over again and again;
And the sad, low words that her white lips said,
Were, 'Company C, William Warren dead.'
The world toiled on through the busy street,
With its aching hearts and unresisting feet;
The night came down to her cold hearth-stone,
And she still the words that her white lips said,
Were, 'Company C, Willlam Warren dead.'
The light of the morning chased the gloom
From the emberless hearth of that attic room,
And the city's pulse throbbed again,
But the mother's heart had forgotten its pain.

She had gone through the gates to the better land,
With that terrible list in her pale, cold hand,
With her white lips parted, as at last she said,
'Company C, William Warren dead.'

SARAH T. BOLTON.

## THE SWORD AND THE PLOW.

SKIRMISH AT HARRISONVILLE, VA.

JULY 25TH, '61.

The Sword came down to the red-brown field,
Where the Plow to the furrow heaved and keeled;
And it looked so proud in its jingling gear,
Said the Plow to the Sword—"What brings you here?"

"Long years ago, ere I was born,
They doubled my grandsire up one morn,
To forge a shire for you, and now
They want him back," said the Sword to the Plow.

The red-brown field glowed a deeper red,
As the gleam of war o'er the landscape sped;
The sabres flashed, the cannons roared,
And, side by side, fought the Plow and the Sword.

ANONYMOUS.

## FORWARD.

### BATTLE AND OCCUPATION OF FORSYTH, MO.

JULY 26TH, '61.

WHAT, again! Does their insolence dare so much?
  Again for our soil do they force us to fight,
Polluting our homes with its poisonous touch?
  Does treason essay so audacious a flight?
To the front! to the front with our glorious flag!
  Our banners by thousands should gladden the air,
The foe in our faces is flaunting his rag
  And he comes not to sue, nor pity, nor spare.

Our friends from the borders are flying in fear,
  Their wives and their little ones faint in the path;
For the foe is behind them—his horsemen are near—
  The smoke of our homesteads foreshadows his wrath.
Too long have we waited, too long have delayed;
  Too long has indifference palsied our hand.
The swift steps of traitors will never be stayed,
  Till the last of the brood is swept out of the land.

United once more, and in earnest at last,
  Let us drive them at once from the soil of the free,
Nor slacken our speed when the danger is past,
  But follow them on to the shores of the sea.
None prate now of peace, when the foeman is near:
  The wrangling and clamour of faction are hushed
When treason triumphantly threatens us here,
  What peace can we have until treason is crushed?

Oh, then, a new oath let us solemnly swear,
  To pause not, to halt not, nor rest on the way,
Till our flag, thro' the whole land, shall glow in the air,
  And treason is buried forever and aye.
Let us move as one man, with the might of the free,
  Though partisans falter and cowards deride,
Till the traitors submit from the gulf to the sea,
  To Union and Freedom—our glory and pride,

EDWARD WILLET.

## AM I FORGOTTEN?

AFTER THE BATTLE OF DUG SPRING, MO.

AUGUST 2D '61.

'MID the clangor of arms and the clash of the battle,
  By Fate, dearest one, is thy fortune now cast;
The hiss of the shell and the musketry's rattle
  Are borne to thine ears on Wars terrible blast:
But as with firm step, unappalled by the danger,
  Led on by the flag of the brave and the free,
Thou treadest the fields where pale death is no stranger,
  O, tell me, my love, think'st thou ever of me?

And tell me, when night's dusky pennon's are waving
  Concealing the free—brooding over the foes—
When the moon the red fields with her silver is laying
  And wrapt in thy mantle thou seekest repose,
Doest thou thro' the dim aisles of the Past ever wander
  And think of the one that's e'er thinking of thee?
Dost thy spirit in dreams over other days ponder,
  And are thy dreams sweeter for being of me?

MONROE G. CARLTON.

## THE PICKET FOUND MISSING.

### SURRENDER OF FORT FILLMORE, TEXAS.

### AUGUST 2D, '61.

THE news of the battle was sent thro' the land,
Ev'ry sentence was read and re-read again;
And our hearts were relieved of a terrible fear,
We found not his name 'mong the wounded or slain.

Day after day we watched for a letter,
And coupled his name with bright glory and fame,
But days, weeks, and months passed swiftly away—
'Twas strange, very strange, yet no letter came.

We heard the report of the soldiers returning,
And knew by the cheers that the heroes were near;
With hearts buoyed up with hope and sweet pleasure,
We rushed to the meeting of him that was dear.

Thro' each column we searched, ev'ry visage scanned,
Hoping, still doubting, o'ercome with despair;
Friends mingled with friends in joyous delight—
All seemed so happy—but he was not there.

The brain 'gan to whirl, and our eyes grew dim—
A terrible dread took the place of our glee;
And our hearts, too, beat wildly in anguish and pain,
Not wounded or slain, then where could he be?

They said he was ordered on duty one night,
The same watch he kept so often before;
And when the grand round challeng'd the pickets, alas!
He was found missing, and ne'er was seen more.

Ah! he was the pride and hope of our household—
A star of bright honor was set on his brow;
His smile was like sunshine, so pleasant and sweet—
Oh! where will we find the "missing one" now.

FRANCIS B. MURTHA.

## THE RELIEF.

AT MANASSAS JUNCTION, VA.

AUGUST 3D, '61.

'TIS Night! The Camp's in sleep profound,
The guardsman tramps his watchful round;
While sentries march with shoulder'd guns,
From post to post the watch cry runs:
"Stand! Who comes there? Pass not the line!"
"A Friend!" "Advance with countersign!"
"The Union Flag!" "Pass, Friend! Good Night!
"The Union Flag!" Pass, Friend! Good night!"

'Tis morn! the sunbeam lopes its light
On glistening gun and bayonet bright;
The wearied sentry treads his rounds,
Till soon the welcome drum resounds!
"Stand? Who comes there? Pass not line!"
"Grand Rounds!" "Advance, with Countersign!"
"The Union Flag!" "Relief! All right!
'The Union Flag!' Relief! All right!"

F. A. SPANGLE.

## RETURNING SOLDIERS.

### RETURN OF THE THREE MONTH'S VOLUNTEERS.

### AUG. 5TH, '61.

WARM welcome home, ye noble northern bands;
We bid you welcome with our hearts and hands,
Always our dear, but now our dearest ones,
Our closest kindred, fathers, brothers, sons.
Warm welcome, soldiers, howsoe'er you come,
Whether you keep step to the stirring drum,
Or maimed and feeble, faltering and slow,
Sad victims of the contest, and the foe,
Or borne on litters with expiring breath,
Or stretched in all the majesty of death.
We bid you welcome, oh, ye gallant braves,
To happy lives or honorable graves.
The dear survivor shall have love and fame,
The loyal dead a consecrated name—
Nor only now; for after years shall tell
The story of your deeds and triumphs well.
The generations that are yet to be,
With flowing eyes, your country's flag shall see,
Emblem of joy, pride, glory, and success,
Without stripe erased, one star the less,
As all its dazzling hues and dots expand
From sea to sea, o'er one united land,
Shall cannonize your memories late and long,
Subjects of eloquence and themes of song,
Martyrs and patriots, whose death sublime
Have made our Union holy for all time!

PARK BENJAMIN.

## THE SOLDIER'S WIDOW.

SKIRMISH AT POINT OF ROCKS, VA.,
AUG. 5TH, '61.

Wo! FOR my vine clad home!
That it should ever be so dark to me,
With its bright threshold and its whispering wee.
That it should ever come,
Fearing the lonely echo of a tread,
Beneath the roof-tree of my glorious dead!

Lead on! my orphan boy!
Thy home is not so desolate to thee,
And the low shiver in the linden tree,
May bring to thee a joy,
But oh! how dark the bright home before thee,
To her who with a joyous spirit bore thee!

Lead on! for thou art now
My sole remaining helper God hath spoken,
And the strong heart I leaned upon is broken;
And I have seen his brow,
The forehead of my upright one, and just,
Trod by the hoof of battle to the dust.

He will not meet thee where
We blessed thee at the eventide, my son,
And when the shadows of the night steal on,
He will not call to prayer.
The lips that melted, giving thee to God,
Are in the icy keeping of the sod!

Aye, my own boy! thy sire
Is with the sleepers of the valley cast,
And the proud glory of my life hath pass'd,
With His high glance of fire.
Wo! that the linden and the vine should bloom,
And a just man be gathered to the tomb.

N. P. WILLIS.

---

## BATTLE EVE.

BEFORE THE BATTLE OF ATHENS, MO.

AUGUST 5TH, '61.

OUR tents gleam soft in the moonlighted mist,
The soldiers slumber as soldiers do,
But I lie awake and look up to the stars,
And remember my love for you.

If the future is dark, yet the past is our own,
And fate cannot alter nor e'en subdue
That passionate dream, and this tender regret,
And the old fond love for you.

Our guns are yet warm on the fortified steep,
To-morrow the carnage we shall renew;
To-morrow night I shall wake to muse
On my old fond love for you?

God knows, God knows! Ere another eve
Yon fields must blush with ruddier dew:
If I never come back, then one heart dies
With an old fond love for you?

## MY COUNTRY—I WEEP FOR THEE.

### BURNING OF THE VILLAGE OF HAMPTON, VA.

AUGUST 8TH, '61

If ever man had cause to weep,
Ay, weep as man—strong man—alone can weep,
That *cause* is now! Now, may he bow his head,
And shade with trembling hand his burning eyes,
While down his cheek the scalding drops of grief
May course their way unchecked and unreproved
By those whose brows serene with shame would glow,
To own the presence of a single tear,
If shed for cause less grevious and sad,
Than this, o'er which shame not e'en they to weep!

When in the gloom of Valley Forge—
'Mid winter's chilling blast, and sleeting storm,—
'Tis said that Washington—our nation's chief—
Oft knelt in prayer before his people's God,
And praying, wept—wept tears of voiceless woe,
Perhaps, as Christ once kneeling, prayed and wept,
In the seclusion of Gethsemanies shade,
Till tears of anguish turned to tears of blood,
So poignant was the agony he felt,
To find the human race so lost to him,
So lost to truth, to virtue, and to God?
Think ye he would not weep as he then wept,
Were he still in our midst in mortal form,—
Thus to behold poor mankind now as lost

To reason's sway, as they then were to God?
Think ye that Washington would shame to weep,
Could he but see—as you and I now see—
The passing scenes and acts of life to-day!
To see the soil once drenched with the warm blood
Of patriot sires, in Freedom's cause arrayed,
Now wet again—not by the blood of foes
From foreign climes transported hence to slay,
But by the liquid life of patriot sons,
Of such brave sires—ay, brothers of one blood,
Met face to face, with gleaming swords upraised,
And glistening bayonets, in war's fierce strife,
Directed 'gainst each other's vengeful breast?
Alas! who would not weep?

There is a time when tears
Belong to other than a maiden's eyes:—
When hearts, bold in the consciousness of might,
May without shame forget their stern manhood,
And like a very child bow down and weep!
Weep for a People's happiness destroyed,
Weep for the dream of promised greatness gone,
Weep for sweet hope departed with the day,
Which 'mid the gloom of night will pass away,
When Freedom's sons prove basely recreant
To the great TRUST their sires in them reposed,
And leave the honered citadel of State—
By four and thirty Pillars vast made strong,—
All shatter'd by the sacrilegious hands,
Of fiends incarnate, who despise all law,
And the pure altar of Fraternal Right
Besmeared with blood, in its defence poured out,
While faith appalled, will disappointed frown,
And Liberty close veil her face and weep!

My country—oh! I weep for thee,
Beside the ruins of thy fall I weep!
Nor shame I for the sacred drops thus shed;
Because each sigh is now a bitter oath,
Each tear a seal, which makes the oath a bond,
*To firm restore thee to thy pristine might,*
*Or with thee fall!* 'Twere well to weep such tears:
They purge the heart, and to the soul give strength,
To do great deeds—when deeds are needed most.
Who loves his country therefore shame not now,
O'er her great woes, with me to weep!

J. HENRY HAYWARD.

## THE HARVEST OF DEATH.

ATTACK ON POTOSI, MO.

AUGUST 9TH, '61.

ALL over our land, our beautiful land
Of meadow and hill and plain,
The golden harvests ripened stand,
And death is reaping the grain.

But not with the crooked hook or the scythe
Does the reaper arm him now;
For a harvest so vast those tools of the past
Would be deemed exceedingly "slow."

He gleans no more for the single stalk,
Nor counts what the stubbles yield;
But he draws from above the bolts of Jove,
And launches them into the field.

Hissing in wrath the red bolts fall,
Gleaming with lurid fire;
And he laughs when he hears the crackling of ears
That meet in the levin's ire.

He strikes not single victims now—
'Twere a labor to great for Death;
For gathered afloat in ship or in boat,
He can blast them all at a breath—

Or smothered below, or aloft they go,
Dispersed in atom and shred;
*N'importe* the amount, for a sorry count
Would he make of the bits of the dead.

An insidious foe is Death no more,
But a conqueror, bold and frank,
Who proudly boasts that he marshals his hosts
And smites them rank by rank.

He drives at the mass with a sulphurous storm
Of leaden and iron rain,
And the screeching shell is the larum and knell
To the hecatombs of slain.

Oh! Death is drunken with rage, and our land
Is red with the blood of his prey:
Not the sorrows of years nor rivers of tears
Will wash the traces away.

OWEN GLENDOWER.

## GONE TO THE WAR.

BEFORE THE BATTLE OF DAVIS CREEK, MO.

AUG. 10TH, '61.

I LOOK no more with longing eyes,
Towards the clouds in the eastern skies,
To watch the coming day;
The days have no pleasure now for me,
The beauties of earth I cannot see,
Since Charlie went away.

He gave a lock of his curling hair,
To his mother and me to wear,
The ones who loved him best;
Then marched away when the summons came,
He said, to win a soldier's fame;—
Our fears—a soldier's rest.

I see the flag now waving high;
How many for that flag will die,
While 'tis proudly flying?
I hear in dreams the cannon's sound,
I see upon the battle ground,
The form of Charlie lying.

My days are filled with anxious dread;
Lest I should hear my darling's dead.
My nights, they know no rest—
But when I see the morn is nigh,
I strive to hush the wailing cry
Which will not be repressed.

His mother's eyes are growing dim
Awaiting for the sight of him,
  Her darling pride and joy.
O, Thou who ever reigns on high,
Wilt thou not hear my earnest cry,
  God keep our soldier boy?

CARRIE C. HALLOCK.

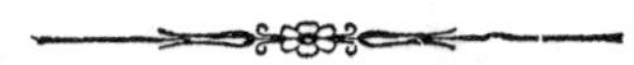

## THE WOUNDED SOLDIER.

AT THE BATTLE OF GRAYTOWN, VA.

AUGUST 13TH, '61.

I'M wounded, Effie, and they say
  I never can get well;
'Twas in the thickest of the fight
  That I got hurt and fell.
It seems to me like ages, yet
  It's but a month to-day
Since you promised you'd wait for me,
  Though I were years away.

Do you remember—oh! how well
  It all comes back to me!—
Our sitting in the bright moonlight,
  Beneath the maple tree;
When first I said I loved you,
  And told you we must part,
For not e'en you could keep me, when
  My country had my heart.

I knew you did not wish it, as
  Your little hand in mine,
You did not try to stay me then
  By either word or sign;
But trying to keep back the tears,
  Although a few would fall,
You bade me trust in God, your God,
  Whatever might befall.

But all my bright ambitious hopes
  Forever now are fled,
The sunlight of to-morrow morn
  Will fall upon me dead;
There'll be one soldier less to fight,
  One less on earth to love,
But there'll be one hand to strike
  The golden harps above.

I have a mother in the skies;
  I wonder if she'll know
The little baby that she left
  So many years ago.
I'm weary, Effie, and can not think:
  Let this your comfort be,
Your love has been the brightest thing
  In all the world to me.

W.

## ONLY A FEW.

### THE ATTACK ON FREDRICKTOWN, MO.

AUGUST 16TH, '61.

How OFTEN we read in the news of the day
Accounts of a fight, or a skirmish, at most,
Where a few of our soldiers held thousands at bay,
Or scattered like chaff a whole rebel host.

And as onward we read the paragraph through,
Our hearts with deep fear and anxiety filled,
Though hotly contested an hour or two,
We find there were only a few soldiers killed.

Yes, "only a few"—yet how little we think
Of the desolate homes, bereft of their light—
Of the hearts that in sorrow and in misery sink,
Being robbed of their hope, their pride and delight.

How lonely and dreary those few homes now are,
Though gratitude honors the glorious dead.
Dimly indeed glory's bright star—
Their noble and high aspirations hath fled.

A few months ago filled with ardent desires,
They shouldered the musket, and bade a good bye;
That *glory* for which every soldier aspires
Nerved them to conquer or gloriously die.

But, oh! who can console those poor mothers now,
Those sisters, those wives, or those children so dear?
Though a bright laurel crown encircles each brow,
Their fame and their glory is dimmed with a tear.

ANONYMOUS.

## THE LOYAL SLAIN.

### FIRST BATTLE AT CHARLESTOWN, MO., AUGUST 18TH, '61.

As WAR's dread tones sound fierce and loud
  On high plateau or river shore,
The grey and fitful rising cloud
Of battle forms a ghastly shroud
  Over dark rivulets of gore.

Where are the loyal slain?—those men
  Who, with patriotic aim,
Marshaled in Freedom's column, when
Black Treason rose, and from his den
  Spread terror, guilt, and crimson shame.

Upon the turf, by shot and steel
  Spirit-robbed, lie these loyal dead;
As each dear heart is stilled, let's feel
A stronger love for Freedom and its weal,
  And cling to Hope, but not to dread.

Yes, fondly search, and mark each grave
  Of these revered and gallant forms;
And from Oblivion's precincts save
The names of all the noble brave,
  As patriot recollection warms.

With prouder flaunt and grander sheen,
  On tower and hill, and o'er the graves
Of our loved warrior-dead, serene,
'Neath heavenly blue, above earth's green,
  Our beauteous star gemmed ensign waves!

WILLIAM J. M'CLURE

## THE PRICE OF VICTORY.

SKIRMISH AT LADY'S FORD, VA.,
AUGUST 18TH, '61.

"A VICTORY!—a victory!"
  Is flashed across the wires;
Speed, speed the news from State to State,
  Light up the signal fires!
Let all the bells from all the towers
  A joyous peal ring out!
We've gained a glorious victory,
  And put the foe to rout!

A mother heard the chiming bells;
  Her joy was mixed with pain.
"Pray God," she said, "my gallant boy
  Be not among the slain."
Alas! for her! that very hour
  Outstretched in death he lay;
The color from his fair young face
  Had hardly passed away.

His nerveless hand still grasped the sword
  He never more might wield,
His eyes were sealed in dreamless sleep
  Upon the bloody field.
The chestnut curls his mother oft
  Had stroked in fondest pride,
Neglected hung in clotted locks,
  With deepest crimson dyed.

Ah! many a mother's heart shall ache,
  And bleed with anguish sore,
When tidings come of him who marched
  So blithely forth to war.
Oh! sad for them—the stricken down
  In manhood's early dawn—
And sadder yet for loving hearts—
  God comfort them that mourn,

Yes, victory has a fearful price
  Our hearts may shrink to pay,
And tears WILL mingle with the joy
  That greets a glorious day.
But he who dies in Freedom's cause,
  We cannot count him lost;
A battle won for truth and right
  Is worth the blood it cost!

Oh! mothers! count it something gained,
  That they for whom you mourn,
Bequeath fair Freedom's heritage
  To millions yet unborn;
And better than a thousand years
  Of base, ignoble breath,
A patriot's fragrant memory,
  A hero's early death.

ANON.

## THE SOLDIER TO HIS BETROTHED.

BEFORE THE FIGHT AT HAWK'S NEST, VA.
AUGUST 20TH, '61.

THE joys of home are dear to me,
  And dearer still thou art;
But I, my country's son must be,
  She calls and we must part.
The stars upon her banner fair,
  That brightly beam above,
My Mary, pure and constant there,
  Are emblems of my love.

No captive in his dungeon's gloom,
  E'er long'd for Freedom's light,
As I shall wish—whate'er my doom—
  For my lov'd Mary's sight.
But better far that she should weep,
  My absence or my fall,
Than here to sleep the coward's sleep,
  Nor heed my country's call.

When in the deadly battle-field,
  The Union's foes we meet;
If dying there my faith is seal'd,
  My death hour will be sweet.
The soldier for his country dies,
  For her his blood he gives;
But if that fate his star denies,
  For thee, and love he lives.

Thine eye's bright beam, thy love's soft smile,
  My best reward shall be,
When turning from the battle's toil,
  And homeward bound to thee.
My Mary! hear the bugle blow,
  And see the banner fly;
Farewell, my Mary—thine I go,
  Thine, it I live or die!

H. ALGER, JR.

## A SON IN THE WAR.

SECOND BATTLE AT CHARLESTOWN, MO.
AUGUST 20TH, '61.

WE gathered 'round the cheerful fires,
  Dismissing every care;
And happy is the household band,
  And every one is there;
Ah, no, there is a vacant seat,
  There is an absent one,
There is a mother's loved boy
  Who to war has gone.

Alone for him she daily mourns,
  Alone for him she daily weeps,
Alone for him in midnight shades
  She constant vigil keeps;
Alone for him when all is joy
  Around the household hearth,
The silent tear is seen to drop
  Adown her withered cheek.

Alone for him at hour of prayer,
  She fondly breathes above
Her soul to God, but to protect
  And keep him in His love!
And when her streaming eyes were closed
  In slumbers of the night,
She fancies that the absent one
  Is present in her sight.

ANONYMOUS.

## THE LAST SUNDAY AT HOME.

BEFORE THE SKIRMISH AT CROSS LANES, VA.
AUGUST 21ST, '61.

ONCE more within the House of God below
  We stand, in rev'rent hope and fear, to pray;
Our hearts, with holy courage burning, glow—
  For duty calls to battle hence away,
    "O, God, preserve our country's life,
    And lead us in the fearful strife—
      To Thee alone the glory."

The Lord is our defense; in Him our might,
  Let battles e'er so fiercely, madly rage;
We fight for Freedom and th'eternal Right,
  And for this land, our holy heritage.
    And if we save our fatherland,
    Hath God not done it through our hand?
      To Him alone the glory.

Ambition soon the ashen fruit shall taste,
  Of impious wrongs which spring from reckless pride,
While Freedom's morn shall light the desert-waste
  Of minds, which, long in night, the day denied.
    For in this struggle, fierce and long,
    God is with us, and we are strong—
      To Him alone the glory.

He calls us now to vict'ry on to press,
  Nor doubt the morning star which lights the way—
His voice is heard in every patriot's breast,
  "Awake! the night is spent; behold the day!"
    Us shall He show, e'en in death's night,
    The golden glow of Freedom's dawning light.
      To Him, our country's God, the glory.

T. H. KORNER.

## THE SILENT ANVIL.

AFTER THE BATTLE OF SOMERSVILLE, VA.
AUGUST 26TH, '61.

I CREPT in the lane at midnight—
  The lane so silent and dead!—
A stagnant calm in the world below,
  And a stagnant calm o'er head;
And Venus was wrapt in a jaundice mist,
  And Mars in his flaming red.

I crept to the door of the smithy,
  And peered through the heavy gloom—
The forge was cold and in ashes,
  And silent the anvil's boom;
And the sledges were laid aside for aye,
  And sooty the furnace-flume.

And I thought how the early morning,
  When it flashed on the window-pane,
And burned with its pleasant fever
  The leaves of the summer lane—
It should bring the little children
  To look at the forge again.

And I pictured their wandering glances,
  And their silence of sharp dismay,
When they missed the smith at the anvil-block,
  And the sound of the sledge's play;
And the hum of the flame in the chimney cold,
  And the pondrous bellow's sway.

And I thought how the herdsmen round about
  Would miss, from the evening sky,
The distant clank of the forgeman's blow,
  The light and the crimson dye
That blazed and burned from the blackened flume,
  Like a beacon raised on high.

And I said: " O forgeman stout of limb,
  Of muscle firm and true,
No more shall your sledges shape the plow,
  Or the will of the farmer do.
There is heavier work for heart and hand—
  There is heavier work for you.

" For, with storms and battle the air is filled,
  And bared is the foeman's steel;
And crash on crash, from the cannon's mouth,
  Make the charging squadrons reel;
And the arts of peace are crushed and ground
  'Neath Havoc's iron heel."

JEREMY BLANC.

## GOD'S BLESSINGS ON THEM,

CAPTURE OF FORTS HATTERAS AND CLARK, N. C.
AUGUST 29TH, '61.

GOD bless the brave ones! in our dearth,
Their lives shall have a trailing glory;
And round the poor man's homely hearth
We'll proudly tell their suffering story.

All savior-souls have sacrificed,
With nought but noble faith for guerdon,
And ere the world hath crowned the Christ,
The man to death hath borne the burden!

The savage broke the glass that brought
The heavens nearer, saith the legend;
Even so the bigots welcomed aught
That makes our visions starrier regioned.

They lay their corner stones in dark,
Deep waters, who uphold in beauty,
On earths old heart their triumphs are,
That crown with glory lives of duty.

And meekly still the martyrs go
To keep with pain their solemn bridal!
And still they walk the fire who bow
Not down to worship Custom's idol.

The heart! the rude dust, dark to-day,
Soars a new lighted sphere to-morrow:
And wings of splendor burst the clay
That clasps us in death's fruitful furrow.

GERALD MASSEY.

## THE WHETTING OF THE SCYTHES.

ATTACK ON LEXINGTON, MO.
AUGUST 29TH, '61.

THE dew laughs on the blossom'd grass,
Like diamonds gem the flow'rs—
And over all the soft winds pass
All fresh from Night's cool bow'rs,
While sharp and clear, upon the ear,
Across the field, we list to hear
The whetting of the scythes !

The laugh and song may float along,
From festive heart and lip,
Where the belles and beaux in joyous throng
The cup of pleasure sip—
But let me hear upon the air
A sweeter sound, more full of cheer—
The whetting of the scythes !

Now, soldiers, mow the rebels down
With blades of tempered steel—
Make, make our Union's power known,
Let them its vengeance feel—
Then home once more from tented plain,
You'll haste to hear in peace again—
The whetting of the scythes !

ANONYMOUS.

## MY MINIE RIFLE.

AT THE FIGHT AT BALL'S CROSS ROADS, VA

AUGUST 30TH, '61.

THE finest friend I ever knew,
  And one with whom I dare not trifle,
Who in all danger sees me through,
Whose aim is ever good and true,
  Is my sweet Minie Rifle.

She gently rests upon my arm,
  Is always ready, always willing;
And though, in general, somewhat calm,
Wakes up, upon the first alarm,
  To show she can be killing.

And she is very fair to see,
  The most fastidious fancy suiting;
Her locks are bright as they can be,
And that her sight is good to me
  Is just as sure as shooting.

Though used to many a firey spark,
  She's never careless in her pleasure;
She always aims to hit the mark,
And when her voice the Sothrons hark,
  They find she's no Secesher.

The heaviest load seems not to weigh
  Upon her more than 'twer a trifle;
She's highly polished; and I'd pray,
Were I bereft of friend this day,
  "Oh! leave my Minie Rifle!"

ANONYMOUS.

## OUR DEAD SOLDIER BOY.

AFTER THE REBEL ATTACK AT DENT CO., MO.,
SEPTEMBER 1ST, '61.

He died before he had reached the field,
  When the battle cry was sounding,
His dear young life he must sadly yield,
  With his comrades in camp surrounding;
"Oh! had he lived" is the mournful cry
  Of the weeping mother that bore him,
"Had he lived on some stricken field to die,
  Less sad would our grief be o'er him."

Not what is done but the wish and the will,
  Not the power but the heart of daring,
These make our pride when the dead lie still,
  And our heaviest grief we're bearing;
He gave to his country the hopes of youth,
  And he sleeps all darkly and lonely,
But our lov'd soldier boy has died for the truth,
  And his patriot grave is holy.

When the strife is o'er in some future year,
  And our nation's light is breaking,
Our soldier boys will be doubly dear,
  Those who died when the land was waking;
Let sweet roses bloom o'er his fair young head,
  And his tomb be honor'd in story,
For not one of the patriot army is dead,
  But has part in the nation's glory.

HENRY MORFORD.

## DEAD IN HIS YOUTH.

AT THE FIGHT AT BOONE COURT HOUSE, VA.,
SEPTEMBER 1ST, '61.

THE earliest ray of morn had brought
  The din of arms to many an ear,
And many a life was quickly bought
  And fitted for the narrow bier.
For hours the flash of muskets gleamed
  Along our ranks, from line to line—
For hours our shining bayonets beamed
  Like shifting spray upon the brine.

The day that flushed the summer sky
  At length had faded into night,
And many a star had risen high
  And dropp'd on earth its rays of light;
The pale moon rose above the hills,
  And coldly smiled upon the plain—
Its rays were riding on each rill,
  And resting on each battle-slain.

But one whose brow was young with years,
  Lies where the moonbeams kiss his brow!
Oh! ye who never shed warm tears,
  Come gaze—and shed them now.
See where the bullet pierced him through,
  And laid him in the pool of gore!
Upon his brow the pearly dew
  Of life will settle there no more.

This lad, he left his vine-clad hills
  To seek the treacherous battle-plain,
Where flows the blood like mountain rills
  From many a stalwart hero slain!
He was the first within the 'fray,
  The dash, the charge, or fight,
But now his brow of marble clay
  In death is ashy, cold and white.

Alas! that cruel death should take
  The life that filled his noble breast.
And sad that such a heart should break
  To take its last and only rest.
When parents watch for his return,
  His vine-clad hills among,
O! how their hearts will beat and burn
  To learn that he will ne'er come home.

Alas! I wonder if that heart will break
  Within his aged mother's breast,
When she shall learn her son's sad fate,
  And where he takes his lonely rest?
Alas! for her, the gentle maid,
  Who lonely waits his fond return!
She soon shall know that 'neath the shade,
  The pine tree is her lover's urn.

ANONYMOUS

## LOYAL AMERICA.

### THE FIRST APPEAL FOR A NATIONAL LOAN.

SEPTEMBER 2D, '61.

AMERICA ! dear Native Land,
I love thee tenderly and true ;
My heart clings to thy verdant strand,
And pines without thy sky of blue ;
Thy hills and vales, and woods and brakes,
Thy falls and rivers, springs and lakes,
Within my heart pure rapture wakes,
And life with new-born joys endue !
Thou art the work of God's own hand,
Sweet home of peace and rest,
I love thee, oh, my Native Land,
Of all the world the best !

America ! dear Native Clime,
My very soul exalts in thee,
When I peruse the Book of Time,
And trace therein thy history ;
The deeds of sire and of son,
The battles fought, the triumphs won,
The power gained, ere thou had'st run
That round of time—one century !
Which is the work of God's own hand,
Sweet home of peace and rest ;
I love thee, oh, my Native Land,
Of all the world the best !

America! dear Natal Place,
  Thy glory is my greatest pride;
Thy arm enwraps the human race,
  And o'er its destinies preside;
Where e'er man's vent'rous foot may wend,
There thine influence doth extend,
And with the foes of Right contend,
  And Despots galling chain divide!
    Such is the work of God's own hand,
    Sweet home of peace and rest,
    I love thee, oh! my Native Land,
    Of all the world the best!

America! dear Place of Birth,
  I turn from all the world to thee,
There is no other spot on earth,
  Where feels my soul that it is free;
Thy beauty is my heart's delight,
Thy power is my manhood's might,
Thy glory is the whole world's light,
  A Nation's hallow'd Trinity!
    All is the work of God's own hand,
    Sweet home of peace and rest;
    I love thee, oh, my Native Land,
    Of all the world the best.

J. HENRY HAYWARD.

## THE SOLDIER'S BRIDE.

BATTLE OF CORNIFEX FERRY, VA.

SEPTEMBER 10TH, '61.

AFAR upon the battle-plain,
  The dewy eve descended,
Where our young Henry dying lay,
  Amid the dead untended.
The pulse of life was ebbing fast,
  His eyes were dim already,
His feeble voice was faint and low,
  *His gory hand unsteady!*

"Oh God!" the dying soldier cried,
  "If she were only here—"
When "Henry! Henry," through the gloom,
  Rang in his dying ear.
Then fondly clasped within her arms,
  She kissed his marble brow,
He only smiled—his spirit passed,
  *For death had claimed him now!*

"Awake! awake! my own beloved!"
  The frantic maiden cried;
Then sorrowing sunk upon his corpse,
  And ere the morn she died!
Now calmly sleeping on that plain,
  They've laid them side by side;
Secure from all the storms of life,
  The soldier and his bride!

W. A. DEVON.

## THE BIVOUAC.

SKIRMISH AT LEWINSVILLE, VA.,
SEPTEMBER 11TH, '61.

THE camp is all quiet—my comrades are sleeping—
They dream of their homes, and loved ones dear,
The slow rising moon, with its light gently creeping,
Shows eyelids now wet with the slow falling tear,

There lays a young soldier—in years but a boy—
His musket beside him—cold pillow of steel—
The weapon to him is a pride and a joy,
As he dreams to the traitor a death it will deal.

And he dreams, too, of hearts that anxiously fear
Each bulletin sad with its grim battle story,
May tell that he, whom they all love so dear,
Is in death lying low in his youth—yet in glory,

A stern visaged man is lying near by—
Fitfully sleeping, and fitfully dreaming—
His country he loves—for that country he'll die—
His brow this reveals in the moonlight's gleaming.

Thus resting in groups, on this now peaceful spot,
Lie father and brother—the lover, the son,
To-morrow to waken 'midst rattling of shot,
The shrieks of the wounded, and war of the gun.

When the next risen sun shall have sunk in the West,
And the next evening stars shine o'er us on high,
Those sleeping here now, will take their last rest
'Neath the sod where they fight but to gallantly die!

ANONYMOUS.

## WITH THE SLAIN.

BATTLE OF ELK WATER, VA.
SEPTEMBER 11TH, '61.

IN homes of affluence and wealth,
'Mid joy and gayety,
Where live the poor and lowly,
In haunts of misery.
In city, town and village,
On mountain hill and dale,
Where sunshine is, or nature blooms,
Is heard the low sad wail.

The young wife anxiously watches,
From morn 'till close of day,
Praying and weeping the whole night long,
For a husband far away.
In vain she sobs his dear loved name,
Tho' hope hath nearly fled,
But still she weeps, and hopes and sighs,
Nor dreams that he is dead,

The mother thinks of her only boy,
Her joy, her hope, and pride,
And pictures scenes of happiness,
Her darling by her side.
But far away from friends and home,
On the dreaded battle plain,
Regardless of all care and strife,
He numbers with the slain.

And fathers, mothers, sisters, all
Sigh, and weep, and mourn
For brothers, lovers, kindred dear,
Friends that will ne'er return.
Our country calls for great rejoicing,
  We've gained a victory,
But who can stay those sighs and tears,
  This grief and misery.

FRANCIS B. MURTHA.

## THE AMERICAN TRAITOR'S CURSE.

DEATH OF THE REBEL COLONEL, JOHN WASHINGTON.
SEPTEMBER 12TH, '61.

GOD of the Just, the True, the Free!
Let now a curse descend from Thee
A curse pure, glorious and grand
As ever breathed for Freedom's land.
God of the Free! O, hurl *Thy* curse
On traitors through the Universe—
The wretches who have dared to strike
  Our Union's Altar and the Laws
That great Columbia's patriots made
  For Liberty's and Virtue's cause!
May famine waste their dastard frames!
May History blast their hated names!
May all their memories be hurled
In horror through the shuddering world,
And let their *praises* only swell
Around the snake-wreathed walls of Hell!

FRANCIS CADDELL.

## THE BIRTH OF OUR BANNER.

DESTRUCTION OF THE U. S. DOCK, PENSACOLA, FLA.

SEPT. 12TH, '61.

WHEN the dawn of creation was breaking,
To usher in bright balmy day,
The Goddess of Light, at her waking,
Was shrouded with curtains of spray,
That rose as the incense of morning,
From valleys resplendent with dew,
To deck the broad ocean of distance
In tints of the Red, White and Blue.

And far in the blue dome of Heaven,
Where stars with a soft, holy ray,
That have shown in an unbroken union
While ages have moldered away:
And Freedom, when journeying hither,
The earth with its blessings to strew,
Has gathered these trophies of glory,
As gems for the Red, White and Blue.

When man braved the wrath of Jehovah
The flood-gates of Heaven arose
To deluge the earth in His anger,
And drive from existence His foes;
Still justice was tempered with mercy—
On cloud-crested banners He drew
His promise to all generations,
In symbols of Red, White and Blue.

And thus is our Banner of Freedom,
  But tints of the glories above
Of Him who has made us a nation,
  And bound us with garlands of love—
Which none on the earth shall dissever,
  But each on our altars renew
The oath of unshaken devotion,
  And trust in the Red, White and Blue.

ROBERT M. HART.

## THE ATTACK AND REPULSE.

REBEL ATTACK AT CHEAT MOUNTAIN, VA.,

SEPTEMBER 12TH, '61.

It is midnight, and a silence
  Hangs about the tented camp,
Only broken in its stillness
  By the watchful sentry's tramp,
By the sighing of the breezes
  Through the branches of the pines,
Or the watchword, softly whispered,
  As we pass along the lines.

Soldiers sleeping, sweetly dreaming,
  Of their homes far, far away,
Where the loved ones, kind and gentle,
  Weary wait and watchful pray—
Resting now for that to-morrow
  Which may call them to the fray—
Gath'ring strength by nature's aiding—
  Strength their brother men to slay.

Day is dawning, dimly, grayly,
  In the border of the sky,
And the bugle soon will banish
  Sleep from ev'ry soldier's eye.
Hark! a roaring like the tempest
  When it breaks among the trees—
Like the simoon when it sweepeth
  O'er the breast of India's seas!

Up and arm ye! Sound the bugle!
  Not the tempest which ye hear:
'Tis the thunder of the war steeds—
  'Tis the sound of foemen near!
Like the whirlwind on they're rushing!
  Like them come, but come to die—
Finding foemen ever ready
  For the fray, but not to fly!

Form battalions, calm and steady;
  Let each aim be sure and true—
Let each "bullet find its billet"—
  They are many, we are few!
There they darken—*fire!* Now hearken
  To the shriek and to the groan—
Fix your bay'nets—charge ye boldly!
  Nobly done—the battle's won!

EDWARD C. JUDSON.

## THE BROTHERS' LAST MEETING.

AT THE ATTACK ON BOONVILLE, MO.,

SEPTEMBER 13TH, '61.

They bore him away from his first red field
  That warrior young and brave,
While the clear starlight of a Southern night
  Fell still on his open grave.

In his cloak they wrapped his slumb'ring form,
  Those comrades stern and grim;
Their steps were slow and their voices low!
  And their eyes with tears were dim.

No mother's kiss on his brow is pressed;
  No sister is weeping by;
No solemn prayer, on the evening air,
  Goes up to the star-gemmed sky.

But tearless and white, in the ghastly light,
  One form beside him stood:
His heart stood still, for his gleaming sword
  Was bathed in a brother's blood.

Through the long, long day had the battle raged,
  And when twilight's veil was drawn,
Like a peaceful dream, over hill and stream,
  Still War's red tide surged on.

Two warriors met by a murmuring rill,
  Now tinged with a crimson hue,
Sol's last rays show but the garb of foe,
  And their words are stern and few.

"Draw and defend!" and the flashing light
  Springs bright from the ringing steel.
Rise not, O moon! for thy light too soon
  Will a fearful scene reveal.

The stars looked down, and a boyish form,
  With his brown hair dim with blood,
'Neath their brightness lay, while fast away
  Life ebbed with the crimson flood.

"Mother"—the tone, with the dying moan,
  From his pale lips floated low
But a fount was stirred, by that voice and word,
  That surged to the victor's brow.

It brought the dream of his childhood back,
  The dream of youth's happy day,
Of a flowery dell, where the shadows fell
  On the streamlets flashing play.

He thought of one who each sport had shared,
  That boy with his mother's brow,
Whose steps had strayed from the roof tree's shade,
  Where, where is that wanderer now?

Sweet thoughts of home, with its softening love,
  Came swift in the twilight's hush,
And he bent him low o'er the fallen foe,
  To stay the life blood's gush.

But Death was there, and the pallid lips
  The smile of childhood bore;
With Crime and Pain, on the battle plain.
  The brothers meet once more.

He sleepeth well, in the silent dell,
  By the Cumberland's blue wave,
But the brother in vain, 'mid the fiery rain,
  Hath sought for a warrior's grave!

ANONYMOUS.

## THE LITTLE SOLDIER.

SKIRMISH AT SHEPARDSTOWN, VA.
SEPTEMBER 14TH, '61.

" O WOULD I were a soldier,"
  Cried little Bertie Lee;
" If I were only older,
  How very brave I'd be:
I'd fear not any danger,
  I'd flee not from the foe,
But where the strife was fiercest
  There I'd be sure to go.

" I'd be the boldest picket,
  Nor fear the darkest night,
Could I but see a rebel,
  How bravely I would fight.
I'd nobly do my duty,
  And soon promoted be—
O, would I were a soldier,"
  Sighed little Bertie Lee.

"But when I'm grown to manhood,
This war will all be o'er;
I cannot join the struggle
Our dear flag to restore.
I may not bleed for Freedom,
That glory's not for me,
My name will not be written
The hero, Herbert Lee."

Then answered Bertie's mother,
In tender, loving tone,
"My darling little Bertie,
You need not thus bemoan.
A noble strife awaits you,
'Tis even now begun,
And you may gain the victory,
If brave and true, my son,

"You are a little soldier,
A picket guard, my boy,
To ward off every evil,
That may your soul annoy.
No earthly foe need vex you;
No midnight sounds alarm—
With Jesus for your leader,
What could my darling harm?

"The noblest of all soldiers
My little son may be,
His name in heaven recorded.
The hero, Herbert Lee.
That were far higher glory
Than any earthly fame;
God grant the list 'promoted'
May bear my Bertie's name."

ARAYLAND.

## DYING ON THE BATTLE-FIELD.

AT BARNESTOWN, MD.

SEPTEMBER, 15TH, '61.

MOTHER, mother—not another
  Can thy holy place supply;
I am pining for the twining
  Of thy arms, once ere I die.
Never my sorrow knew a morrow
  When thy love shone on thy boy;
Tear-drops vanished—pain was banished—
  Patience by thy side was joy.

Mother, mother—haste, sweet mother!
  Bend beside my cot the knee;
Lift entreaty—Heaven will pity;
  Help me in this agony.
In the rattle of the battle
  Fought I well the trait'rous foe;
O, my gleaming blade was streaming—
  Loyalty sent home each blow.

Come, then, mother! there's no other
  Touch like thine for my poor brow!
Lowly sighing, I am dying—
  Lay thy dear hand on me now.
Mem'ry's bringing soft thy singing,
  As on childhood's ear it fell;
Love most gracious—now so precious—
  Hark! "HE doeth all things well."

LAURA ELMER.

## WAITING FOR NEWS.

### CAPTURE OF CAMP TALBOT, MO.

### SEPTEMBER 16TH, '61.

WAITING, O Father! a fond mother waiting,
Waiting *so* anxious, the dark tide's abating!
Waiting all breathless, in agonized anguish,
Living by heart-throbs that spring up—then languish;
Catching each sound that comes back from the battle,
Dark shrieks and groans and the lonely death rattle,
Imagining visions of feverish thirsting—
Hearts in their utterest lonliness bursting!

Thinking of *him* late the babe of her bosom,
Fair-faced and blue-eyed, love's tenderest blossom,
Dashing along 'mid the carnage around him,
Fearless as Mars 'mid the balls that surround him,
Changed as by magic, from home's tender brother,
Lovingest son both to father and mother—
Changed to a man, to a stern, noble soldier—
None in the field that is braver or bolder!
Writing: "I'm proud of the name, dearest mother!
Craven is he who would hold any other
While our loved standard of freedom's in danger,
May he forever be held as a stranger!"
Such are the words in his last noble letter!
What fifteen years that could write any better?
Now I am waiting to know if he's wounded—
Waiting to know—how my fears must be bounded:
Closed his eyes *may* be to sorrow and danger—
Dead he *may* be in the land of the stranger!

God of the desolate—Rachael's Consoler!
Light of the universe—Nature's Controller!
Pity me, pity me! Send consolation!
Let not my heart feel this deep desolation!
He is *so* young and he loves me so truly—
Scourge me not, Father! so deep—so unduly!
Leave him! to lighten my life-load of sorrow!
Leave him to brighten the clouds of my morrow!
Leave him to love me when other loves fail me,
Leave him to strengthen when rude storms assail me!
Leave him—so kind, both as son and as brother;
Leave him, a future of hope to his mother!
God of all battles, speed, speed this decision!
Let us not look, as afar, at a vision!
Send to our soldiers the true men to lead them!
*They* have the courage, do Thou guide and speed them!
Then shall our sisters, our wives, and our mothers,
Feel that our husbands, our sons, and our brothers,
Though they may fall, are not led to the altar,
Heedless and reckless, like beasts by the halter!
Then we may feel, though their dear blood is staining
Freedom's fair banner, a *country* we're gaining!
Then we may look, though with eyes dim and burning,
Some day or other, their blessed returning!
Or we may see, though with eyes dim with weeping,
Freedom's bird hover in love o'er their sleeping:
Feeling, though sorrow may make our heads hoary,
They are not victims of weakness, but glory!

J. C. DAVIS.

## OUR COUNTRY'S DEAD.

AT BLUE MILLS LANDING, MO.

SEPTEMBER 17TH, '61.

THEY live to God, they live to God,
  Though gone from human sight!
The good and brave, who left their homes
  To battle for the right.

To thee, O God, they still live on,
  Though ceased their mortal strife;
And wait the triumph of the cause,
  More dear to them than life,

In sight of men they seem to die,
  And perish from the earth;
But Thou dost give them, even here,
  A new, immortal birth.

Though chastened for a little time,
  Thou dost reward their pain;
To die, to suffer for the right,
  Is, e'en on earth, a gain.

For to their Country still they live,
  And, on her roll of fame,
Recorded shall forever stand
  Each brave and honored name.

D. C. BROWN.

## THE EMPTY SLEEVE.

AFTER THE BATTLE OF MARIATOWN, MO.

SEPTEMBER 17TH, '61.

BY the moon's pale light, to a gazing throng
Let me tell one tale, let me sing one song;
'Tis a tale devoid of an aim or plan,
'Tis a simple song of a one-armed man.
Till this very hour I could ne'er believe
What a tell-tale thing is an empty sleeve,
What a weird, queer thing is an empty sleeve.

It tells in a silent tone, to all,
Of a country's need, and a country's call,
Of a kiss and a tear for a child and wife,
And a hurried march for a nation's life;
Till this very hour who could e'er believe
What a tell-tale thing is an empty sleeve,
What a weird, queer thing is an empty sleeve?

It tells of a battle-field of gore—
Of the sabre's clash—of the cannon's roar—
Of the deadly charge—of the bugle's note—
Of the gurgling sound in a foeman's throat—
Of the whizzing grape—of the fiery shell—
Of a scene that mimics the scenes of hell.
Till this very hour would you e'er believe
What a weird, queer thing is an empty sleeve?

Though it points to myriad wounds and scars,
Yet it tells that a flag, with the stripes and stars,
In God's own chosen time will take
Each place of the rag with the rattlesnake;
And it points to a time when that flag shall wave
O'er land where there breathes no cowering slave,
To the top of the skies let us all then heave
One proud huzza for the empty sleeve—
For the one-armed man with the empty sleeve!

WILMOT.

## THINK OF ME, DEAREST.

SKIRMISH NEAR COLUMBUS, KY.
SEPTEMBER 18TH, '61.

"Think of me, dearest," the young soldier said,
As he clasped a fair maid to his resolute heart,
"It is but for a time, a very short time,
I'll come back again, never more to depart;
And I'll think of you, darling, when far, far away,
I march to the time of the drum and the fife,
Your smiles like bright sunbeams will brighten my path
Where ever I go, sweet pearl of my life.

"The war-cry is raised from the East to the West,
Our country's in danger and needs every arm,
Though terrors surround me, I'll still struggle on,
Your prayers my dear girl will shield me from harm.
Oh! how happy the dawning of that sunny morn,
That will welcome me back to friends and to thee,
With America's name still unblemished and pure,
'The home of the brave and the land of the free.'"

FRANCIS B. MURTHA.

## MOTHER, I'VE COME HOME TO DIE.

AFTER THE CAPITULATION OF LEXINGTON, MO.,
SEPTEMBER 20TH, '61.

DEAR mother, I remember well
  The parting kiss you gave to me,
When merry rang the village bell,
  My heart was full of joy and glee;
I did not dream that one short year
  Would crush the hopes that soar'd so high!
Oh, mother dear, draw near to me,
  Dear mother, I've come home to die.

Hark! mother, 'tis the village bell,
  I can no longer with thee stay;
My country calls to arms, to arms,
  The foe advance in fierce array!
The vision's past—I feel that now
  For country I can only sigh;
Oh, mother dear, draw near to me,
  Dear mother, I've come home to die.

Dear mother, sister, brother, all,
  One parting kiss, to all good-bye;
Weep not, but clasp your hand in mine,
  And let me like a soldier die!
I've met the foe upon the field
  Where kindred fiercely did defy;
I fought for right. God bless the flag!
  Dear mother, I've come home to die.

G. W. H. GRIFFIN.

## TOGETHER.

STORMING OF THE TOWN OF ROMNEY, VA.

SEPTEMBER 24TH, '61.

TOGETHER! together! Oh, why should we part?
Together in hand, together in heart!
Shoulder to shoulder, as ever before,
Oh, still let us strive for the Union of yore!

Oh, well may we bleed, as our forefathers bled,
For Liberty dies when the Union is dead.
Then, still let us cling to the Union of old;
It is better than all of our lives and our gold.

Northerner, Southerner, still you are one,
Spite of the foul deeds that traitors have done—
Spite of your bloodshed and spite of your hate!
Living or dying you are joined in your fate.

As one you have risen: as one you must fall;
And one flag or no flag must float over all,
For better or worse we've plighted our troth,
And the ruins of Union must bury us both.

Then bloody and long though the contest may be,
Our freemen must fight for the cause of the Free,
Though rivers of blood may yet deluge the land,
Our heart must not fail us, nor slacken our hand.

No counting the cost! for the Union is worth
All the lives of the South and lives of the North;
For what is of value to you and to me,
If the stars shall be torn from the flag of the Free?

Together! together! Join hands once again!
Though years be before us of toil and of pain.
Together! together! we conquer or fall;
For one flag or no flag must float over all!

ANONYMOUS

---

## THE DEVASTATION OF WAR.

SKIRMISH NEAR CHAPMANSVILLE, VA.,

SEPTEMBER 25TH, '61.

By the blue Potomac waters',
By the Rappahannock's line,
By the sunny Southern rivers,
'Neath the holly and the pine.
Falling in the shock of battle,
Wounded, in their blood they lie—
Pining with the dark malaria—
So our wounded patriots die.

In the city, in the village,
In the hamlet far away,
Sits the mothers, watching waiting
For their soldier boys to-day.
They are coming—daily coming,
One by one, and score by score,
In their leaden casings folded,
Underneath the flag they bore.

Thinks the mother, weeping, wailing,
  And expectant all the day—
When his regiment was summoned,
  How her soldier went away;
With his bayonet a-gleaming,
  With his knapsack on his back,
With his blanket strapped and folded—
  And his home-filled haversack.

Thinking of the courage swelling,
  In his eye and in his heart,
Though a manly tear was rolling,
  When he kissed her to depart;
Thinking of his precious letters
  Written by the Camp-fires glow,
Rich in love of home and country,
  And for her who made him go.

Counting now the lagging moments
  For the knocking at the door;
For the shuffling and the tramping
  Feet of strangers on the floor;
Bringing in their precious burden,
  Leaving her to grief and tears;
To the sorrow and the mourning,
  Darkening all the coming years.

DARLING.

## OUR BIRTH-RIGHT—LIBERTY.

A NATIONAL ANTHEM.

FIRST NATIONAL FAST DAY.

SEPTEMBER 26TH, '61.

GOD of Heaven, kind and mighty,
  Thou who gave us Liberty;
Still watch o'er us as thy People,
  And sustain us ever free;
Oh, preserve the Constitution,
  And intact the Union keep,
Sacred as the soil where lieth
  Washington in tranquil sleep!

Lord of Hosts, whose grace endureth,
  Thro' all time, forever more,
Let Thy wisdom guide our nation
  Safely thro' the gloom of war;
Let Thy glory be our glory,
  And thy might our power be,
To preserve our hope—the Union,
  And our Birthright—Liberty!

J. HENRY HAYWARD.

## THE END OF GLORY.

FIGHT AT LUCAS' BEND, KY.,
SEPTEMBER 26TH, '61.

"How hot the night! Its stifling breath
Seems charg'd with pestilential death;
The drowsy night winds scarcely stir
The plumy tassels of the fir.
Scarce flaps the curtains of my tent,
Thro' whose loop'd folds the firmament
With all its soft, celestial light
Shines on my feverish sense to-night.
Here in my tent I lie at last,
While life's dull surge is ebbing fast,
This is the ending of the dream
That lured me with its pageant gleam;
Touch'd my young spirit with the flame
Of glory and immortal fame.
Yet I repine not. It was sweet
That onward march thro' square and street;
The rolling of the war-like drum;
The shout of multitudes—the hum
Of crowds—the flaunt of banners gay,
While votive garlands strew'd the way;
All this was glorious—yet I mourn
I ne'er as victor may return."

"'Tis well nigh o'er! The damps I feel
Of death upon my senses steal;
Scarce can my fading, glazing eye
The tent, the flag, the heavens descry,
And yet o'er fancy's mystic glass
Old scenes in long procession pass;
Friends, father, mother, kindred bend
Above me, drawing to my end!
Was it the whisper of the breeze
That sobb'd and shivered o'er the trees,
That stirr'd the flapping tent but now,
And seem'd to breathe upon my brow?
Or rather was it not the sigh
Of home, that whispered, fluttering by?
O! mother, give one last caress,
Bend o'er these pallid lips to press;
I know the fervor of thy love,
Come, then, like angel from above;
Yield one embrace, one parting prayer,
To waft my spirit thro' the air.
A vain delusion! Far away
In Northern lands my brethren play;
Full many a long mile lies between
My kindred and this final scene;
I know that never more may fall
My footsteps in my father's hall!"
He died—then Carolina's grave
Closed o'er the ashes of the brave.
His comrades bore him to his rest,
While battle-flags drooped o'er his breast,
The muffled drum its requiem paid,
"Dust unto dust," the Chaplain said,
The volleying shot above him rose,
And the dead slumber'd in repose.

ISAAC M'CLELLAN.

## LETTERS FROM HOME.

BATTLE AT FALLS CHURCH, VA.,

SEPTEMBER 29TH, '61.

The day is passed with its march or drill,
  And the soldiers, tired of their lot in life,
Have gathered together, rare castles to build
  Of the times, when peace shall finish the strife;
Their sunburnt and bearded faces glow
  Hard and unmoved by the camp-fires bright;
They seem to be proof against hardships and woe,
  And their hearts to be callous to love and light.

But, hark! they hear some familiar sound,
  And quickly they hush the loud laugh and jest;
And yonder group drop their cards to the ground.
  And their pipes from their mouths to turn and list,
The mail has come! and quick to his feet
  The strong man springs like an eager child;
Is there naught for me? yes, here it is; sweet
  And cheering almost, as an old friend's smile.

But his smiles soon turn to groans, alas!
  As he reads that his loved one is ending her life,
And vainly calling for him to the last,
  And he murmurs, "O God! help the soldier's wife."
Near by stands one, reading, his face all aglow,
  Loving words from his own brave, true little wife;
There a boy, scarce twenty, whose unbidden tears flow,
  At his mother's warm prayers, for his welfare and life.

Here one reads that another is wooing his lady,
  And he clenches his fists with ferocious scowls;
Pat there, has his sheet, telling how little Teddy
  And the *other* pigs grow, bless their dear little souls.
But there stands one with an anxious face,
  Is there none for me? almost breathless he speaks,
No, that was the last; and he turns away,
  Ashamed of the tears on his sunburnt cheeks.

Would you deem a man less noble and brave,
  That the tears could stand upon his cheek?
The One who descended our souls to save,
  Did not disdain for sinners to weep.
The soldiers afar from their homes and their friends,
  Our prayers and our sympathies daily need.
O, do what you can to make them amends,
  For the life which, for our country, they lead.

O, write to them often! our brave soldier boys!
  Wives, mothers, and sisters, and sweethearts dear!
Write cheering and hopeful, of love, and the joys
  That await them again when peace shall reign here.
A letter from home hath a magic spell,
  To make them forget, for a time, all care,
In the thought that loved ones at home wish them well,
  And remember them often in thought and in prayer.

ANONYMOUS.

## LISTEN.

AFTER THE BATTLE OF GREEN BRIAR. VA.
OCTOBER 3D, '61.

LISTEN! did ye not hear that sound
Echoing from afar.
Faintly o'er the distant hills
Like some funeral car?
Did ye not hear that mournful cry
That agonizing prayer,
Which from many a burdened heart
Ascends in deep despair?

Listen! that same sad, mournful cry,
That same bewailing prayer,
Extends its cries from shore to shore,
With anguish rends the air!
For on yon blood-stained field
Full many a brother lies,
With upturned face and pleading look
The noble hero dies!

Listen! from yon battalions height
Each distant grassy plain
Where lie the gasping multitude
Of vanquished heroes slain!
That prayer doth rise in louder strains
With accents still more deep!
It is a plea for Heaven to aid
The *dear old flag* to keep.

Listen! along the garden walks
Of yonder cottage low,
A maiden treads the vine clad bower
With lingering steps, and slow,
A paper in her hand she holds
Which tells of victories won, and lost,
Of hard-earned fame, and manly toil,
Which blood and treasure both have cost.

Listen! she's reading the list of those
Who fell in the deadly strife,
Of those who in their country's cause
Delivered up their life.
But lo! her brother's name she spies
Ere half the list is read;
Her brother's name—Great God! is there,
Down with the ghastly dead!

Listen! a cry of deep despair,
A mournful cry of pain
She utters, while in tears she shrieks:
"My brother too, is slain!"
And then she glances once again
Upon the precious name,
Alas! there can be no mistake,
Her brother too, is slain!

Listen! how many, many groans
Are borne upon the air,
From hearts that's tasted of the cup
Of bitterest despair!
Great God! how long must we behold
Such bloody times as these?
How long ere Truth shall reign o'er all,
And Freedom kiss the breeze?

J. R. PENHOLLOW.

## MOTHER IS THE BATTLE OVER?

BATTLE OF BUFFALO HILL, KY.,

OCTOBER 3D, '61.

"MOTHER, is the battle over?
Thousands have been slain, they say,
Is my father coming?—tell me,
Have our soldiers gained the day?
Is he well, or is he wounded—
Mother, do you think he's slain?
If you know, I pray you, tell me,
Will my father come again?"

"Mother, dear, you're always sighing
Since you last the paper read,
Tell me why you now are crying,
Why that cap is on your head?
Ah!—I see you cannot tell me,
Father's one among the slain,
'Though he loved us very dearly,
He will ne'er come home again."

"Yes, my boy, your noble father
Is one numbered with the slain;
We no more on earth shall see him,
But in Heaven we'll meet again,
He died for the Union's glory,
Our day may not be far between,
But I hope, at the last moment,
That we all shall meet again."

SAWYER.

## "ONLY A PRIVATE KILLED."

### REBEL ATTACK ON SANTA ROSA ISLAND, FLA. OCTOBER 9TH, '61.

"WE'VE had a fight," a captain said,
"Much rebel blood we've spilled;
We've put the saucy foe to flight,
Our loss—but a private killed!"
"Ah, yes," said a sergeant on the spot,
As he drew a long deep breath,
"Poor fellow, he was badly shot,
Then bayoneted to death!"

When again was hushed the martial din,
And back the foe had fled,
They brought the private's body in;
I went to see the dead.
For I could not think the rebel foe,
Though under curse and ban,
So vaunting of their chivalry,
Could kill a wounded man.

A minie ball had broke his thigh,
A frightful, crushing wound,
And then with savage bayonets,
They pinned him to the ground.
One stab was through the abdomen,
Another through the head;
The last was through the pulseless breast,
Done after he was dead.

His hair was matted with his gore,
His hands were clenched with might,
As though he still his musket bore
So firmly in the fight:
He had grasped the foeman's bayonet,
His bosom to defend,
They raised the coat-cape from his face—
My God! it was my friend!

As, little he thought, that soldier brave,
So near his journey's goal,
That God had sent a messenger
To claim his Christian soul.
But he fell like a hero, fighting,
And hearts with grief are filled,
And honor is his, tho' our chief shall say,
"Only a private killed."

I knew him well, he was my friend;
He loved our land and laws;
And he fell a blessed martyr
To our country's holy cause.
And, soldiers, the time will come, perhaps,
When *our* blood will thus be spilled,
And then of us our chief will say,
"Only a private killed."

But we fight our country's battles,
And our hopes are not forlorn,
And our death shall be a blessing
To "millions yet unborn."
To our children and their children!
Then as each grave is filled,
What care we if our chief shall say,
"Only a private killed."

DEARTRAM.

## IN THE HOSPITAL.

### AFTER THE BATTLE OF LEBANON, MO.

### OCTOBER 13TH, '61.

Here is a hospital; its every floor
  Is thickly piled with dying and with dead;
And still they come, and there is room for more,
  To fill the place of those whom death has sped.
Each comer finds the sheets already warm
  With his last life breath who, a moment since,
Was carried out a corpse, whose broken form
  Upon the yielding couch has left its prints.

Shaded by lofty trees, shut in by swamps,
  A monster graveyard stretches out from here;
A pestilential spot, whose poisonous damps
  Press on the brain, and chill the heart with fear.
Daily it grows, and daily it claims its prey,
  Daily it opens wide its ravenous mouth,
A hundred men are added every day
  To this new, silent City of the South.

The air is heavy with the groans and sighs
  The tortur'd frames from stoutest hearts will force,
O God of peace, behold the sacrifice!
  Let the Peace-angel hither wing his course!
All do not die. Some struggle home again,
  With lopped-off limbs, a piteous sight to see,
And linger out a weary life of pain,
  Eating the bitter bread of charity.

ANONYMOUS.

## I AM WITH THEE.

CAPTURE OF LINN CREEK, MO.,

OCTOBER 14TH, '61

BROTHER, dearest, I am with thee,
  On thy marches long and drear,
And whatever fate betide thee,
  Think! O, think that I am near.

For I love thee, darling brother,
  With a sister's holy love;
Now we're parted from each other,
  But will never part above.

Brother, life hath many changes,
  Sad, and often hard to bear,
In the world much sorrow ranges,
  And we each must have a share.

Once my joy thou could'st not measure,
  Life had many charms for me,
Now I see the darker picture,
  Which I never dreamed I'd see.

May'st thou never know the sorrow,
  Never feel the pangs I've borne,
May sweet hope beam on each morrow,
  And thou ne'er have cause to mourn.

Know, then, brother, I am with thee,
  In the battle's dreadful strife,
And to save *thee* I would gladly,
  Willingly, yield up my life.

When the last dread battle's ended,
  And our glorious cause is won,
To the dear home thou'st defended
  Hasten, for thy work is done.

ANONYMOUS.

---

## VOLUNTEERED.

BEFORE THE FIGHT AT FREDERICK, MO.

OCTOBER 15TH, '61.

I KNOW the sun shines, and the lilacs are blowing,
  And Summer sends kisses by beautiful May—
Oh! to see all the treasures the Spring is bestowing,
  And think—my boy Willie enlisted to-day!

It seems but a day since at twilight low humming,
  I rocked him to sleep with his cheek upon mine,
While Robby the four-year old watched for the coming
  Of father, adown the street's indistinct line.

It is many a year since my Harry departed,
  To come back no more in the twilight or dawn;
And Robby grew weary of watching, and started
  Alone, on the journey his father had gone.

It is many a year—and this afternoon, sitting
  At Robby's old window, I heard the band play,
And suddenly ceased dreaming over my knitting
  To recollect Willie is twenty to-day;

That, standing beside him this soft May-day morning,
The sun making gold of his wreathed cigar-smoke,
I saw in his sweet eyes and lips a faint warning,
And choked down the tears when he eagerly spoke:

"Dear mother, you know those traitors are crowing,
They trample the folds of our flag in the dust;
The boys are all fire; and they wish I were going—"
He stopped, but his eyes said, "Oh say if I must!"

I smiled on the boy though my heart seemed breaking:
My eyes filled with tears, so I turned them away,
And answered him, "Willie, 'tis well you are waking,
Go, act as your father would bid you, to-day!"

I sit in the window and see the flags flying,
And dreamly list to the roll of the drum,
And smother the pain in my heart that is lying,
And bid all the fears in my bosom be dumb.

I shall sit in the window when Summer is lying
Out over the fields, and the honey-bees' hum,
Lulls the rose at the porch from tremulous sighing,
And watch for the face of my darling to come.

And if he should fall—his young life he has given
For Freedom's sweet sake—and for me I will pray
Once more with my Harry, and Robby in Heaven,
To meet the dear boy that enlisted to-day.

N. P. WILLIS.

## WHEN THIS CRUEL WAR IS OVER.

RECAPTURE OF THE CITY OF LEXINGTON, MO., OCTOBER 16TH, '61.

DEAREST love, do you remember,
 When we last did meet,
How you told me that you loved me,
 Kneeling at my feet?
Oh! how proud you stood before me
 In your suit of blue,
When you vow'd to me and country
 Ever to be true.

When the summer breeze is sighing
 Mournfully along;
Or when autumn leaves are falling,
 Sadly breaths the song.
Oft in dreams I see thee lying
 On the battle plain,
Lonely, wounded, even dying,
 Calling, but in vain.

If amid the din of battle
 Nobly you should fall,
Far away from those who love you,
 None to hear you call—
Who would whisper words of comfort?
 Who would soothe your pain?
Ah! the many cruel fancies
 Ever in my brain.

But our country called you, darling,
  Angels cheer your way;
While our nation's sons are fighting,
  We can only pray.
Nobly strike for God and Freedom,
  Let all nations see
How we love the starry banner,
  Emblem of the free.
    Weeping sad and lonely,
      Hopes and fears how vain!
    When this cruel war is over,
      Praying that we meet again.

CHARLES C. SAWYER.

## BURY HIM LOW AND DEEP.

AFTER THE ENGAGEMENT AT BOLIVAR HIGHTS, VA., OCTOBER 16TH, '61.

Bury him low and deep,
  Where the storm winds ne'er can find him,
To trouble his body's sleep,
  And of his lost world remind him.
Bury him low and deep.
  Nearer the promised to-morrow;
Over his form we will weep,—
  E'en soldiers may weep in sorrow.
Bury him low and deep.
  A lock of his hair first sever,
His mother would like to keep
  This relic of one gone forever.
Bury him low and deep!

GEORGE W. BIRDSEYE.

## GOD REAPS HIS JUDGMENT.

BATTLE OF PILOT KNOB, MO.

OCTOBER 16TH, '61.

GOD reaps his judgment-field to-day,
  And sifts the darnel from the wheat:
A whirlwind sweeps the chaff away,
  And fire the refuge of deceit.

In vain a nation's bloody sweat,
  The sob of myriad hearts in vain,
If the scotched snake may live to set
  Its venom in our flesh again.

The lords of treason and the whip
  Have called us to the dread appeal,
From the loud cannon's fevered lip,
  And the wide flash of bristling steel.

If now the echo of that voice
  Shake down their prison house of wrong,
They have their own perfidious choice,
  For God is good, and Truth is strong.

Their steel draws lightning, and the bolt
  But fires their own volcanic mine;
God in their vineyard of Revolt
  Treads out his sacramental wine!

GEORGE S. BURLEIGH.

## FAREWELL.

SECOND FIGHT AT LYNN CREEK, MO.

OCTOBER 17TH '61.

Farewell ! farewell ! is often said
  By parting friends and lovers dear,
When hearts are full of holy love
  And naught but peace or joy is near.
'Tis sad at most e'en for a time,
  To part with those we highly prize,
But still more sad, when angels come
  Like clouds across the summer skies.

The cannon's roar, the steel's loud clash,
  The bugle's sound, the heavy tramp,
The chill bivouac, the lonely watch,
  The ambush, too, in marshy swamp,
Such thoughts as these shoot thro' the brain,
  When now we hear the sad good-bye,
The heart beats wild with dread and fear,
  And tears stand trembling in the eye.

It may, perhaps, be the last farewell,
  For ne'er may they return again,
But fall before the battle's breath,
  Numbered with the glorious slain.
Farewell ! farewell ! alas ! it sends
  A chill through every vital part
And dark forebodings creep around
  Deep in the altar of the heart.

FRANCIS B. MURTHA.

## COUNTRY OF WASHINGTON.

FIGHT AT BIG HURRICANE CREEK, MO.
OCTOBER 20TH. '61.

HAIL ! brightest banner that floats on the gale !
Flag of the country of Washington, hail!
Red are thy stripes with the blood of the brave,
Bright are thy stars as the sun on the wave ;
Wrapt in thy folds are the hopes of the Free;
Banner of Washington ! blessings on thee !

Mountain-tops mingle the sky with their snow;
Prairies lie smiling in sunshine below;
Rivers, as broad as the sea in their pride,
Border thine Empires, but do not DIVIDE;
Niagara's voice far out-anthems the sea ;
Land of Sublimity ! blessings on thee !

Hope of the World! on thy mission sublime,
When thou didst burst on the pathway of time,
Millions from darkness and bondage awoke;
Music was born when Liberty spoke ;
Millions to come yet shall join in the glee ;
Land of the Pilgrim's hope! blessings on thee;

Traitors shall perish, and treason shall fail;
Kingdoms and thrones in thy glory grow pale !
Thou shall live on, and thy people shall own,
Loyalty's sweet, where each heart is thy throne ;
UNION and FREEDOM thine heritage be ;
Country of Washington ! blessings on thee !

WILLIAM E. ROBINSON.

## THE HERO.

BATTLE OF BALLS' BLUFF, VA
OCTOBER 21ST, '61.

Rear high the banners on the city domes,
  Let trumpets sound and martial drums loud beat,
For lo! on prancing steed a hero comes
  To lay his triumphs at a nation's feet!

Along his pathway spread the cloth of gold,
  Fresh buds and leaves before his footsteps fling,
About his august person sagely fold
  The robe of State, and loud proclaim him King!

No envied gift of human Church or State,
  Is more than ye 'pon him must now bestow,
For he has bravely fought and conquered fate,
  And waded through vast seas of blood and woe!

His noble brow with laurels green entwine,
  His honored name on slabs of stone engrave,
Let him not die—who worship the sublime,
  E'en though his form sinks in a mortal grave!

Yea, he must fill a grave—as all must fill,
  No homage ye confer can cheat old Death,
He, seeking honor, did not pause to kill
  Though pausing cost him but an empty breath!

He did not count the tears of anguish shed
  O'er graves, the imprint of his martial heel,
Why, then, should ye thus worship, who have bled,
  And weep for one, who for ye would not feel?

I marvel not, that fiends in human shape.
  Play with your passions, temper with your laws,
For one the issue to ye *lace* or *crape*,
  He always meets the popular applause!

And so will it continue while ye bow
  Your humble heads before the shrine of Mars,
Ye need expect naught else until ye vow
  To brand the Hero *as the cause of wars!*

J. HENRY HAYWARD.

---

## "IS THAT MOTHER."

### AT THE BATTLE OF FREDERICKTOWN, MO.

### OCTOBER, 21ST, '61

Is that mother bending o'er me,
  As she sang my cradle hymn—
Kneeling there in tears before me,
  Say?— my sight is growing dim.

Mother! oh, we bravely battled—
  Battled till the day was done;
While the leaden hail storm rattled—
  Man to man, and gun to gun.

But we failed—and I am dying—
  Dying in my boyhood's years—
There—no weeping—self-denying,
  Noble deaths demand no tears!

Fold your arms again around me;
  Press again my aching head,
Sing the lullaby you sang me—
  Kiss me, mother, ere I'm dead.

E. BOWERS.

## THE ORDERLY.

BEFORE THE BATTLE AT CAMP WILD CAT, MO.,
OCTOBER 21ST, '61.

"The corn is growing full, dear John,
The harvest moon more round;
Ere you come back the nuts will strew
The brown and barren ground.
But the husking will no frolic bring,
The nuts ungathered lie,
For I would not know them for the tears
Between them and mine eye.

"You're going to the war dear John
Far, far from love and me;
Would that I too, thy lot might share,—
O take me, John, with thee!"
He stooped his head for that caress
Her fair arms climbed to seek,
And fondly kissed where tears had plucked
The roses from her cheek!

Then lightly laughed, her fears to quell,
Till she smiled through her tears,
And gaily said, "How queer, to take
A maid of tender years?
Fitter some sturdy farmer lad,
To braid his horse's mane,
And other work that he would love,
And hold his bridle rein."

Loud is the boom and bright the flash,
  By that dark river's tide,
And wild the shriek, where hand to hand
  Fall brothers side by side.
Now seems the earth to lose its course
  'Neath the column's thundering charge;
While death rides swift on the leaden ball,
  With the freeman's breast its targe.

Out crawled a figure, bleeding, frail,
  Slow moving midst the slain;
And still it moaned and still it called:
  "O, tell me where he's lain!
She found him at the eventide,
  Sank on his shattered breast,
Laid low her cheek by his, and moaned:
  "I am weary, let me rest!"

Then came a dying whisper low:
  Don't be angry, will you, John?
I could not stay and pine at home
  When you and all were gone.
I only came to do your will—
  To hold your bridle rain,
And think I served my lover well
  When I combed his horse's mane."

His wavering breath was failing fast;
  Yet love has wondrous power,
And sometimes calls the fleeting life
  Back at the final hour.
"God bless you!" then his sad lips closed,
  His hand no more caressed;
And she who so had watched his life
  Lay dead upon his breast.

GRAMPUS GLOWARD.

## THE BADGE I WEAR.

ENGAGEMENT AT WEST LIBERTY, MO.,

OCTOBER 23D, '61.

Oh! dearer than life is the badge that I wear,
With its star knit of gold from my lady-love's hair!
Close over my heart like a blossom it grows—
Tri-colored, inodorous, gold-hearted rose!

When the bells of our village tolled out their alarms,
And the drums beat the music that called us to arms,
My darling, with steady, white hands, pinned it there,
While she said in a voice that was tender as prayer,

Its silver unjared by a shiver of fear:
"I give you to God and to Liberty, dear!
In the pride of your years, and strength of your youth,
My heart gives you up to the battle for truth."

To test her, I said: "When I go to my grave,
I'd rather my sweetheart were loving than brave.
Leave courage for men, but for women are fears,
The duty of prayers and the weakness of tears;"

"True love never dooms with so tranquill a pride,
Its objects to danger." She clung to my side;
All the patriot blood to her face leaped like flame
"True love, O my life, cannot clasp hands with shame!"

Our star-spangled flag shall not trail in the dust;
Live for me if you can, die for that if you must,
God make me a widow before I am wife,
If I prize not your honor as more than your life!"

Still further to try her, I took from its place
Her gift. The proud glow faded out of her face.
"Excuse me my dear, but your love's so divine,
It climbs quite beyond the discernment of mine.

"For your gift, many thanks! Tie it to your waist!
I have seen the same colors much more to my taste
In a different shape." Oh, her scorn, her surprise!
Oh, the lightnings that glowed in her beautiful eyes!

And after the lightnings flashed, torrents of rain,
And her voice smote my heart silver-sharp with pain.
"O traitor!" she cried, "may the Father above
Cast you out from His peace as I do from my love;

"May the land you desert never yield you a grave,
Or heaven claim the soul of so craven a slave!
False to Freedom—" I caught the words from her lips,
And kissed the wet eyes into sudden eclipse.

"Nay, listen dear love, to my plea," I replied,
"And spare me the rest of your anger and pride.
May God deal by me, as in purpose and deed,
By my country I deal in this hour of her need,

"But the mouth that touched mine just a moment ago,
These little soft hands that are colder than snow;
These eyes, rayed like stars, my kisses have pressed,
Are the red, white and blue in the shape I love best."

Oh! dearer than life is the badge that I wear,
With its star knit of gold from my lady-love's hair!
No traitor shall gather my tri-colored rose,
Except thro' my heart, the red soil where it grows.

God bless our dear country, and save her from spoil,
From the greedy home-vultures who blacken her soil;
In the name of these colors, all others above.
Of the lips, hands and eyes of the woman I love.

J. S. HUNT.

## A BATTLE HYMN FOR MIDSUMMER.

FIGHT AT SPRINGFIELD, MO.

OCTOBER 25TH, '61.

KING of the sword and shield,
Throned on each battle field;
    Hopeful and strong:
Look through the battle smoke,
Guide thou the battle stroke,
God who of yore hast broke
    The red ranks of Wrong.

Deeds crown our prayers with might;
Soldiers, strong in His right;
    Victory he leads:
War is His awful form,
Vengeance in our blood made warm,
'Gainst God in battle's storm
    Men are but reeds.

Close up your silent ranks,
Ransomed nations crown with thanks
Real soldiers bold;
Here is the gleaming steel,
Here is the cannon's peal,
Foes reel from those who kneel;
Strife for life is old.

One thought for home and land,
For them in Thy right hand
Our lives are given :
May peace with laurels bind,
Lives, loves in blood now signed;
They who lose life shall find
The life of Heaven.

Charge with a line of fire!
Charge to the sounding lyre
Of battle's shock;
Hands red with blood are white
In Duty's holy light;
God is the patriot's might,
The martyr's Rock.

God of our father's fame,
Save sons by battle flame
From Freedom's night;
One flag o'er Fatherland;
One realm from strand to strand;
One fame of Freedom's band,
God speed the right!

REV. N. N. CHAMBERLAIN.

## THE VOLUNTEER'S RETURN.

AFTER THE BATTLE OF WOODBURY, KY.,

OCTOBER 29TH, '61.

Sweet home! Young father, wert thou here,
To look upon your latest born,
'Twould be the happiest of the years,
This fresh and smiling April morn.
Young mother! pale and wan thou art,
'Tis hard to suffer thus alone.
Thank God that hope yet fills thy heart,
That prayer can mingle with thy moan.

Well may thy mother cherish thee,
Sweet baby-boy, whose infant prattle
Shall please him when from duty free,
And perils of the camp and battle,
He seeks his quiet home again,
And, numbering o'er thy childish charms,
Forgets his former toil and pain,
Unheeding war or war's alarms!

Next June will surely see him here,
Forever free of camps and wars;
And will he be a jot less dear,
If worn, and maimed, and gashed with scars?
Ah, no! though lopped and bruised his frame,
Our tears of joy will blind our eyes,
If they but leave his heart the same,
They leave enough for us to prize.

EDWARD WILLIS.

## OMNIBUS AND COUPE.

ATTACK ON MORGANTOWN, KY.

OCTOBER 31st, '61.

We were school-fellows once, Madame!
In many a struggle we bore the palm:
Our hands were in girlish friendship knit,
Our hearts with unselfish lore were lit.
When we talked of the future we twain were one,
In a common channel our dreams would run,
Of Love as pure as the purest gold,
Of Friendship that never was bought nor sold,
Till we floated along on the stream of Time
Fast linked together as rhyme with rhyme.
But I ride in an omnibus down Broadway,
While you dash by in your grand coupe.

You married, I hear, a millionaire,
Your house is fine and your jewels are rare;
Misty with lace or rich with shawls,
You lounge through concerts or float through balls.
When men address you, they speak in tune;
To hold your fan is a precious boon;
And it seems as if Nature was half unkind
That it does not perfume the very wind
That blows about you, and softens down
To music the roar of the noisy town.
But I am not envious to see you gay,
And happy, and rich, in your grand coupe.

I married Charlie, your husband's clerk,
Whose life was duty, honor, and work,
And we somehow contrived, in our humble way,
To be very happy, and free, and gay;
For my husband was honest, and brave, and kind,
With a delicate heart, and a cultured mind;
And the gifts he gave me, though few and cheap,
Were set in a frame-work rich and deep—
A frame-work of Love that never grows old,
But was clear as diamond and solid as gold:
So I do not envy in any way
Your wealthy husband or grand coupe.

Your husband every day, Madame,
Drives down to business well-dressed and calm;
But my Charlie is off where the muskets shine,
And the picket stretches his sleepless line,
And the sullen ring of the distant gun
Tells of a battery lost and won.
It was hard to part while our love was new,
But the country called him—what could I do?
So I kissed his lips, and bade him go,
And strike for our banner one hearty blow;
And I am prouder of him, in his honest gray,
Than you of your husband and grand coupe.

ANONYMOUS

## THE SOLDIER'S DREAM.

EVE OF THE BATTLE AT PLATTE CITY, MO.
NOVEMBER 2D, '61.

HE lay in his tent,
With his blanket around him,
While visions of home
Were thronging his brain,
Till his eyelids grew heavy,
And the goddess of slumber
Threw round him her fetters—
Her soft rosy chain.

His couch was a hard one,
His knapsack a pillow,
And the cold wind was whistling
Around him so drear,
But he heeded them not,
For again he was crossing
The threshold where gathered
The loved ones so dear.

How they start at the sound
Of the dearly loved footstep,
And spring to his arms
With a glad cry of joy;
The father, the mother,
The dearly loved sisters;
How gladly they welcome
Their dear soldier boy.

The wind whistles still,
And the camp fires are burning,
And gleaming far out
On the dark troubled sky.
But *another* fond heart
'Gainst his own is now beating,
And rapture lights up
Each fond loving eye.

Soft arms are around him,
And eyes gently beaming
Look into his own
With their soft loving light;
The mother's soft voice,
Her glad tearful greeting,
Thrill his heart with emotions
Of purest delight,

How familiar is all
In that dear home dwelling;
How brightly the fire
Gleams out on the wall;
How tempting the viands
Spread out on the table,
As in olden times round it
Now gather they all.

Ah, the soldier boy now
Has forgotten the morrow;
His dreams are so vivid,
His slumber so deep,
Forgotten that perils
And hardships surround him,
That the morrow perhaps
The foe he may meet.

Ah, soldier boy, soldier boy,
Dreaming on still,
How blissful, how real,
Thy visions now seem;
The sweet gentle face
Upturned to thine own—
Ah, can it be? can it be
Only a dream?

Aye, hark now, the sound
Of the clear shrill trumpet
Arousing the sleepers
From a soft pleasant dream.
He starts—ah the change;
Around and above him
The camp-fires shine out
With their wild lurid gleam.

Stern hearts are around him;
The tread of the warriors,
The clanking of arms.
Now fall on his ear;
His blanket is 'round him
His knapsack a pillow;
And far from his home
And his loved ones, so dear.

SARAH L. MILES.

## WHEN HE IS AWAY.

CAPTURE OF HOUSTON, MO,

OCTOBER 4TH, '61.

OUR dear, loving Charlie has gone from us now,
He has left his white cottage, his babe, and his plow;
And although Hattie laughs in her cradle at play,
She only reminds me that he is away.

His portrait hangs up, and so gay on the wall,
With his steel-buttoned coat, and his sword, cap and all;
And his tall, gallant form to his sword gives display—
But, oh, I am lonely when he is away.

There's bushwackers and rebels—a riótous crew,
And our Uuion they'd rend it and cleave it in two;
But Charles is for Union, though cost what it may,
And from home, wife, and cottage, it calls him away

During each bloody fight I have quaked in my fear,
For I know in his heart he would long to be there;
And although they have sung him in fame's gallant lay,
My heart still has languished, for he was away.

We've Génerals and Colonels, and Privates, and all,
And although he may rival, yet still he may fall;
And although fame and glory may now be his pay,
Their glare shines but dimly, for he's far away,

But now this dark war—oh, when shall it cease,
And all mustered home to their friends and at peace?
Then Hattie will kiss him, and smiling she'll say,
"Ma is weeping for gladness, for pa's not away."

GERSHOM WIBORN.

## A MOTHER'S OFFERING TO HER COUNTRY.

### AT THE BATTLE OF BELMONT, MO.

NOVEMBER 6TH, '61,

'TIS very hard to let thee go, my son,
And when I think of all which thou must meet—
The peril and the dangers thou must face—
My heart grows faint and bleeds with agony,
And I reach out my clasping arms to hold
Thee back; and while I press the tenderly,
Close to the breast that nourished thee, my child,
I cry, "O, God! I cannot, *cannot* let him go."

And yet, how can I bid thee *stay*, my son?
For when thou wast a little prattling boy
I made a little silken flag for thee,
And, while, with eager joy, you flung its folds
High out into the morning breeze and laughed,
And shouted out, "Hurrah! hurrah! hurrah!"
I told you what its wondrous meaning was,
And how our fathers fought and died for it;
And while you listened, I could see your heart
Throb'd bravely, and your brown eyes grew bright.

Your little form expanded proudly when
I said, "My son must love his country well;
So well that he would rather *die* than see
Its flag dishonored—trampled in the dust

By traitors!" Then, with firm and steady hand
You pressed its silken folds unto your lips,
And cried, "Hurrah! old flag, I'll sooner die
Than see you trampled 'neath a traitor's foot!"

And so I cannot bid thee stay with me,
In this dark hour of peril, though my heart
Is almost breaking with its weight of fear,
Of what may be, of what may come to thee
While thou'rt away.

I give thee up, my child,
My only child—and I a widow, too—
And if thou never should'st come back to me,
But fall a sacrifice unto thy love
Of our dear country, I will try to say,
"Thy will be done, O, God!" 'mid smiles of joy,
That I was blest with such a son to give.

CORA MAY.

## THE BANNER OF THE SEA.

AT THE CAPTURE OF PORT ROYAL, S. C.
NOVEMBER 7TH, '61.

Of all the flags that float aloft
O'er Neptune's gallant tars,
That wave on high in victory,
Above the sons of Mars,
Give us THE flag—Columbia's flag—
The emblem of the free,
Whose flashing stars blazed through our wars
For Truth and Liberty.

Beneath its folds we fear no foe,
  Our hearts shall never quail,
With bosoms bare the storm we'll dare,
  And brave the battle-gale;
And though the cannon plough our decks,
  The planks with gore run red,
Still through the 'fray our flag alway
  Shall gleam far overhead.

On every wave, to every shore,
  Columbia's flag shall go,
And through all time its fame sublime
  With brighter hues shall glow:
For Freedom's standard is our flag,
  Its guardians, Freedom's sons,
And woe betide the insulter's pride,
  When we unloose our guns.

Its enemies our own shall be,
  Upon the land or main;
Its starry light shall gild the fight,
  And guide our iron rain.
Nor foreign power nor treason's arts
  Shall shake our patriot love,
While with our life, in peace or strife,
  We'll keep that flag above
    Then dip it lads in ocean's brine,
      And give it three times three,
    And fling it out 'mid song and shout,
      The Banner of the Sea.

ANONYMOUS.

## BURIAL HYMN FOR THE UNION SOLDIERS.

AFTER THE BATTLE OF PIKETON, KY.

NOVEMBER 8TH, '61.

Cypress shall not o'er thee wave ;—
Laurel only for thy grave ;
Muffled drums shall never sound ;
But the trumpet thrill around;
Crape shall not our Banner shroud
It shall rustle bright and proud.
Even all the tears that fall,
Only gem thy glorious pall!

For such death as thine is great
Roses filled the hands of Fate ;
Honor proudly towered by,
Lightning leaping from her eye ;
Glory smiled upon thy form,
Falling in the Battle-Storm ;
Sacred heroes of the Past
Swelled thy name upon the blast !

Soldier of the Union, rest !
Lo ! a Nation guards thy breast !
With a larger, grand desire,
Freedom sweeps her mighty lyre
Lo ! the Immortal in her bloom
Writes upon thy sacred tomb,
"*Honor, Glory,* Union, *wave*
*Wreaths eternal o'er thy grave!*"

WILLIAM ROSS WALLACE.

## VIVA L'AMERICA.

SKIRMISH IN THE KANAWHA VALLEY, VA.,

NOVEMBER 10TH, '61.

NOBLE Republic! happiest of lands,
Foremost of nations Columbia stands;
Freedom's proud banner floats in the skies,
Where shouts of Liberty daily arise.
"United we stand, divided we fall,"
Union forever—freedom to all.
  Throughout the world our motto shall be,
  Viva l'America, land of the free.

Should ever traitors rise in the land,
Curs'd be his homestead, wither'd his hand;
Shame be his mem'ry, scorn be his lot,
Exile his heritage, his name a blot;
" United we stand, divided we fall,"
Granting a home and freedom to all.
  Throughout the world our motto shall be,
  Viva l'America, land of the free

To all her heroes, Justice and Fame,
To all her foes, a traitor's foul name;
Our "Stars and Stripes" still proudly shall wave
Emblem of Liberty, flag of the brave.
"United we stand, divided we fall,"
Gladly we'll die at our country's call.
  Throughout the world our motto shall be,
  Viva l'America, land of the free.

MILLARD

## OH! SENTRY! TELL ME OF THE NIGHT.

AT THE DESTRUCTION OF WARRINGTON, FLA.,
NOVEMBER 23D, '61.

OH, sentry, tell me of the night,
How dawns the slow approaching day?
Will darkness e'er give place to light?
Will this drear gloom ne'er pass away?
Can you discern a single star
Amid the low'ring clouds on high?
Is there no hope of *coming day?*
Oh! tell me sentry, ere I die!

Have courage, comrade! courage, man—
For though the night is dark and drear,
Tho' light'ning's flash and thunder's roll
Proclaim the howling storm is near.
Still 'neath the frowning clouds I see,
A faint streak in the north'ren sky;
While far and near on every hand,
I hear the picket's watchful cry.

Yes, sentry, 'tis the cry that woke
The north'ren legions from their sleep,
Then ev'ry heart cried—" Wake!—to arms,"
While mothers bow'd their heads to weep—
To think their children North and South,
Were thus arrayed in mortal fray;
But oh! my wounds—they bleed afresh,
Oh! tell me, sentry, of the day.

"Have courage, comrade: day is nigh,
  Tho' its approach is slow indeed,
And your unsightly bleeding wounds
  A mother's tender care must need:
But, see!—amid the threat'ning clouds,
  While earth with heaven's thunder jars,
I now behold amid the light,
  A *Constellation* of bright *Stars!*"

"I thank you, sentry, for those words,
  For eased would be my dying pain,
Could I but see the light of day
  Or those bright *Stars* shine once again.
But then, alas! I see no light,
  Except the rebel foe's watch fire,
These bleeding wounds obscure my sight,
  Tell me—of day—e'er I expire!"

"Have courage, comrade, look again;
  The light, which there your dim'd eyes greet,
Proceeds man, from the *burning stores*
  Of our base foe in wild retreat!
The Constellation of bright Stars,
  Which 'mid the clouds are shining thro',
Are those upon the Union Flag,
  As our brave boys the foe pursue!"

"Joy then is mine!—the day is ours!
  The sun of vict'ry soon will shine,
Again upon our country loved,
  And rescued by God's hand divine!
Oh! raise me, sentry, to my feet,
  Let me behold the foe's dismay,
There—gently—so:—I see them now—
  And our bright "Stars" Hurray!—Hurray!"

With that last cry of heart-felt joy
  The wounded soldier gave up life
To wake no more at reveille—
  To mingle never more in strife!
For him, shame not to drop a tear,
  Nor value light the fame he won,
*For men who thus their country serve*
  *Are quite as great as* WASHINGTON!

J. HENRY HAYWARD.

---

## THE BATTLE ARMOR.

BEFORE THE BATTLE AT LANCASTER, MO., NOVEMBER 24TH, '61.

THERE was deep and wond'rous meaning
  In the Northern legend old,
That when Eric forged his armor,
  From his lips an anthem rolled—
Rolled above the sounding anvil
  Diapasons high and brave,
Telling of the victor's laurel,
  Telling of the hero's grave.

There he stood, the swart and earnest,
  Turning in his brawny hands
Many a helmet on his anvil,
  For the knights of many lands;
And the high, heroic music,
  Mingling with the hammer's peal,
Gave to Eric's armor virtue
  Never known before to steel.

Over all shone Eric's helmets,
  In the van, like warrior-stars;
Dazzling, flashing, his sacred armor
  On the battle's sounding cars;
Helm and haukbert were enchanted
  In that old and wond'rous time—
For he made his simple smithy
  Glorious with the gallant rhyme.

Let us learn from that grand armor
  By the earnest Northman made,
What the loyal soul must fashion
  When the battle is arrayed—
When the Constitution's threatened,
  When the traitor-shadow falls,
When the trump of Truth is sounding
  Many a charge on Treason's walls.

'Tis the patriot's mighty armor:
  Forge it, nurse the gallant thought—
Thought to which a Stark and Warren
  All their mighty armor wrought;
Sword and cannon then enchanted
  By the patriotic flame,
Shall triumphant, bear us over
  Every dastard traitor's frame!

WILLIAM ROSS WALLACE.

## I DREAMED MY BOY WAS HOME AGAIN.

SECOND FIGHT AT VIENNA, VA.,

NOVEMBER 26TH, '61.

LONELY, weary, broken hearted,
  As I laid me down to sleep,
Thinking of the day we parted,
  When you told me not to weep,
Soon I dreamed that peaceful Angels
  Hovered o'er the battle-plain,
Singing songs of joy and gladness,
  For my boy was home again.

Tears were changed to loud rejoicing,
  Night was turned to endless day,
Lovely birds were sweetly singing,
  Flowers bloomed in light array;
Old and young seemed light and cheerful,
  Peace seemed everywhere to reign,
My poor heart forgot its sorrow;
  For my boy was home again!

But the dream is past: and with it
  All my happiness is gone;
Cheerful thoughts of joy have vanished,
  I must still in sorrow mourn.
Soon may peace, with all its blessings,
  Our unhappy land reclaim;
Then my tears will cease her flowing,
  And my boy be home again!

CHARLES CARROLL SAWYER.

## WITH "VICTOR" ON HIS CREST.

AT THE BATTLE OF BLACK WALNUT CREEK, MO.,
NOVEMBER 27TH '61.

Ay! Leave the Stripes and Stars
Above him, with the precious cap and sash;
The mute mementos of the battle crash,
And of a hero's scars.

Rest, gallant soldier, rest!
Ennobled e'en in dying; Christ's true knight
Is now a king, in royal glory bright,
With "Victor" on his crest.

And yet—God giveth sleep;
No earthly victor's laurels ever shed,
A glory like the halo round his head,
Ye loved him—should you weep?

Say ye, "His life is lost;
Our home's sweet comfort, and our crown of hope?"
Nay, friends! His life has now a grander scope,
A living holocaust.

To God, and Truth, and Right,
It aye hath been; and if the gleaming coal
On God's own altar hath unborne the soul
In fiery chariot bright.

'Mid battle roar and strife;
If to the fearless soldier, God's release
Came swiftly with the seal of perfect peace
Upon his earthly life.

Ay, though it sorely crush
The hearts that clung to him, poor hearts that ache,
With yearning sense of loss—oh, for his sake
Each wail of anguish hush!

And yet, ye well may weep,
As those who mourned the holy martyr erst,
On whose glad eyes Heaven's waiting glories burst,
Before "he fell asleep."

A hero-heart is still,
And eyes are sealed; and loving lips are mute,
Which bore on earth the Spirit's golden fruit,
But peace! It was God's will.

And for our precious land—
The land he loved, and died for in her need.
The blood of heroes is the country's seed,
As he stood, let us stand.

The Lord of hosts doth reign.
He crowned our soldiers, "dying at their guns."
Oh be the nation worthy of such sons—
The noble-hearted slain,

And so we sadly lay,
Yet not so sadly, though with tearful eyes,
A little nameless flower where he lies,
And gently steal away.

M. E. LEE.

## LEFT ON THE BATTLE-FIELD.

AT THE FIGHT AT SALEM, MO.,

DECEMBER 3D, '61.

WHAT, was it a dream? am I all alone,
In the dreary night and the drizzling rain?
Hist!—ah, it was only the river's moan;
They have left me behind with the mangled slain.

Yes, now I remember it all too well!
We met, from the battling ranks apart;
Together our weapons flashed and fell,
And mine was sheathed in his quivering heart.

In the cypress gloom where the deed was done,
It was all too dark to see his face;
But I heard his death-groans, one by one,
And he holds me still in a cold embrace.

He spoke but once, and I could not hear
The words he said for the cannon's roar;
But my heart grew cold with a deadly fear—
O God! I had heard that voice before!

Had heard it before, at our mother's knee,
When we lisped the words of our evening prayer!
My brother! would I had died for thee—
This burden is more than my soul can bear!

I pressed my lips to his death cold cheek,
  And begged him to show me, by word or sign,
That he knew and forgave me; he could not speak,
  But he nestled his poor cold face to mine.

The blood flowed fast from my wounded side,
  And then for a while I forgot my pain,
And over the lakelet we seemed to glide
  In our little boat, two boys again.

And then, in my dream, we stood alone,
  On a forest path where the shadows fell;
And I heard again in the tremulous tone,
  And the tender words of his last farewell.

But that parting was years, long years ago,
  He wandered away to a foreign land;
And our dear old mother will never know
  That he died to-night by his brother's hand."

The soldiers who buried the dead next day,
  Disturbed not the clasp of that last embrace,
But laid them to sleep till the Judgment day,
  Heart folded to heart, and face to face.

## THE PICKET-GUARD.

FIGHT AT DAM NO. 5, UPPER POTOMAC.
DECEMBER 8TH, '61.

"ALL quiet along the Potomac," they say,
"Except, now and then, a stray picket
Is shot as he walks on his beat to and fro,
By a rifleman hid in the thicket.
'Tis nothing—a private or two, now and then,
Will not count in the news of the battle;
Not an officer lost—only one of the men
Moaning out, all alone, the death-rattle."

All quiet along the Potomac to-night,
Where the soldiers lie peacefully dreaming;
Their tents, in the rays of the clear autumn moon
Or the light of the watch-fire, gleaming.
A tremulous sigh, as the gentle night-wind
Through the forest-leaves softly is creeping;
While stars up above, with their glittering eyes,
Keep guard—for the army is sleeping.

There's only the sound of the lone sentry's tread
As he tramps from the rock to the fountain,
And thinks of the two in the low trundle-bed,
Far away in the cot on the mountain.
His musket falls back—his face, dark and grim,
Grows gentle with memories tender,
As he mutters a prayer for the children asleep—
For their mother—may Heaven defend her!

The moon seems to shine just as brightly as then,
  That night when the love yet unspoken
Leaped up to his lips—when low murmured vows
  Were pledged to be never unbroken.
Then drawing his sleeve roughly over his eyes,
  He dashes off tears that are welling,
And gathers his gun closer up to its place,
  As if to keep down the heart-swelling.

He passes the fountain, the blasted pine-tree,
  The footstep is lagging and weary;
Yet onward he goes, thro' the broad belt of light,
  Toward the shade of the forest so dreary.
Hark! was it the night-wind that rustled the leaves?
  Was it moonlight so wond'rously flashing?
It looked like a rifle— "Ha! Mary, good-by!"
  And the life-blood is ebbing and plashing.

All quiet along the Potomac to-night,
No sound save the rush of the river;
While soft falls the dew on the face of the dead—
  The picket's off duty forever!

E. B.

## THERE IS NO SEPULCHRE.

FIGHT AT CAMP ALLEGHANY, VA.,
DECEMBER 13TH, '61.

THERE is no sepulchre for those who perish
Before the cannon's mouth that speaks for WRONG;
Their names art embalmed in hearts that cherish
Them with devotion infinite and strong.
He who their burning impress would efface,
Must first exterminate their kindred race.

But there's a grave for recreants who nourish
The dragon's teeth with mercenary aim,
Till realms of bloom, plague-smitten, cease to flourish,
As war's volcano belches lava flame—
A grave fit outpost of the place where goes
The soul to reap the hurricane it sows.

*But not a place of rest;* for it is haunted
By spectral remnants of the brave and fair—
Brave oaks that stood before the axe undaunted,
Fair flowers that mutely languished in despair—
Once guarding and adorning their green land,
Before the viper stung the fost'ring hand.

No softened hearts as daylight closes linger,
No grass nor violet spring beside that grave;
Tradition there directs a warning finger
Where the rank night-shade's lurid blossoms wave.
Though not a stone denotes the burial-sod,
It's not unmarked by an avenging God.

## THE VOLUNTEER.

### AFTER THE FIGHT AT MUNFORDSVILLE, KY., DECEMBER 17TH, '61.

"YOUR arm—your arm! help me across the street,
Or the crowd will trample 'neath their feet
One who their cause sustained at night
On picket guard by camp-fire's light;
With eye of fire and nerve of steel,
I made the crouching foeman feel
The lightning shock of the Minie ball
That whizzed through the brain at his final fall.

"As many comrades around him close,
I stand the chance of outnumbering foes,
Who shatter my leg and break my arm,
Ere the advance-guard catch the sound of alarm.
Faint and exhausted with loss of blood,
I crawled to the verge of a running flood
To slake my thirst and ease my pain:
Nor know how long I there had lain,
Save what they told me the following morn
In the midst of a terrible thunder-storm.

We heard the signal gun last night
With cheerful hearts and spirits bright;
Our company full, they, *now are ten*,
Honest and staunch true-hearted men.
Your brother, in the foremost rank,
Turning the foe's deceptive flank,
Fell, riddled with unseen musketry
Concealed in the branch of a distant tree,

We well avenged him on the spot—
All those that fired—*now or not;*
No tree nor shrub o'ertops the grass
Near the place which we named *The Bloody Pass.*

"With sullen thoughts and burning brain,
I heard the tale of my comrades slain,
And sprang from the damp unfeathered bed,
When my wounds oozed anew, afresh they bled;
The life-blood fell on my fevered hands,
Moistened, as water, the parched lands,
A torrent at last came, I could not smother,
But sobbing aloud "*My brother—brother!*"

"Exhausted nature sank to rest,
Again the wooden pillow pressed;
I dreamt of home and peaceful lands,
Of social, kindred, friendly bands,
*Then*, striving to quell a family feud,
Our hands were all with *blood* imbued,
Defeat or Victory were the same,
Each struggle added grief and pain."

"Pardon, my story seems quite old
You've heard the same so often told
Since war has through our country rung,
And glorious deeds so oft been sung,
That pity long has ceased to reign
For wounded misery—bleeding—slain."

*Friend*—"Brother soldier, say not so,
Tears daily for our wounded flow,
While charity, with open hand,
Plays hostess through the suffering land;
Those dames now passing yonder way,
The hospitals have seen to-day,
And to the feverish-suffering there

Have ministered the tenderest care.
Come, courage, man, don't droop again,
The brave will die ere shrink at pain;
This carriage enter—come with me—
My home and family you shall see;
True hospitality and rest
Be thine, my country's worthy guest."

A spacious house in street Thirteen,
With trees that placed a shade between
Received the wounded Volunteer,
Where smiles of welcome beamed to cheer.

The chamber set for guests apart,
Gave comfort to an aching heart,
And ne'er in battle's raging strife;
Contention, tried to save a life!
More earnestly than woman's care
Strove to preserve the Volunteer.
But all in vain. The Doctor came
To freshly dress his wounds again:
The feeble pulse and flighty brain,
Gave tokens true—skill was in vain.

He rallied through the live long night,
With wandering thoughts and absent sight,
Seeming to mourn his comrades slain,
And muttering, "Boys, we'll meet again
At taps." Then with a feeble air,
And moan that seemed a parting song,
He raised his dying hands in prayer
And sung, "*We're Marching On.*"

Small the effects and lean the store
Of those—the *wounded*, *weak* and *poor*—
His knapsack graced the battle-field,

When serving for a bayonet shield;
His gun had in the river sank,
When it had helped him to its bank;
A miniature all stained with gore
Upon his manly breast he bore,
But whether of mother, or loving wife,
Sister, or a betrothed in life,
We ne'er shall know—the crimson stain
Left woman only—thoughts remain,
That even now with silent tear
Some maiden mourns her volunteer.

A lock of hair on his person found,
With some withered flowers clinging 'round,
And lines from a brother now no more,
Were all the contents of his pocket's store.
The hair, if we judge from its glossy flow,
Crowned the brow of a maiden pure as snow;
The flowers contained one blooming spot,
'Twas the emblem of love, "*forget-me-not.*"
The brother's lines—their history tell—
*Both died* for the land *beloved so well!*
If ever valor stamped repose,
If ever wounds from duty rose
If ever death a glory cast,
To lead the future—name the past,
'Twas that which heralded the bier
Of our departed *Volunteer.*
The family of the stranger friend
That led him home, and saw his end,
Were there—and soldiers lined the grave,
Who three loud warlike vollies gave,
Then left him quietly abed
In the gorged city of the *dead.*

G. C. HOWARD.

## TOUCH THE ELBOW.

CAPTURE OF MILFORD, MO.,

DECEMBER 18TH, '61.

Where battle-music greets our ear
  Our guns are sighted at the foe,
Then nerve the hand and banish fear,
  And, comrades, touch the elbow!

Home and country, patriots fire,
  Kindle our souls with fervid glow,
And Southern traitors shall retire
  When Northmen touch the elbow!

A cannon shot may plow our rank,
  And through it strike its deadly blow;
Close up the space the ball made blank,
  And, comrades, touch the elbow!

Though many brave men bite the sod,
  And crimson heart's blood freely flow,
Shout, as their spirits soar to God,
  On, comrades, touch the elbow!

Now, show the steel of which you're made,
  The General signals march: Halloo!
Double the quickstep, First Brigade—
  Charge, comrades, touch the elbow!

Touch the elbow now, my boys,
  Comrades, touch the elbow;
Double the quickstep, First Brigade—
  Charge, comrades, touch the elbow!

BRIG. GEN. MARTINDALE, U. S. V.

## THE SOLDIER'S SOLILOQUY.

CAPTURE OF CAMP SHAWNEE MOUND, MO.,
DECEMBER 18TH, '61.

THE heath this night must be my bed,
The bracken curtain for my head,
My lullaby the warder's tread,
        Far, far from love and thee, Mary.
To-morrow eve more stilly laid,
My couch may be my bloody plaid,
My vesper song thy wail, sweet maid;
        It will not waken me, Mary.

I may not, dare not, fancy now!
The grief that clouds thy lovely brow,
I dare not think upon thy vow,
        And all it promised me, Mary.
No fond regrets must Norman know;
When bursts Clan Alpine on the foe,
His heart must be like bended bow,
        His foot like arrow free, Mary.

A time will come with feeling fraught;
For if I fall in battle fought,
Thy hapless lover's dying thought,
        Shall be a thought on thee, Mary.
And if returned from conquered foes,
How blithely will the evening close,
How sweet the linnet sing repose
        To my young bride and me, Mary,

A. C. SHERMAN.

## I'LL COME BACK AGAIN.

BEFORE THE SECOND BATTLE AT HUDSON, MO., DECEMBER 20TH, '61.

FAREWELL, my dear Katty, my own darling Katty,
The time it has come and I must depart;
But to know that you will think of me, darling,
'Mid peril and danger will cheer my sad heart.
For your bright smile of kindness will ever be near me,
To soften my sorrow and relieve every pain;
And if fortune but spares me, my own darling Katty,
When the war is all over I'll come back again.

Farewell, my dear Katty, my own darling Katty,
The sun it is up, and I must away;
The boys now are marching and handkerchiefs waving,
So, farewell, dear Katty, I'll no longer delay.
You'll think of me sometimes, and pray for me, too,
When you hear an account of the wounded and slain;
And if God only spares me, my own darling Katty,
When the war is all over, I'll come back again.

Farewell, my dear Katty, my own darling Katty,
One kiss now at parting, and then I'll be gone;
The drums are a-beating, the music is playing,
While friends with kind words are cheering us on.
We are fighting for honor and glory, my darling
The rebels for plunder, and booty, and gain;
So, when we have whipp'd them back into submission,
And restored the old Union, I'll come back again.

FRANCIS B. MURTHA.

## WHEN THE DIN OF WAR IS ENDED.

BATTLE OF DRANESVILLE, VA.,

DECEMBER 20TH, '61.

Rolling drums and thundering cannon,
  Cheerful hearts with smiling faces,
Fire and sword, and fearful terrors,
  Pleasant dreams of heavenly places—
*Traitors*, *demons*, perfect *devils*,
  Loyal patriotic souls,
Broken hearts and ruined prospects,
  Fortunes caught in gilded bowls—
Bubble, bubble, toil and trouble,
  Pleasure, calmness, and delight,
Lights and shadows how they double,
  No alternative but fight.
Hear the dying groans of brothers;
  And again the songs of mirth;
Hear the shrieks of mangled soldiers,
  And the gladsome songs of earth—
Blooming fields and waving blossoms,
  Gardens filled with blessings rare,
Man destroys what God bequeathed him,
  And rejects the good and fair—
When the din of war is ended,
  And the sound of battle's strife,
When our hope to live contented,
  And be happy hence through life—
Hasten on, oh, God, that coming;
  Let thy righteous ways of peace,
Spread their flowery paths before us,
  And command that war shall cease.

H. A. M.

## WE WILL FIGHT AS OF OLD.

THE STONE BLOCKADE OF CHARLESTON HARBOR, S. C.

DECEMBER 21ST, '61.

WHEN rebellion first swept, with its pestilent breath,
Through our dear native land, causing terror and death.
We vowed by the martyrs who fought and who fell,
That no foreign assistance its fury should quell.
Let the trumpet and drum sound all over the land,
Let us muster with rifle, with cannon and brand!
And teach those proud nations, far over the sea,
We'll fight as of old for the home of the free!

Oh, shades of our sires! Sacred spirits impart
Strength and courage to nerve each arm and heart!
With a Patriot's zeal, and fidelity true,
To conquer or die for "the red, white and blue."
The quarrel's our own—we'll adjust it at home;
No false foreign power interfering shall come;
Then never, we swear, while the sun sheds its light,
Shall foreign exaction set our quarrels aright.

Our blades have to often been fleshed to the hilt;
In the forms of our kindred, what blood we have spilt,
In this terrible strife! thus proclaiming to all,
When we fight for the right we conquer or fall.
Sound trumpet and drum all over the land:
Join together in love each true heart and hand—
North and South, East and West, O, God! we implore,
Our glorious Union again to restore.

H. WILTON, U. S. N.

## FORWARD AGAIN.

FIGHT AT NEWPORT NEWS, VA.,
DECEMBER 22ND, '61.

WAVE all your plumes, O lordly Northern pines,
Again to conflict like the north wind's blast;
By all the power that Honor's self defines,
By all the mem'ries of th' historic past.

Onward to meet the foe—again press on!
Hurtling the iron rain, and flashing sword;
On! for your battle-fields by valor won,
Ring out the battle-cry with fierce accord.

On, for the heritage of unborn men,
On, for the ashes of your buried sires;
Bid each bright star blaze in its field again,
And warm the martial pulse with patriot fires!

Men of the North! your hands are on the plow!
Will ye turn back or lie down in the furrow
That ye have made? saying: "Not now, O, not now;
But in the golden splendor of to-morrow,

"We'll do such deeds, that tyrants on their thrones
Shall thrill with terror, and the grain shall grow
To winnowed be ere yet it is high noon,
Upon the earth's threshing floor! But O, not now.

'A little longer; we must bide our time,
He who runs fast, is sure to catch a fall."
Men of the North! Treason is in its prime,
And must be crushed to fragments. Know that all

The logic of great minds would fail to gain
  One single convert. Traitors are not born,
But spring, full grown, from out some lusty brain,
  Armed cap-a-pie, unshaven, and unshorn.

Men of the North, this is no game of chance,
  A toss up—e'en or odd—and one must win.
As victors for the Right, we must advance,
  Or fold our hands, the waiting chains within.

God to the Rescue! be the battle-cry,
  From Maine's pine-forests to the Golden Gate,
While for the star of Promise in our sky,
  A stricken people hopeful watch and wait.

MRS. N. ORR.

## THE WAR CHRISTIAN'S THANKSGIVING.

CAMP CELEBRATION OF CHRISTMAS DAY,
1861.

Oh! God of Battles! once again,
  With banner, trump and drum,
And garments in Thy wine press dyed,
  To give Thee thanks we come.

No goats or bullocks garlanded,
  Unto thy altars go;
With brother's blood, by brothers shed,
  Our glad libations flow.

From pest-house and from dungeon foul,
  Where maimed and torn they die;
From gory trench and charnel house,
  Where heap on heap they lie.

We thank Thee for the sabre's gash,
  The cannon's havoc wild;
We bless Thee for the widow's tears,
  The want that starves her child.

We give Thee praise that Thou hast lit
  The torch and fanned the flame;
That lust and rapine hunt their prey,
  Kind Father, in Thy name!

That for the songs of idle joy,
  False angels sang of yore,
Thou sendest war on earth: ill will
  To man forever more!

We know that wisdom, truth and right
  To us and ours are given,
That Thou hast clothed us with the wrath
  To do the work of Heaven.

We know that plains and cities waste,
  Are pleasant in Thine eyes;
Thou lovest a hearth stone desolate,
  Thou lovest the mourner's cry.

Teach us to hate—as Jesus taught
  Fond fools of yore, to love—
Give us Thy vengeance as our own—
  Thy pity hide above!

Where'er we tread may deserts spring,
  Till none are left to slay,
And when the last red drop is shed,
  We'll kneel again and pray.

DARLING.

## WILL THEY WEEP FOR ME AT HOME.

AT THE BATTLE OF MOUNT SION, MO.,

DECEMBER 28TH, '61.

WILL they weep for me at home,
When they hear of my sad end?
Oh! perchance they think me well,
With each gay and jovial friend?
Here I lie among the slain,
Dearest friend as well as foe.
Oh! this weary burning pain!
Oh! these painful hours of woe!

Do they wait at home for me,
My sweet wife and children dear.
I shall never see them more—
For my life-blood ebbs out here.
For my country I shall die;
To her cause my life I yield;
Hark! our men have gained the day,
Our Flag alone is on the field.

Farewell, dear beloved wife!
Death is taking me now hence—
Freely now I give my life:
For, our Country's loved defence!
Then, success attend our cause;
May we always gain the day,
And each traitor meet his death,
Till the last is swept away!

WALTER WARREN.

## THE OLD THIRTEEN.

BATTLE ON PORT ROYAL ISLAND, S. C.,

JANUARY 1ST, '62.

GOD bless the good old thirteen states;
  God bless the young ones too;
Who cares for musty birth-day dates—
  God bless them, old and new.
The old ones first our freedom gained,
  In bloody fight of yore;
The young ones have their right maintained,
  As the old ones did before.

No South or North, no East or West,
  Twin sisters all they be;
One mother nursed them on her breast,
  And that was Liberty.
And may the wretch whose hand shall first
  The bond that binds them *shake*,
Be ever among men accursed—
  Oh, may it never *break!*

Oh! may that banner wide extend
  O'er every land and sea,
Without beginning, without end,
  And conquer to set free:
Till Freedom's banner floats alone,
  A beacon in the sky,
And man no other lord shall own
  But Him who rules on high.

ANONYMOUS.

## OUR COMRADE.

DESTRUCTION OF FORT BARRANCAS, FLA.

JANUARY 2D, '62.

Where tangled boughs of fadeless evergreen,
Their emerald canopy o'er earth out-spread,
Shielding his pale face from the sun's bright sheen,
Our Willie lay, with pale and bloodless mien,
There with the mangled dead.

The wind that through the tangled cedars sighed,
Back from his pallid brow, swept the brown hair,
And kissed his cheek, as oft, bending beside
His couch, his mother kissed her boy, her pride,
And blessed him, sleeping there.

No mother blessed him when his young life fled,
But on the chilly earth his warm blood flowed,
And on his couch of death no tears were shed—
To his loved ones no farewell words were said—
No parting kiss bestowed.

We laid him there within his narrow grave,
And heaped the damp earth o'er his lifeless form;
He sleeps beside a comrade true and brave,
Who with his last look saw our banner wave
In the fierce battle-storm.

No more the startling bugle greets his ear;
The rolling drum calls him to come no more,
When its loud notes bespeak the foeman near;
No more will he the shouts of victory hear—
His warfare now is o'er.

ELRINE MAY.

## MY COUNTRY-WOMEN.

CAPTURE OF BIG BETHEL, VA.,

JANUARY 3D, '62.

THINK ye to night of the poor weary soldier
Lying wounded, and bleeding, far, far from his home?
With the dreams of his youth, the hopes of his manhood,
O'ershadowed, and chill'd by the gloom of the tomb.

For his country he left the dear home of his childhood
And wandered afar, over mountain and plain;
The sun's burning rays and the cold dew of evening
Relaxed his strong muscles and fevered his brain.

From the long weary march he rushed into battle
To fight for our freedom—our Nation to save;
The carnage was fearful, and deadly the struggle,
Ere he fell as a warrior, so faithful and brave.

Oh, Sisters! how holy and blessed our mission—
To comfort the hearts that have bled for us all,
To whisper the words of Divine consolation
To soldiers just resting, before their last call,—

To fight the dread battle, where man must surrender
To Death, his relentless, unchangeable foe,
No fond arm of mother or sister upholds him,
As he sinks in the anguish of silence and woe.

ANONYMOUS.

## THE TWO SHARPSHOOTERS.

BATTLE OF HUTTONSVILLE, W. VA.,
JANUARY 4TH, '62.

Two men went out from the fire-lit camp
In the autumn midnight gray;
Over the quaking, croaking swamp
To the edge of the woodland still and damp,
With rifle and spade went they.

A hunting owl wailed out to its young,
And the picket stood as still
In the meadow below as the shadows flung
By the beaded tent lights thickly strung
On the silver-threaded rill.

'Twas long ere the picket moved away,
And there was no time to lose;
The pits must be dug by dawn of day:
Said one, "We are digging graves, I say;"
And the other whispered, "Whose?"

With the morning light a column of steel
Moved upward along the hill
Toward the hidden pits, but a double peal
Close in the front made the column reel
A moment, and then stand still.

The check won a battle-field that day;
On the morrow the dead were laid
Head to foot in a trench of clay;
But two apart in the front that lay
Were buried without a spade.

W. H. LONGFELLOW.

## WHAT PA THINKS.

BEFORE THE BATTLE OF SILVER CREEK, MO.,
JANUARY 8TH, '62.

PA thinks of Bloomy toddling down
Before 'tis fairly light,
In his night-cap and loose night-gown,
And wishes for a sight.
With clean-washed face, smooth-combed hair,
Pa thinks 'twould him delight,
To see his Bloomy place each chair
Around the table right.

And then to see him seated there,
By pancake good and light,
Buttered and *lassied*, cut up square,
Pa thinks would be a sight.
Pa thinks of prayer time, and the kiss
That does each one delight,
And wishes he could share the bliss
Of taste as well as sight.

Or with Romy going to the barn,
To see if all is right,
And feed the geese a little corn,
Were worth a cent a sight;
Pa 'd march thro' mud, march thro' rain,
By darkness and day-light,
If he could only get again
Of his two boys a sight.

A PRIVATE OF 110TH N. Y. S. V.

## WHEN MY LOVER RETURNS.

### AFTER THE BATTLE OF BLUE GAP, VA., JANUARY 9TH, '62.

OH, my bird, my beautiful bird!
  Sing no more to-day;
The saddest maiden under the sun
I must be, till this weary war is done;
  For my lover has gone away.

Ah! your voice could never drop as it does
  Down through those slender bars;
If you ever had loved a soldier lad,
And he was all the friend you had,
  And was gone away to the wars.

You are quiet now! too quiet, my bird,
  To suit my restless mood;
'Tis fearful to feel the house so still,
Sing out again, till you sing your fill;
  I shall die with solitude!

Yet low, sing low, while he is gone
  To fight for the stripes and stars;
I would not hear your voice ring out,
Till it blends itself with the nation's shout,
  When my lover comes from the wars.

You must sing for us both in that blessed day,
  When I welcome my soldier boy;
For my eyes will be dim with the happy tear,
And my heart will come to my lip so near,
  That I cannot speak for joy!

PHEBE CARY.

## THE DYING DRUMMER BOY.

AFTER THE BATTLE OF CEDAR KEYS, FLA., JANUARY 13TH, '62.

"I AM dying comrades, raise my head
  And place it on my drum,
I've long time feared, and yet I hoped,
  This time might never come.
'Tis not because I fear to die—
  No!—I would rather yield
A thousand lives, if they were mine,
  Than we should lose the field.

"But 'tis because within my home,
  Now many miles away,
I see my aged mother kneel
  At eventide to pray.
And 'tis for me, her only son,
  She offers up that prayer;
She prays that He who reigns above—
  Her only child will spare.

"She little thinks that on the field,
  All wet with crimson gore,
Her darling boy is dying now—
  She ne'er will see him more.
But, comrades, tell her, ere she dies,
  What were my last words here—
(And then he raised his glassy eyes)
  I'll watch for her up there."

LOUISA.

## WHAT TIDINGS FROM THE CAMP.

BATTLE OF MILL SPRINGS, KY.,

JANUARY 19TH, '62.

MY brother and loved soldier friend,
How farest thou in the camp to-night?
To thee love's greetings now I send,
As from my peaceful home I write.
Within thy tent, or out "on guard"—
On "picket" guard, God shield thee e'er;
Or in the battle raging hard,
God shield thee still shall be my prayer.

What tidings are there from the camp,
What news from the seat of war, to night?
Dost hear the sentry's measured tramp?
Dost sit beside the camp-fire bright?
O, brother mine, and soldier-friend,
I charge thee tell how speeds the fight?
Is Treason's might soon to have end?
Will it soon dawn Freedom's day-light?

What tidings are there from the war?
What do our troops—and what the foe?
O, by all things which righteous are,
Strike!—to give Treason its death blow!
Advance our standards!—forward, march!
Forward to battle and to fame!
And 'neath Heaven's blue, ethereal arch,
Act valor worthy of our name.

JAMES A. C. O'CONNOR.

## WHAT NEWS FROM THE WEST.

### CAPTURE OF FORT HENRY, TENN., FEBRUARY 6TH, '62.

"DID'ST hear the news, just from the West?"
 In thrilling tones salute the ear;
The traitors that our land infest,
 Are driven back with groan and fear—
And Mississippi with the streams,
 That pour their life into her flood,
Reflect our flag in victory's beams,
 Sustained by men of loyal blood.

The Sun of Liberty now shines
 With lustre bright and unsubdued,
And blasted are the dark designs
 Of *all* promoters of the feud.
From prairie-homes the warriors come,
 From homes upon the lakes green banks,
To render treason fearful, dumb,
 And terrify Rebellion's ranks.

Fort Henry's ramparts 'neath the folds
 Of Freedom's emblem nobly stand;
And where the battle's thunder rolls
 To tell of Victory to our land,
What glad event was it that woke
 All patriot hearts from mount to shore?
It was the fight that Treason broke,
 The grandest onset of the war!

THO. ELLIS.

## OR FILL AN OCEAN GRAVE.

### THE CAPTURE OF ROANOKE ISLAND, FEBRUARY 8TH, '62.

THOUGH many a year of Peace has come,
Since on the wat'ry plain,
We wrenched the trident from
The Empress of the main:

Since Lawrence, with his ebbing breath,
Inspir'd his gallant crew,
Or over Erie, dark with death,
Our Perry's thunder flew:

The blood of valiant men that wet
Our battle-decks of yore,
Leaps in our ocean-warriors yet,
When naval thunders roar.

Off Carolina's coast our fleet,
By brave men's skill controlled,
O'er Roanoke's forts, the standard sheet
Of Union has unrolled.

Yet, 'mid our triumphs, let us weep
For Monteil and the brave,
Who, 'neath the sands of Roanoke sleep,
Or fill an ocean grave.

C. F. B.

## ARM FOR THE FIGHT!

CAPTURE OF ELIZABETH CITY, N. C.,
FEBRUARY 11TH, '62.

ARM for the fight! The cry goes forth,
Thro' the Eastern States, thro' the West and North,
As loud as the surge of the mighty sea
It bursts from the lips of the brave and free,
  Strike for God and the Right!
Traitors shall never Our Union sever,
Our Flag shall wave o'er the land forever,
  Patriots! Arm for the fight!

Arm for the fight! There has blood been shed,
And vengeance must fall on the traitor's head;
We have sued for peace—but we sue no more—
That vain hope is past, that dream is o'er.
  Strike for God and the Right!
Unfurl your flag to the winds of Heaven,
And let three cheers as it floats be given,
  Patriots! Arm for the fight!

Arm for the fight! Hear the eagle cry,
As wounded he soars 'mid the clouds on high;
From his trembling pinions drips the gore,
And it falls on the City of Baltimore—
  Strike for God and the Right!
By the force of arms keep Our Nation free;
Let our country's flag wave o'er land and sea,
  Patriots! Arm for the fight!

L. AUGUSTUS JONES.

## WHERE MY COMRADE IS SLEEPING.

CAPTURE OF EDENTON AND PLYMOUTH CITY, N. C., FEBRUARY 12TH, '62.

SOFTLY now the shades of evening
Gently fall through twilight air,
Nature drapes the sun in darkness,
As some weary maiden fair
Droops with sleep her jetty lashes
O'er her eye, so piercing bright,
While afar on distant mountains
Sweep the noiseless wings of Night.

Lonely dreams now pass before me,
Dismal hues my thoughts assume,
While the deep'ning stealthy shadows
Stamp my soul with half their gloom;
And I mourn my dearest comrade,
Sleeping in his silent grave,
'Neath the shadow of that fortress
Looming o'er the Southern wave.

Have ye seen a Northern cottage,
Underneath whose hanging eaves
Gleam the sceptres which old Winter
There in sparkling beauty leaves?
Saw ye sunbeams in the morning,
Quench their life blood with their fire?
As they melt they gleam the brighter,
Smiling sweetly, they expire.

Thus the soul of the departed
  Saw in death no hideous gloom—
Shudder'd not to see before him
  A short pathway to the tomb.
Fixed his eyes on bright-winged seraphs,
  Saw their crowns of starry hue,
Smiled to hear their shouts of welcome,
  As his glad soul upwards flew.

Like the breast of some huge sea-bird,
  Sleeping on the tossing foam,
Crowned with plumes of shining emerald
  Climbs to Heav'n—his island home.
There, with tear-wet eyes, a mother,
  Long with ceaseless grief will mourn,
And her gray hairs grow yet whiter,
  Weeping for her brave first born.

Take, oh grave, the earthen casket
  To its kindred dust again,
But the gem that gave it beauty,
  Sparkles now where seraphs reign;
Should the gold forever glitter
  Undisturbed, in native clay?
Rather cleanse it, till its brightness
  Pictures back the heavenly ray.

W. E. CREDESLEY.

## THE NIGHT GUARD.

CAPTURE OF SPRINGFIELD, MO.,

FEBRUARY 13TH, '62.

THE march was o'er—the toilsome march,
Through forest dark, and tangled wild—
Each soldier sought his couch of leaves,
And slumbered like a wearied child.
The swift Potomac coursed along
Beside them, like a silver thread,
And mingling with its rushing tide
Came echoes of the sentry's tread.

The watch-fire's out—no tell-tale light
Must point the foe to where they lay,
While thus they slept beneath the trees,
And dreamed the starry night away.
In hours like these, of hurried rest,
In whom to trust they knew full well;
They slept in peace beneath the care
Of tried and trusted sentinel.

He, with careful, steady step,
Walked to and fro among the trees,
With eager ear to catch each sound
That reached him coming with the breeze.
The rustling branches, sighing winds,
Each dying leaf that slowly fell,
Were heard, and not a sound escaped
The trusted watchful sentinel.

GEO. F. BOURNE.

## ONE TO BE FOREVER MORE.

CAPTURE OF BOWLING GREEN, KY.,
FEBRUARY 14TH, '62

FREEMEN! one more sacred pleasure
  Should our festal day employ;
Seraph voices, tuneful measure
  To express a nation's joy.
Bright eyes gleaming, banners streaming,
  Gay bells pealing through the land;
All uniting, all are plighting
  Heart to heart, and hand to hand;

For our country undivided,
  For the pledge our fathers signed,
For that law supreme provided
  Race and sect as one to bind.
And though treasure without measure
  We must lavish to defend,—
And though perish all we cherish,
  We will neither yield nor bend,—

Till our flag, in honor planted,
  Float again o'er sea and shore,
And what rebel hands have flaunted
  Shall usurp its place no more!
Then regretting and forgetting
  Fancied wrongs and needless war,
God that made us one, will aid us
  One to be forever more.

ANONYMOUS.

## LEFT WOUNDED ON THE FIELD.

### AT THE CAPTURE OF FORT DONELSON, TENN., FEBRUARY 16TH, '61.

How like a mighty avalanche
Our brave boys sweep upon the foe,
Regardless of the fearful fire,
Which lays so many heroes low!
On! on! into the storm of death!
Up! up! before those iron throats,
Which pour destruction in their ranks,
And shake the earth with thunder notes!

Great, fearful gaps are in their lines,
The slain in heaps lie in their track,
Yet not a sign of faltering—
Yet not a thought of turning back!
On, on they press, 'till hand to hand
The soldiers struggle in the fight,
God give our men the victory,
God give the battle to the right!

But human valor cannot stand
Such awful carnage as they meet;
And then is given the command
To cease the combat, and retreat.
Amid the rebels' hideous yells,
And fearful shouts of victory,
Our shattered forces leave the field,
Where they have fought so gallantly.

There, on that awful battle plain,
  Our dead and wounded soldiers lie,
With none to bind their bleeding wounds,
  Or hear their last words ere they die.
We hear their piteous cries for drink,
  Born to our ears in dying tones—
We hear their feeble calls for help,
  But cannot heed their dying groans.!

The cruel foe with dev'lish hate,
  Watch closely all who leave a trench,
To minister to wounded friends,
  And seek their burning thirst to quench,
And from their strongholds quickly send,
  A bullet which may fatal prove,
To all who venture on the field,
  Upon this holy work of love!

Half-way between us and the foe,
  Our leader brave, disabled laid,
And oh! 'twas truely terrible,
  To hear his agonizing cries for aid.
He called for drink incessantly;
  But who could ease his dreadful woe?
'Twas certain death to venture there—
  And who will venture there to go?

A man stepped forth— a martyr brave—
  To give his life for noble deed;
And all his comrades gathered 'round,
  To bid the noble youth God speed!
His features glowed with calm resolve,
  And tears were seen in many eyes,
He grasped their hands and turned away,
  Amid the soldier's sad "good byes."

J

How anxiously they on him gaze,
  As 'mid the fallen ones he treads;
Will he return to them again,
  Or sleep with them on gory beds?
Will he succeed and gain the side
  Of him who led them on to-day?
Will he relieve the sufferer,
  Before his life is snatched away?

Still safe he bravely pushes on
  Amid a storm of leaden hail!
He's almost there—one moment more—
  Will he succeed? or will he fail?
See, see, he kneels, and places now
  His canteen to the soldier's lips—
God grant our leader may imbibe
  New life with every drop he sips.

Our hero rises! can it be
  He'll safely yet return to us?
Oh, God of battles! we now pray
  That Thou wilt kindly will it thus!
Another shower of bullets fall—
  Will he escape this as before?
Alas! behold him stagger—fall!
  Ah! Heaven has gained one martyr more!

The days passed on—we toiled away,
  Assured the fortress soon must fall;
And how we cheered when we beheld
  The white flags wave along the wall.
The place was ours! and victory
  Had perched upon our banner bright,
Treason was humbled in the dust
  Before the all-triumphant Right!

J. GORDON EMMONS.

## THE DYING SOLDIER.

DESTRUCTION OF WINTON VILLAGE, N. C.,
FEBRUARY 19TH, '62.

THE grim-visaged cannon had ceased to roar,
  And hushed was the musketry's rattle;
The bright-flashing sabre, all dripping with gore,
  Lay in peace on the red field of battle;
The warm golden sunlight flooded the plain;
  The night-wind was mournfully sighing,
And bore on its bosom, again and again,
  The groans of the wounded and dying.

On blood-crimsoned turf, with bright eyes upturned
  To the smoke-hidden heavens above him,
A dying youth lay, while his manly heart yearned
  For his home and the friends who had loved him;
Yet firmly he clings to his sabre red,
  Though sharp are the pains through him darting;
And the glaze o'er his eyes, which shuts out the dead
  Tells that body and spirit are parting.

A smile wreathes the lips that once were so sad,
  As he looks on the smoky cloud o'er him;
Life's shadowing twilight flits o'er his head,
  And visions of home dance before him.
His father, with tottering step, he sees,
  And hears the sweet voice of his mother;
And, fronting the door, the wide-spreading trees,
  Where he played with his sister and brother.

Yet another vision now meets his gaze,
With joy it advances to meet him;
The loved playmate of his youthful days
Comes forth, with her parents, to greet him.
The blood-stained sabre now falls from his hand
To his feet in triumph he started;
And then, with a groan, fell back to the sand,
While his spirit, to meet them, departed!

S. H. POTTER.

## THE LAST MAN AT HIS GUN.

### AT THE BATTLE OF FORT GRAIG, NEW MEXICO.

Alone, amid his comrades slain,
Upon the crimson battle field,
'Mid death and dire destruction's reign—
He will not fly—he will not yield!
But coolly sits, upon his gun,
Now silent in the battle's roar
His duty nobly, bravely done—
He falls—the last—one martyr more!
Will ever traitors perish thus,
Or stand before such a foe as he,
With such brave men to fight for us,
Base treason's doomed eternally!
Ah! hero brave! thy noble name
We'll breathe around our peaceful fires—
Tell childrens' children of thy fame,
When we are old and white-haired sires!

J. GORDON EMMONS.

## MY GRANDFATHER'S SWORD.

CELEBRATION OF WASHINGTON'S BIRTH-DAY

FEBRUARY 22D, '62.

How I used to love, when a happy boy,
To roam through these old halls
In my father's house, and wondering gaze
At the portraits on the walls.
But there was *one thing* I loved more than all
Of the relics around me stored.
'Twas the rusty old weapon that hung on the wall,
My grandfather's old heavy sword.

Cheerless and cold was this lonely hall,
Cheerless and dark as night,
And oft have I crept along the wall
And opened a shutter to let in light;
Then I'd climb on a chair, with cautious air,
Fearing I might be heard,
With trembling hand unclasp the band,
And take down my grandfather's sword.

With awe I would gaze and hold my breath,
As I drew from its scabbard the blade,
And think of the old man's fearful death,
And the grave where he was laid
I looked on the weapon in fond delight;
I thought of the tales I adored,
How my grandsire fell on Bunker Hill's height,
Waving that blood-stained sword.

When I hung it up I'd steal away
  To the "green," where the school boys used to play,
And tell the boys of our country's foes,
  Who fell in the strife 'neath my grandsires blows.
How my heart throbs now while I think of home,
  And memory's tears all silently come
When I think of the hall with old trophies stored,
  I sigh when I gaze on my grandfather's sword

L. AUGUSTUS JONES.

## THE SPECTRAL WARRIOR.

CAPTURE OF NASHVILLE, TENN.,

FEBRUARY 23D, '62.

A MAIDEN mused as the day grew dim,
  And the stars encamped in the West;
The pine tree flourished its dusky limb,
As if beating time as the breeze's hymn,
  Seemed chanting a soul to rest.
The wires were warm with the news of strife
  On Virginia's stricken sod;
And she thought of one who had pledged his life,
Whose scarlet sash for his battle-knife,
  She had girt with a prayer to God.
Like blasted figs on a sterile shore,
  Life's flowers bestrewed her heart:
The Past unfolded a radiant store,
But the blossoms were sore that the Future bore,
  And she saw its last depart.
Her soul was wrung into tears, and she wept;
  Hope gilded her thoughts no more;
When midnight came at the lattice she slept,
And a calm o'er her soul as softly crept,
  As the moonlight over the floor,

Did leaves rustle then! they're mute as the dew;
  The moonlight fled from the floor,
As a phantom warrior, clad in blue,
A weird and a sombre shadow threw,
  As he entered the closed door.
Like a fire that glows in a darkling cave,
  Or cannon flame from a fort,
His eye from its sunken socket gave
Unearthly light—the badge of the grave,
  With a mystic meaning fraught.
With a banner grasped in his bony hand,
  And the scarlet sash she bound,
She saw her spectral lover stand,
With a mortal wound where the Southern brand,
  His life-stream sought and found.
He waved his hand; with a sound as before,
  He vanished like April's flake;
The moonlight slumbered again on the floor,
But the calm returned to her soul no more,
  And she shrieked herself awake.
She knew the worst; and her eye was clear
  When she stood at the village well,
And a wounded soldier she chanced to hear
Relate with many an honest tear,
  How her Spartan lover fell.
The colors he bore through the fiery sleet,
  Ere the foe was put to rout,
And planted it at the foeman's feet,
Where he smiling sank, and his dying heat
  Was poured in a battle-shout.
Above to graves in the twilight dim,
  Like a mourner sore opprest;
The pine tree tosses its dusky limb,
And is beating time as the breeze's hymn,
  Is chanting two souls to rest.

CLARENCE F. BUHLER.

## WE LOOKED AGAIN UPON HIS FACE.

CAPTURE OF FAYETTEVILLE, ARK.,

FEBRUARY 24TH, '62.

SAY is one's country dearer than one's husband?
I scarce can tell you even now,
Tho' livelong months the grave sod has been folded
Across my husband's marble brow.
I know it was a sunny day in August,
Though I scarce saw its brightness then,
With a firm step and proud high bearing,
He joined those files of noble men.

Who, loving their grand country better
Than life, or home, or aught else dear,
Went forward, in their hands their young life holding,
With sense of duty, such as conquers fear.
I sometimes thought that if in glorious battle
His name was written on the list of killed,
As 'twas for country, so no murmur should escape me,
No eyes drop tears, though ever so well filled.

But not his fate to die for country quickly,
With crimson life blood oozing from his breast,
But in the dreary wards of far-off hospital,
At Danville he at last found rest.
And when his father tried to get him a short furlough
I thought that they would surely grant him this,
He brought not him, but a closely fastened coffin,
That held a soldier's form, but 'twas not his.

Slow, weary aays went on, then came a message;
  "Come now, and you shall have your son;"
The words once brought hope, but then I only waited—
  I knew that his life-work was done.
We looked again upon his face, and calm and smiling
  Was the look his features wore,
It was the peace from his bright soul reflected,
  Amid the glories of the further shore.

My little boy upon my knee begins to babble now,
  And asks me when his papa will come home,
And I can only weep, and sob, and turn away,
  And cannot tell him he will never come.
And so I fold him closer to my heart, and sit
  Within the lengthen'd shadow of that grave,
But I will struggle on thro' life alone content,
  If lives like his can our lov'd country save.

C. H. HANNUM.

## I WOULD SEND YOU A KISS.

BATTLE OF BIRD'S POINT, MO.,
FEBRUARY 28, '62.

I WOULD send you a kiss dear daughter,
  As pure from a fond father's lips,
And as chaste as the drop of water,
  That fresh from an icicle drips;
But kisses thus sent in a letter
  Would lose all their sweetness for thee,
And I know it would please thee far better
  To receive a few "greenbacks" from me:
I therefore send you this nice little sonnet,
Instead of the greenbacks to buy a new bonnet.

## THE MONARCH OF THE WEST.

### AT THE CAPTURE OF BRUNSWICK. GA., MARCH 2D, '62.

THE war-cloud crossed the battle plain,
And heroes bloody in the fight,
Pushed on among the mangled slain,
To strike for Liberty and Right!
Of all the banners waving there,
Was one more honored than the rest—
The Stars and Stripes, that kissed the air,
And sang, "I'm Monarch of the West!"

Columbia's Eagle in the sky,
Peered down upon the smoky plain;
And as the war shouts rose on high,
He "victory" echoed back again!
Then Heaven's archways loudly rung
With melodies from those at rest,
And angel-voices sweetly sung,
"Long reign the 'Monarch of the West.'"

Then Peace came pleading on the field,
To stop the fearful scenes of woe;
And Mercy, she had gently kneeled,
To soothe the dying friend or foe;
And while our banner waved on high,
With "Victory" written on its crest—
A nation's prayers sped to the sky,
"God bless the 'Monarch of the West.'"

Thus when a thousand years have passed,
  And this fair land is gray with age,
Shall not these deeds of glory last,
  As jewels on Time's mighty page?—
And all the earth resound with praise,
  For those who bravely stood the test,
Thus perilled all, in darker days,
  To save the "Monarch of the West!"

ROBERT M. HART.

## THE EXTRA.

AFTER THE CAPTURE OF COLUMBUS, KY,
MARCH 3D, '62.

The day had passed, and stillness reigned,
  Where all was toil, and care, and strife;
Grim twilight drew her shadows o'er
  The varied scenes of busy life.
One by one the stars peeped forth;
  High in the heavens the moon arose,
Covering the earth with silv'ry light,
  While wearied nature woo'd repose.

Sleep sought the couch of rich and poor,
  Relieving sorrow's poignant smart;
For a time at least, peace held full sway;
  Contentment cheer'd each restless heart.
Through happy dream-land fancy stray'd,
  Culling flowers of brightest hue,
For all seemed fair—but nature slept
  To wake again with grief anew.

One by one the hours passed by
  Twelve o'clock, and all seemed well;
On the watchman's ear most solemnly
  Fell the strokes of the midnight bell;
When suddenly, as if by magic,
  Loud shouting came from far and near;
People leap'd to the windows quick,
  And trembling stood in dread and fear.

"Extra," "extra," "extra," "extra,"
  "Another glorious victory!"
Cried the newsboy, madly running
  Thro' the silent, slumb'ring city.
In eager haste the news was read,
  Describing how they fought and died;
Another battle had been fought and won,
  And thousands killed on either side.

No names were given. The bulletin
  Said all had fought as fight the brave,
For country, home, and liberty;
  Each gain'd a soldier's honored grave.
And many a prayer was said that night
  For trusty friends, and lovers dear,
And callous hearts, in pity moved,
  E'en shed the sympathetic tear.

Far away from home and kindred,
  Ne'er to see the light of day;
Far away from those that loved them,
  Cold and ghastly now they lay.
No useless coffins to enclose them,
  Neither hearse nor funeral train,
Not e'en a stone to mark the spot,
  Where nobly fighting they were slain.

FRANCIS B. MURTHA.

## THE EAGLE'S REPLY—AN ALLEGORY.

AT THE BATTLE OF PEA RIDGE, ARK.,

MARCH 7TH, '62.

I'VE bathed my plumes in the golden rays
  Of the day-god's morning beam,
And slept on the clouds as they idly lay
  Like fairies in a dream.
I've screamed aloud with the tempest too
  Since God first gave us light,
I've ever been to the brave and true
  A talisman for right.

I've sailed above in the ether blue,
  When the world was calm below;
From mountain tops I've sipped the dew,
  Or played with the glistening snow.
I've slowly sailed o'er the battle-field,
  When the day of strife was o'er,
And saw on the dying soldier's shield,
  The bird of their native shore.

But I've *never* placed my weary feet
  'Neath the roof of a temple high,
Where *traitor* hearts each Sabbath meet,
  And our banner does not fly.
I've *never* bent my back to hold
  That sacred book of earth,
Where priests with sermons dark and cold,
  Can *never* know its worth.

I claim no kin to the Alta's bird,
  But hold it in disdain,
And ask the while if it ever heard
  Columbia's melting strain.
And the Nation's flag shall *ever* wave
  While I part the airs of heaven,
And I'll ever be to the loyal brave
  Their emblem God has given.

ZORA.

---

## THE LORD IS IN THE STRIFE.

CAPTURE OF FORT CLINCH, ST. MARY'S, FLA.

MARCH 7TH, '62.

MINE eyes have seen the glory of
  The coming of the Lord,
He is trampling out the vintage,
  Where the grapes of wrath are stored;
And hath loosed the fearful lightning
  Of his terrible swift sword.

I have see Him in the watchfires
  Of a hundred circling camps;
They have builded him an altar,
  In the evening dews and damps;
I can read His righteous sentence
  By the dim and flaring lamps.

ANONYMOUS.

## DEATH OF HIS SON.

SINKING OF THE U. S. FRIGATE CUMBERLAND,
AT HAMPTON ROADS, VA.,
MARCH 8TH, '62.

AT anchor in Hampton Roads we lay,
On board of the Cumberland sloop-of-war;
And at times from the fortress across the bay
The alarum of drums swept past,
Or a bugle-blast
From the camp on shore.

Then far away to the South uprose
A little feather of snow-white smoke,
And we knew that the iron ship of our foes
Was steadily steering its course
To try the force
Of our ribs of oak.

Down upon us heavily runs,
Silent and sullen, the floating fort;
Then comes a puff of smoke from her guns,
And leaps the terrible death,
With fiery breath,
From each open port.

We are not idle, but send her straight
Defiance back in a full broadside!
As hail rebounds from a roof of slate,
Rebounds our heavier hail
From each iron scale
Of the monster's hide.

"Strike your flag!" the rebel cries,
In his arrogant old plantation strain.
"Never!" our gallant Hero replies;
"It is better to sink than to yield!"
And the whole air pealed
With the cheers of our men.

Then, like a kraken huge and black,
She crushed our ribs in her iron grasp!
Down went the Cumberland all a wreck,
With a sudden shudder of death,
And the cannon's breath
For her dying gasp.

Next morn, as the sun rose over the bay,
Still floated our flag at the mainmast-head.
Lord, how beautiful was that day!
Every waft of the air
Was a whisper of prayer,
Or a dirge for the dead.

Ho! brave hearts that went down in the seas!
Ye are at peace in the troubled stream.
Ho! brave land! with hearts like these,
Thy flag, that is rent in twain,
Shall be one again,
And without a seam!

W. HENRY LONGFELLOW.

## THE MONITOR AND MERRIMAC.

NAVAL ENGAGEMENT OFF NEWPORT NEWS, VA., MARCH 9TH, '62.

OH, comrades, come gather and join in my ditty,
It's of a terrible battle which happened of late,
Let each Union tar drop a sad tear of pity,
While I think on the once gallant Cumberland's fate,
On the 9th day of March told a terrible story,
And many a brave tar to this world bid adieu,
Our flag it was wrapped in a mantle of glory
By the heroic deeds of the Cumberland's crew.

On that ill-fated day, about ten in the morning,
The sky it was cloudless, and bright shone the sun,
When the drums of the Cumberland sounded a warning
Which told every seaman to stand by his gun;
Then an iron-clad frigate down on us came bearing,
And it high in the air the rebel flag flew,
The penant of treason she proudly was wearing,
Determined to conquer the Cumberland's crew.

Up steps our bold captain with stern resolution,
Says, boys at this monster we'll ne'er be dismayed,
We swore to maintain our beloved Constitution,
And to fight for our country we are not afraid,
We'll fight for the Union, for our cause it is glorious,
To the Stars and the Stripes we'll ever prove true,
We will sink at our quarters or conquer victorious,
He was answered by cheers of the Cumberland crew.

Our gallant ship opened, her guns roared like thunder,
  Her broadside like hail on the rebels did pour,
The people gazed, and struck with terror and wonder,
  When the shots struck her side and they glanced o'er.
But the pride of our navy ne'er could be daunted,
  Tho' dead and wounded on the decks were strew,
The Flag of our Union; it boldly was planted,
  Sustained by the blood of the Cumberland's crew.

When the traitors found cannon could not avail them,
  While fighting our heroes with God on our side,
The power of Secessia had no power to quail them,
  Tho' blood from her scuppers crimsoned the tide.
She struck her amid ships, her plank she did sever,
  With sharp iron prow, pierced our noble ship thro';
But still, as she sunk in the dark rolling river,
  We'll die at our guns, cried the Cumberland's crew.

Oh! slowly they sank in Virginia's waters,
  Their voices on earth will never be heard more,
They will be wept for by Columbia's sons and daughters
  May their blood be avenged on Virginia shore,
In that blood stained grave they are silently lying,
  And their soul has forever to this world bid adieu;
Yet the Star Spangled Banner above them is flying,
  It was nailed to the mast by the Cumberland's crew.

Oh! Columbia the birth right of freedom's communion
  Our flag never floated so proudly before,
For the spirit of those who died for the Union,
  Above its broad folds does exultingly soar.
And whenever in battle, our sailors assemble,
  God bless our dear banner the Red, White and Blue,
Beneath its bright stars we'll cause tyrants to tremble
  Or die at our guns, like the Cumberland's crew

ONE OF THE CREW.

## TWO ARMIES, BUT ONE NATION STILL.

BEFORE THE EVACUATION OF MANASSAS JUNCTION, VA., MARCH 10TH, '62.

LAY before me now the volume,
Let me search it o'er and o'er,
From the Alpha to Omega,
Thro' the course of peace and war—
Through the history of nations
Who have raised and passed away—
That I may find a precedent
Equaled by this of to-day!

Here we have two armies standing
Face to face, prepared for fight;
Neither falt'ring, neither fearing,
Both declaring for the RIGHT!
Cry it to the waiting nations
Till the sound the world shall fill:
Proves it not, *tho' war divides us,*
*We are human brothers still?*

Here we have two armies waiting
On their arms, prepared for strife,
Ready at the first stern order
To destroy each other's life!
Why is this?—why not the order
Which with war the land shall fill?
Is it not *that love of Union*
*Pleads between the brothers still?*

Here we have two armies halting,
  Waiting but the word "Engage,"
To shake the earth with their fierce battle,
  And the heavens jar with rage!
What forbids the lips to utter
  To the armies that command?
Is it not *dear Freedom pleading*
  *For the welfare of her land?*

Ah, 'tis Equity and Justice
  Interposing for the Laws!
It is Liberty and mercy
  Pleading with the God of wars!
Cry *this* to the *waiting* nations,
  Who with blood the land would fill:
Tho' internal strife divides us,
  *We are human brothers still!*

Ground your arms! rebellious brothers,
  And let Reason take the lead;
Angels will applaud the action,
  God will smile upon the deed!
Mankind will sing songs, rejoicing,
  And the sound all space shall fill:
Cry *this* to the *waiting nations*—
  Echo it, each *native hill!*

J. HENRY HAYWARD.

## UNDER THE WASHINGTON ELM, CAMBRIDGE,

### ENGAGEMENT AT PARIS, TENN., APRIL 12TH, '62.

Eighty years have passed, and more,
Since under the brave old tree
Our fathers gathered in arms and swore
They would follow the sign their banners bore,
And fight till the land was free.

Half their work was done,
Half is left to do—
Cambridge, and Concord, and Lexington!
When the battle is fought and won
What shall be told of you?

Hark!—'tis the South wind mourns—
Who are the martyrs down!
Ah, the marrow was true in your children's bones
That sprinkled with blood the cursed stones
Of the murder-haunted town!

What if the storm clouds blow?
What if the green leaves fall?
Better the crushing tempest's throe
Than the army of worms that gnawed below:
Trample them one and all!

Then, when the battle is won,
And the land from traitors free,
Our children shall tell of the strife begun
When Liberty's second April sun
Was bright on our brave old tree!

OLIVER WENDELL HOLMES.

## THE SOLDIER'S WIFE.

CAPTURE OF THE FORTS AT NEW MADRID, MO., MARCH 13TH, '62.

How wearily the days go by,
  How silence sits a guest at home,
While she, with listless step and eye,
  Still waits for one who does not come!
The sunshine streams across the floor,
  A golden, solitary track;
The flies hum in and out the door;
  The olden clock goes click-a-clack!
And baby sitting wonder-eyed,
  Watches the kitten's noiseless play;
Till sleep comes gently, and she lies
  At rest through half the summer day.

When twilight cometh, dim and gray,
  She sits a-near the open door;
Before her lies the graveled way,
  O'erhung by ancient sycamore;
And through the eve she hears the cry
  Of whip-poor-wills, that shun the light;
She sees the star of evening die;
  And all around her broods the night.
Then, "By-lo-baby, baby-by!"
  She sings her little one to rest;
And muses, with its rosy face
  Held warm and close against her breast.

Beside her couch she weary kneels,
  And clasps her hands before her face—
Ah, only Christ knows what she feels,
  A lonely supplicant for grace!
She prays for one who does not come;
  And draws an answer from her hopes,
The while above her silent home,
  The stars slide down night's silvery slopes.

A. B.

---

## LIGHT.

BATTLE OF NEWBERN, N. C.,

MARCH 14TH, '62.

Lo! from the distant West a glorious light
Breaks on the darkness of the nation's night!
It mingles with the dawn of victory,
Which gilds the eastern sky so brilliantly,
Until the day is beaming full and clear
Where until now was gloom, and doubt, and fear!
Now in this hour of joy!—this happy day
Our gratitude to God we humbly pay!
He ever gives the battle to the *right!*
And wrong cannot prevail with all its *might!*
May He protect the widow and the child,
And soothe their anguish with His blessings mild!
May He be near the wounded heroes too,
And succor those who fought so brave and true!
May he receive the spirit of the slain,
Where they can never know of war again!
A grateful land reveres their memory,
Which shall endure through all Eternity!

J. GORDON EMMONS.

## WHO WILL CARE FOR MOTHER NOW?

AFTER THE BATTLE OF VALLE RANCHE, NEW MEXICO, MARCH 28TH, '62.

WHY am I so weak and weary,
  See how faint my heated breath,
All around to me seems darkness,
  Tell me, comrades—is this Death?
Ah! how well I know your answer,
  To my fate I meekly bow,
If you'll only tell me truly
  Who will care for mother now.

Who will comfort her in sorrow,
  Who will dry the falling tear,
Gently smooth her wrinkled forehead?
  Who will whisper words of cheer?
Even now I think I see her
  Kneeling, praying for me! how
Can I leave her thus in anguish?
  Who will care for mother now?

Let this knapsack be my pillow,
  And my mantle be the sky;
Hasten, comrades, to the battle!
  I will like a soldier die.
Soon with angel's I'll be marching,
  With bright laurels on my brow;
I have for my country fallen,
  Who will care for mother now?

C. C. SAWYER.

## GOD WILL CARE FOR MOTHER NOW.

CAPTURE OF UNION CITY, TENN.,
MARCH 31ST, '62.

QUELL, oh! quell your fears, my darling;
  Think not of your Mother, child;
Though I never cease my weeping,
  Though my thoughts are fierce and wild,
I will try to bear up nobly,
  To God's decree humbly bow,
If you'll only cease your asking:
  Who will care for Mother now?

When you cross the river Jordan,
  Let no anxious thoughts arise:
I am coming, coming after,
  Angels bear me to the skies,
Let no thoughts of coming sorrow
  Cloud your placid, peaceful brow;
You can confidently answer:
  God will care for mother now!

Oh! when in death those eyelids close,
  When they bear thee to the tomb:
When life's arduous work is done:
  When your Maker calls you home:
And when again to dust you turn,
  When in Heaven rise again:
There, where no earthly sorrows come:
  God will guard your Mother then.

C. G. STREVAL.

## FATHER SHIELD HIM FROM THE SHOT.

AT THE BATTLE OF FARMINGTON, VA.,
APRIL 4TH, '62.

O LORD of Hosts! his Country called,
And nobly to her voice he sprung,
While o'er his brow our banner flashed,
Where chargers neighed and trumpets rung;
There were no tremors in his eye,
When putting on his warrior-crest;
And but a tear—it was when he
Was clasped unto his mother's breast!

O Father! shield him from the shot;
But if it is his doom to die,
May he with shouts of triumph round,
Bend on our flag his closing eye—
And feeling that his mother's soul
Is watching on the field of death;
Where, though it weeps, yet gives a smile
Unto her brave boy's last wild breath.

O proudly will his mother see
Her Country wreath his hero-tomb,
And many a Spring nurse tenderly
With Nature's tears the garland's bloom!
How sweet will be the song of praise,
Where his dear relics peaceful lie!
How grand—away exultant thoughts!
O God! he must not, MUST NOT die!

WILLIAM ROSS WALLACE.

## RECRUITING.

BEFORE THE BATTLE OF PITTSBURG LANDING, MISS., APRIL 6TH, '62.

HARK! from the South the startling cry,
Seize, Patriots, seize your arms
And to your country's rescue fly,
Avert the threat'ning storm,
Rebellion's red, malignant star
Has risen on our land,
And treason wages deadly war
And waves his bloody wand.

Stand not aloof, your brother's blood
Cries vengeance, from the glade,
Press forward like a mighty flood,
Unsheath the glittering blade;
Press forward to the battle-field,
Do battle for the right
Till all the hosts of treason yield,
Subdu'd by loyal might.

It must not be, it cannot be,
Our country still must live;
Sustained by hands both strong and free
Our flag respected wave,
And Union strong again restor'd,
Our suffering land shall bless—
Our ship of State securely moor'd
Anchored again in peace.

Your banner now give to the wind,
 Rush to the field of war,
Linger no longer here behind,
 Your brothers cry from far.
Rush forward, sons of Michigan,
 From workshop, field, and fold,
Fill up their ranks, let every man
 The good old flag uphold.

W. A.

## THE STAR OF THE OCEAN.

CAPTURE OF ISLAND NO. 10, MISS.,

APRIL 7TH, '62.

It decks the ocean's pathless blue,
 And floats on every tide;
It cheers the hardy sailor's view,
 Our flag, our country's pride.

It ran aloft on England's coast,
 And kissed the moonlight free,
When Jones smote down proud Britain's boast
 That "England rules the sea."

It shone in beauty o'er the waves,
 When France struck at its stars;
But they in ocean found their graves,
 Swept down by our brave tars.

Decatur, 'midst the battle storm,
  Its starry folds unswung,
And as the wild winds caught its form,
  Triumphantly be sung.

With blushing smiles it lit the fleet,
  When Lawrence led the fight;
He went the enemy to meet,
  Just at the dawn of light.

He stood within his ocean nest,
  And bravely fought that day;
But ere the sun had sunk to rest,
  It mantled his cold clay.

It slept within a thunder cloud,
  By Perry on the lake,
When with wild shouts which rung aloud,
  He did his strong foe break.

It saw with pleasure o'er Champlain,
  Its proud opponent flee;
And floated with the English slain,
  The dwellers of the sea.

Still may it shine in grandeur far,
  The emblem of the brave;
Still may it float the world's great star,
  Till all sleep in the grave.

E.

## DIED IN THE SERVICE.

AFTER THE CAPTURE OF FORT PULASKI, S. C.,
APRIL 12TH, '62.

HE died—the noble volunteer—at morn,
By sickness faded—by sorrow worn;
A smile still plays on his pale lips,
But his eyes are darkened in death's eclipse;
His beautiful hair still shines like gold,
But the heart is still, and the form is cold;
For an angel hand has softly borne
The soldier away to a brighter morn.

Alas! no kind sister's arm caressed,
His cheek no tender mother pressed;
No pitying friend was by his side,
As lonely, far from home he died;
Let your tears fall gently down!
His eyes have watched in vain,
For the loved one far away,
That he ne'er could see again.

Brave comrades he has shared the fight
Up many a well-fought field;
A braver and a nobler knight,
Never the sword did wield.
Sleep, soldier sleep! from sorrow free,
And sin and strife, 'tis well with thee;
It is well, though many a tear
Laments the fallen volunteer

Gather roses white and red,
And scatter them softly on his breast—
Now some barkspurs deeply blue
There the colors for his rest!
Days, months and years shall circle away,
The ocean of time to eternity roll,
Thou art lost to earth's loved ones, forever and aye,
Soldier and brother, peace to thy soul.

J. H. B.

## CONTRABAND.

FIRST BATTLE AT YORKTOWN, VA.,
APRIL 16TH, '62.

LOUD and long the battle thundered,
  Clashing steel and muttering drum,
While the serried ranks, though sundered,
  To the fear of death were dumb;
When our banners, dim and tattered,
  Shone an emblem of our land,
And the foe were widely scattered,
  Leaving us war's Contraband:

In the hush of after battle,
  Came a negro old and gray,
Years of toil had lent the rattle,
  And obscured his reason's ray;
Bent and feeble, proud in freedom,
  Emblamatic of his band,
From afar he said he "seed'em"
  Battling for the Contraband.

And a woman, yes, a mother,
  Wandered to our silent camp,
Shedding tears she could not smother,
  Telling how she heard the tramp
Of our army drawing nearer,
  Kissing oft our soldiers' hands,
For her children—woman's dearer
  Blessings—too, were Contrabands.

Yet a maiden told her story,
  And our hearts with grief were mute,
The new empire of our glory
  Did its pathos oft dispute,
And our souls were sick with seeing,
  In the downcast of our land,
Virtue ravished—all for being
  Color of the Contraband.

C. FRENCH RICHARDS.

## THE CAVALRY CHARGE.

AT THE FIRST BATTLE OF FREDERICKSBURG,

APRIL 18TH, '62,

O'ER all the fields, o'er all the plain
In seried ranks they come:
With martial music's stirring strains,
With bugle blast and tap of drum.
And now in colums long and straight
And glittering in the sun,
A hundred thousand arms await,
The fearful charge— the watchword, "on."

At length resounding o'er the throng,
In peeling tones from post to post—
On the morning air 'tis borne along,
The signal to this gallant host.
The trumpet call—the hurrying feet—
The neighing steed—the clashing shield;
Then face to face in death they meet,
More proud to die, than basely yield.

One beardless cheek, one youthful form
With 'kerchief wipes a tear away—
He cares not for the battle's storm,
Nor fears to meet yon proud array,
But away beside the granite steep,
With tottering steps, by age bowed down,
An anxious mother waits and weeps,
For him, her last—her only one.

Ah! who shall tell the mournful tale,
How sank he on that bloody plain,
How fought—how fell—amidst the wail
Of wounded, and of dying men.
In whispers lowly breathe his name,
Call up no more the battle's fray,
The last link of an honored name
Sleeps where ten thousand heroes lay.

## HE HATH SOUNDED FORTH THE TRUMPET.

BATTLE OF CAMDEN, N. C.,
APRIL 19TH, '62.

I HAVE read a fiery gospel,
Writ in burnished rows of steel:
"As ye deal with my contemners,
So with you my grace shall deal;
Let the hero born of woman,
Crush the serpent with his heel."

He hath sounded forth the trumpet,
That shall never call retreat;
He is sifting out the hearts of men
Before His judgment seat;
Oh, be swift to give Him answer!
And be jubilant, my feet!

In the beauty of the lilies,
Christ was born across the sea,
With a glory in His bosom,
That transfigures you and me:
As He died to make men holy,
Let us die to keep men free!

J. E. RICHARDS.

## HE WOULD NOT SAY GOOD-BYE.

BEFORE THE BATTLE OF PARATTA, N. M.,
APRIL 23D, '62.

I'M looking at the misty wreaths,
As they gather all around,
And touch with fairy finger
Every bramble on the ground;
Shedding halos light and airy,
Round the dancing, dewy leaves,
And bringing objects nearer,
By the mystic web it weaves,
And I'm thinking, softly thinking,
And not without a sigh,
Of the time he said "Good morning,
I will not say good-bye."

I am looking at the mist-wreaths,
And they seem to thicker grow,
And circle round the tree-tops,
With a motion sad and slow,
As if some spirit bade them press
The earth still closer in,
And cover with their sweetness
Every trace of mortal sin;
And I'm thinking, softly thinking
Of the happy days gone by,
Of the time he said, "Good morning,
I will not say good-bye."

Still I'm looking at the mist-wreaths,
  Bright spirits of the air!
In their gossamer apparel,
  How they flutter everywhere,
And I'm thinking should his country
  Take the sacrifice he gave,
I should like the mist to wreath like this
  Above his lonely grave,
And bring whispers from his spirit,
  From out the starry sky,
To the one who said "good morning,"
  But would not say "good-bye."

SUSIE.

---

## THE BRIDE'S LAMENT.

CAPTURE OF FORTS JACKSON AND ST. PHILIP, FLA.,
APRIL 24TH, '62.

I DID not dream, when last I said farewell to thee,
  I should not look upon thy face again;
That thou so soon would'st lay thine armor by,
And slumber 'neath a Western sky,
  On that dark, and bloody plain.

I gazed upon thy proud and manly form,
  And joyed to think thy heart was true;
Though born beneath a Southern sky,
I knew that sooner thou would'st die
  Than tarnish thy fair name.

And I who loved thee, oh, far more than life!
  And naught beside to which my heart could cling,
Sent thee, with blessings forth, to deadly strife,
Ere scarce thy lips had whispered—wife,
  They breathed a sad farewell.

Could I have sat by thee and bathed thy noble brow,
  When the dark angel came for thee;
Have pillowed thy dear head upon my breast,
And fondly thy dear lips have pressed,
  I could have borne it well.

And yet I'd rather be thy widowed bride,
  Than aught earth now could give to me.
Honored in life, and thy dear name
Is numbered with the gallant slain,
  *That nobly fought and died.*

My heart is heavy with its great and bitter grief,
  Since I no more can welcome thee.
Alone life's dreary round I now must tread,
Unknowing where thy cherished head
  Rests in its lowly grave!

SARAH L. MILES.

## WAITING FOR OUR SOLDIERS.

AFTER THE CAPTURE OF FORT MACON, N. C.,
APRIL 25TH, '62.

IN the city, in the village,
  In the hamlet far away,
Sit the mothers, watching, waiting,
  For their soldier-boys to-day:
They are coming—daily coming,
  One by one, and score by score,
In their leaden casings folded,
  Underneath the flag they bore.

Thinks the mother, weeping, waiting,
  And expectant all the day,—
When his regiment was summoned
  How her soldier went away;
With his bayonet a-gleaming,
  With his knapsack on his back,
With his blanket strapped and folded,—
  And his home-filled haversack.

Thinking of the courage swelling
  In his eye and in his heart.
Though a manly tear was welling,
  When he kissed her to depart.
Thinking of the precious letters
  Written by the camp fire's glow,
Rich in love of home and country,
  And of her who bade him go.

Counting now the lagging moments
  For the knocking at the door,
For the shuffling and the tramping
  Feet of strangers on the floor;
Bringing in their precious burden,
  Leaving her to grief and tears,
To the sorrow and the mourning
  Darkening all the coming years.

## THE COUNTERSIGN.

SECOND BATTLE AT YORKTOWN, VA.,

APRIL 26TH, '61.

ALAS! the weary hours pass slow,
  The night is very dark and still,
And in the marshes far below,
  I hear the bearded whip-poor-will;
I scarce can see a yard ahead,
  My ears are strained to catch each sound—
I hear the leaves about me shed,
  And the springs bubbling through the ground.

Along the beaten path I pace,
  Where white rags mark my sentry's track,
In formless shrubs I seem to trace
  The foeman's form, with bending back;
I think I see him crouching low—
  I stop and list—I stoop and peer,
Until the neighboring hillocks grow
  To groups of soldiers far and near.

With ready piece I wait and watch,
Until my eyes familiar grown,
Detect each harmless earthen notch,
And turn guerillas into stone:
And then amid the lonely gloom,
Beneath the tall old chestnut trees,
My silent marches I resume,
And think of other times than these.

"Halt! Who goes there?" My challenge cry,
It rings along the watchful line;
"Relief!" I hear a voice reply—
"Advance, and give the countersign!"
With bayonet at the charge I wait—
The corporal the word doth tell,
With arms aport I charge my mate,
Then onward pass, and all is well.

But in the tent that night, awake,
I ask, if in the fray I fall,
Can I the mystic answer make
When the angelic sentries call?
And pray that Heaven may so ordain,
Where'er I go, what fate be mine,
Whether in pleasure or in pain,
I still may have my countersign.

FOUND ON THE FIELD.

## THE VACANT CHAIR.

AFTER THE CAPTURE OF NEW ORLEANS LA.,

APRIL 28TH., 1862.

WE shall meet, but we shall miss him,
 There will be one vacant chair;
We shall linger to caress him
 While we breathe our evening prayer.
When a year ago we gathered,
 Joy was in his bright blue eye,
But a golden cord is severed,
 And our hopes in ruin lie.

At our fire-side, sad and lonely,
 Often will the bosom swell
At remembrance of the story,
 How our noble Willie fell;
How he strove to bear our banner
 Through the thickest of the fight,
And upheld our country's honor
 In the strength of mankind's might.

True, they tell us wreaths of glory
 Evermore will deck his brow,
But this soothes the anguish only
 Weeping o'er our heart strings now.
Sleep, to-day, O early fallen,
 In the green and narrow bed,
Dirges from the pine and cypress
 Mingle with the tears we shed.

ANONYMOUS.

## THE PARTING.

BEFORE THE BATTLE OF MONTEREY, TENN.,

MAY 3D, '62.

THE parting adieus were spoken,
 And he slowly arose to go;
And yet he wistfully lingered,
 And I wondered what troubled him so·
For his eyes shot forth fiery glances,
 And the cause of it I didn't know.

We slowly walked down to the gate,
 And yet he seemed loth to depart.
He gazed on the moon and on me,
 And his glance pierced mine like a dart;
And, 'tis strange, but I cannot tell why,
 I felt a great flutter at my heart.

We lingered, but said not a word,
 And gazed on the silvery moon,
'Till slowly it awoke in the West,
 Behind the hill tops all too soon,
And we thought and dreamed of the future,
 And gazed where we had last seen the moon.

And I saw the field of battle,
  And the precious blood on the ground spilled;
And with mother's and dear ones, darling;
  The shallow graves hurriedly filled;
And a low wall went up through my heart
  As I thought, oh if he should be killed!

I shuddered, and crept nearer to him,
  And sent up a silent prayer,
For God to watch o'er and guard him,
  And take him under his loving care;
And softly he pressed me to his heart,
  And, somehow, I liked to rest there.

He whispered loved words in my ear
  'Till his face was lit with love's glow;
And my heart quickly went pit-a-pat,
  And I could'nt tell why it did so,
Unless it wanted to fly to him,
  And I'm sure it was his long ago.

On the battle-fields in the far South,
  He is acting his part in the strife,
And if it pleases Our Father
  To spare unto me his dear life,
When the snows of the winter shall come,
  I have promised to be his own wife.

CHERRY BLOSSOM.

## THE FIELD OF THE DEAD.

EVACUATION OF YORKTOWN, VA.,

MAY 4TH, '62.

The wild battle is over, and lo! on the plain,
Like the glebe 'neath the plowshare, lies piles of dead.
Where the conflict was fiercest hecatombs slain,
Lies the death-gathered chaplet for Victory's head.

It is chaos confused, like the ebb of the flood
When all nature seemed wild, and the gore spotted sun,
Like *Bellona*, sinks down 'mid the banquet of blood,
Whence *Mars* has long fled, since the glory was won.

Who saw the red lightnings the cannons belch'd forth?
Who heard the wild shriek when the rifle shot pealed?
And the cheer? And the charge? when hosts of the North
Like mowers at harvest, laid swathes on the field.

It was glorious at noon when the triumph was green,
And the laurel-browed victors were radient with pride;
But alas for the night, and the horrors unseen,
That wild blood o'er the ground where our heroes died!

See! the clouds hover low as to screen the sad sight
From Infinity's eye. See the battle smoke spread,
Like the foul fumes of hell, and the mantle of night—
It stifles the dying and covers the dead.

There the friend and the foe on the same sod repose.
And the steed and his rider blood-mingled may rest;
And the self-shattered cannon no iron wrath throws,
But has murdered its master, and crushes his breast,

Though there's nought but the canopy of Heaven
O'er the dark sulphured ground where they lie:
And no pageantry gleams round the patriot dead,
While each his own monument lingers untombed,

No crusading Knight-hero, all armored and blest,
E'er enshrined in Cathedral, beneath his broad shield:
In his effigied marble and monument crest,
With its tales of the Moslem and Palestine's field:

No gold-armored *Charlemagne* king-robed or crowned,
Nor e'en great "*Cœur de Lion*" of silver-urned heart,—
Or the crypted *Napoleon*, in consecrate ground,—
In their sepulchred royalty, flattered by art,—

Rests in glory untainted as those who are laid
On the cold sodded field, their life-blood yet flows;
Where they fought for the land of their fathers, betray'd
By its weak-hearted friends and its base-hearted foes.

Then all glory be theirs who have offered their lives,
On the altars of Liberty: sacred to fame,
Let the theme be immortal, while gratitude lives—
May the page and the tablet bear every proud name.

Their deeds shall be emblazoned in diamonds and gold;
The young children shall sing of the glorious day,—
And the tale of the triumph of *Freedom* be told,
'Till the last of the nations have wasted away!

WILLIAM H. INGERSOLL L. L. B.

## THE CRIMSON PATCH.

### AT THE BATTLE OF WILLIAMSBURG, VA.

MAY 5TH, '62.

WHEN the storm of treason burst,
  Pouring horror o'er the land,
You brave men among the first
  Met Rebellion hand to hand.
Treason vainly fought in fight
  Your brave Riflemen to match—
The rebels met a fearful sight
  When they saw the Crimson Patch.

Lords and Kings their 'scutcheons have,
  Men of science, men of worth,
But the 'scutcheon of the brave
  Is the noblest badge on earth.
It is not worn in gilded halls,
  Nor where priests or artists teach,
But mid bullets, shells, and balls,
  There you wore your Crimson Patch.

Oft 'round it the battle smoke
  Fringe of darkest war clouds shed,
When the foemens column broke,
  Dying it a deeper red.
But the Stars and Stripes o'er head
  Foeman's grasp could never catch—
Victory's shouts its proud folds spread,
  When 'twas o'er the Crimson Patch.

Think of Williamsburg—the day
  Richmond trembled in her walls—
When, if you but heard "away!"
  Down the Rebel fortress falls.
Think when thousands tracked your path,
  Seeking you o'er powered to catch,
How you piled them in your wrath,
  Soldiers of the Crimson Patch.

On! for nothing yet is done!
  While there's aught remains to do
Finish what you well begun—
  Crush the trembling traitor crew.
We, your brethren, to you cry,
  Come our deeds and daring match—
Come and share our victory,
  Soldiers of the Crimson Patch.

Come! you're called on by the dead;
  Can you e'er the brave forget?
Their brave blood vile rebels shed—
  Seas of blood it calls for yet.
You beheld our heroes fall!
  Two such heroes who can match?
Now they on their followers call,
  Those who wear the Crimson Patch.

Come and let your rifles ring,
  Levelling foes with every shot—
To the breeze your banners fling
  Flags that never knew a spot.
Vicksburg's taken without you;
  We the rebels soon we'll catch;
Richmond we will thunder through—
  Let's meet there, the Crimson Patch.

DR. REYNOLDS, 63D N. Y. V.

## GAY AND HAPPY.

BATTLE OF WEST POINT, VA.,
MAY 7TH, '62.

WE'RE the boys most gay and happy,
  Though we're tented in the field;
With our nation's banner o'er us,
  And its honor for a shield.

Friends at home, be gay and happy,
  Never blush to speak our name;
If our comrades fall in battle,
  They shall share a soldier's fame.

Girls at home be gay and happy,
  Show that you have woman's pride;
Never wed a home-sick coward—
  Wait and be a soldier's bride.

Gay and happy, hear the answer,
  None but fools get married now;
Valiant men have all enlisted,
  And to cowards we'll not bow.

We're the girls so gay and happy,
  Waiting for the end of strife;
Better share a soldier's rations,
  Than to be a coward's wife.

For the gay, and for the happy,
  We're as constant as the dove;
But the man who does not soldier,
  Never can attain our love.

W. M. J. CO. C, 7TH WIS. VOL.

## THE UNKNOWN BRAVE.

BATTLE OF FORT WRIGHT, MISS.,

MAY 10TH, '62.

A SOLDIER lay low on the field of his pride,
  Life's hard battle o'er, and a long peace before him;
And he who so often grim Death had defied
  Felt the chilly blast from his wings rushing o'er him.

The dark crimson tide burst in deadlier stream,
  As with his last strength his faint body he raised;
And the light of his eyes gave a flickering gleam
  As for the last time on the fair world he gazed.

How lovely it seemed to his sight, waning dim!
  Tho' around him the dead and wounded were lying,
And oh! 'twas a thousand times dearer to him,
  The thought of his *country* for which he was dying.

Then came the sad thought of his home—of his wife,
  Children, and friends he should never see more;
And a tear streamed down his wan cheek, not for life,
  But for those left behind him, his death to deplore.

He turned his last look to the bright golden West,
  Where sun and world were just bidding farewell;
With his last murmured breath his country he blest,
  Then in death's peaceful sleep on the battle-field fell.

Ah! many a true-hearted hero and brave,
As any whom FAME's mighty trumpet has blown,
Has sunk, thus unhonored, alone in his grave,
His name and his deeds to his fellows unknown.

Green, green grows the grass o'er his cold, earthy bed!
May the wild flowers of Nature the monument be
Of the patriot who thus for his country has bled,
And drawn his last breath in the cause of the free!'

## THE PARTING HOUR IS DARK, MOTHER.

CAPTURE OF NORFOLK, VA.,

MAY 10TH, 1862.

THE parting hour is dark, mother,
The saddest I have known—
Oh, what a crushing spell of grief
Upon my heart is thrown!
I grieve to think that I, mother,
Must wonder far from thee,
And thy sad features show that thou
Art grieving, too, for me.

Tumultuous are the thoughts, mother,
That in my bosom swell,
As now I leave my early home,
And breathe the sad farewell.
But, Oh! if I should fall mother,
Grieve not too much for me—
Remember that I fall beneath
The banner of the free.

One long last fond embrace mother,
  One kiss upon my brow—
I feel it in the battle's heat,
  E'en as I feel it now.
One pressure of the hand—one look—
  Now broken is the spell
That holds me to thy loving breast;
  My mother dear, farewell.

RICHARD H. LENT.

## NEVER OR NOW.

### DESTRUCTION OF THE MERRIMAC, OFF NORFOLK, VA., MAY 11TH, '62.

LISTEN, young heroes! your country is calling!
  Time strikes the hour for the brave and the true,
Now while the foremost are fighting and falling,
  Fill up the ranks that have opened for you!

You whom the fathers made free and defended,
  Stain not the scroll that emblazons their fame;
You whose fair heritage spotless descended,
  Leave not your children a birth-right of shame.

Stay not for questions while Freedom stand gasping!
  Wait not till Honor lies wrapt in his pall!
Brief the lips' meeting be, swift the hand clasping—
  "Off for the wars" is enough for them all!

Break from the arms that would fondly caress you!
  Hark! 'tis the bugle blast! sabres are drawn!
Mother shall pray for you, father shall bless you,
  Maidens shall weep for you when you are gone.

Never or now! cries the blood of a nation
  Poured on the turf where the red rose shall bloom;
Now is the day and the hour of salvation;
  Never or now! peals the trumpet of doom!

Never or now! roars the hoarse-throated cannon
  Through the black canopy blotting the skies!
Never or now! flaps the shell-blasted pennon
  O'er the deep ooze where the Cumberland lies;

From the foul dens where our brothers are dying,
  Aliens and foes in the land of their birth,
From the rank swamps were our martyrs are lying
  Pleading in vain for a handful of earth;

From the hot plains where they perish outnumbered,
  Furrowed and ridged with the battle-field's plow
Comes the loud summons: Too long you have slumbr'ed
  Hear the last Angel-trump—NEVER OR NOW!

ANONYMOUS.

## GO FORTH MY SON.

BEFORE THE CAPTURE OF NATCHEZ, MISS., MAY 13TH, '62.

Go forth, my son, your country calls
You to the tented field!
Go forth, and battle for her cause,
And only dying yield!
I much will miss your presence here,
Yet to just Heaven trust,
That you'll return, when Treason's flag
Lies humbled in the dust!

When in the dreary Southern gloom
You pace the night guards round,
When all is silent as the tomb,
And lurking foes surround,
Be stout of heart, my darling boy,
Be watchful, and be true,
A mother's prayers will guard you then,
The weary night-watch through!

And when the hour of strife arrives,
And drums to arms doth call;
When sabres flash and cannons roar,
And friend and foe doth fall!
March forward with the foremost rank—
Where danger is, there go;
For I would rather have thee die
Than *fail* to meet the foe!

J. HENRY HAYWARD.

## THE STANDARD BEARER.

BATTLE OF FORT DARLING, VA.,
MAY 16TH, '62.

And the brave standard-bearer, blood mantled and torn
With the wounds of the conflict, that strove for his prize
But wrapped in the banner whose glory life-borne
Now emblazons his bosom, still honored he lies.

There are eyes that are stony, blood-blotted in glare,
And the home-mem'ried tear may yet cling to the lash,
While on lips that are dumb is a death chiselled prayer
That was sealed to its fount by the last deadly crash.

Some are locked in the grapple that struggled to gain
And yet clutches for vict'ry reeking with gore,
As they fell when their powers were urged to the main,
And they sank to the sward, and the battle gave o'er.

Many smiled at the glory achieved ere they died,
Or the frown of defeat may yet mark some cold brow,
Or the grimace of agony still may abide,
While the unfettered spirit has fled from below.

The father lies stark 'neath the grim monster's heel,
And the soft cheek of youth may be covered with dew,
The brow of stern manhood lies crushed by the wheel
Of the death-belching cannon, where wild legions flew.

The most faithful commmander e'er true to his trust,
With his patriot hand he still clutches the blade—
That he pledged to his country till buried in dust,
And upon her fair bosom the warrior is laid.

WM. H. INGERSOLL, L. L. D.

## YES, MY BOY, THE BATTLE'S OVER.

BATTLE OF LITTLE RED RIVER, ARK.,
MAY 18TH, '62.

YES, my boy, the battle's over:
  Brave men, by thousands, have been slain;
Your father's one, among the number;
  We shall not see him here again;
He is well, but is not wounded,
  Still he's one among the slain;
Yet the battle brings us sadness
  To know he'll never come again.

Yes, dear Son, I'm always sighing
  Of what I in the paper read;
You ask me: why I now am crying,
  And why this cap is on my head?
You say, dear child, I cannot tell you,
  Because you think your father's slain;
We know he loved us very dearly,
  But he will never come again.

Yes, mother, my noble father,
  It breaks my heart to think he's slain;
Though, on earth, we shall not see him,
  In Heaven, I hope we'll meet again;
His name will always be remembered
  By those true Patriots to his cause,
The cause of God and our dear Country;
  For, many loved ones now are gone.

ANONYMOUS.

## THE MOTHERS OF 1862.

AFTER THE BATTLE OF BOTTOM'S BRIDGE, VA.,
MAY 24TH, '62.

THEY call for "able bodied men."
  Now there's our Roger, strong and stout,
  He'd beat his comrades out and out
In feats of strength and skill—what then?

What then? why, only this: you see
  He's made out of just that sort of stuff
  They want on battle-fields; enough!
What choice was left for him and me?

So when he asked me yesterweek,
  "Your blessing, mother!"—did I heed
  The great sob of my heart, or need
Another word that he should speak?

Should I sit down and mope and croon,
  And hug my selfishness and cry
  "Not him, my first-born!"—no, not I!
Thank heaven I pipe a nobler tune.

And yet, I love him like my life,
  This stalwart, handsome lad of mine!
  I'll warrant me, he'll take the shine
Off half who follow drum and fife.

Now, God forgive, how I prate!
  Ah, but the MOTHER will leap out
  Whatever folds we wrap about
Our foolish hearts, or soon or late.

No doubt 'tis weakness—mother lip
  Extolling its own flesh and blood—
  A trick of weakly womanhood
That we should scourge with thong and whip.

No doubt—and yet I should not dare
  Lay an unloved, cheap offering
  Upon my country's shrine, nor bring
Aught but was noble sweet and fair.

And so I bring my boy—too glad
  That he is worthy, and that I,
  Who bore him once in agony,
Such glorious recompense have had.

Take him, my country! he is true
  And brave and good; his deeds will tell
  More than my foolish words—'tis well;
God's love be with the lad and you.

God's love and care—and when he comes
  Back from the war, and through the street
  The crazy people flock to meet
My hero, with great shouts, and drums.

And silver trumpets braying loud,
  And silken banners, starry, gay;
  'Twill be to me no prouder day
Than this; nay, not half so proud.

And if—God help me—if, instead
  They flash this word from some red field;
  "His brave sweet soul that would not yield
Leaped upward, and they wrote him '*dead*'"

—I'll turn my white face to the wall,
  And bear my grief as best I may,
  For Roger's sake, and only say,
"He knoweth best who knoweth all."

And when the neighbors come to weep,
  Saying "Alas the bitter blow!"
  I'll answer, Nay, dear friends, not so!
Better my Roger's hero sleep,

And nobler far such lot, than his
  Who dare not strike, with heart and hand,
  For Freedom and dear Fatherland,
Where death's dark missiles crash and whiz.

And Roger's mother has no tear
  So bitter as her tears would be,
  If from the battles of the free
Her son shrank back in craven fear.

CAROLINE A. MASON.

## THE BATTLE-FIELD.

AFTER THE BATTLE OF FRONT ROYAL.
MAY 24TH, '62.

I WANDERED o'er a battle-field,
  One of a thousand such, or more,
That blot the land. The trampled turf
  Was red and wet with slippery gore.
I scarce could pick my path among
  The heaps of slaughtered men and brutes,
Piled thick around me everywhere,
  The bloody battle's rotting fruits.

And these were all—these broken things
  Were all the fruits the battle had.
It was for this a thousand died;
  For this ten thousand hearts are sad.
No longer foemen, blues and grays
  Lay stretched as they were stabbed or shot.
Whoever gained a victory there,
  'Twas very plain that these did not.

They by the stoutest of all foes
  Were stricken and were gathered in,
A foe who wears no shoulder-straps,
  Whose triumphs need no bulletin.
Two years ago, how full of life,
  And strength, and hope, were all these dead!
How fresh and green this battle-field,
  'Ere brother's blood had dyed it red!

By Northern lead and Southern steel,
  Fresh slaughtered, there the victims lay;
For Night and Death had quenched the hate
  That flamed and scorched that fearful day.
Not all are dead. Some feebly drag
  Their broken limbs across the plain,
To seek a quiet spot to die,
  A shelter from the driving rain.

Among the corpses piled and pale,
  A few are living here and there;
A few, with fast abating breath,
  Can shriek a curse or moan a prayer.
A few, through chilling rain and sleet,
  Upturn their slowly glaring eyes;
But see no beam of hope above,
  No rainbow in the sullen skies.

Across the misty, sodden field,
  Vainly their aching sight they strain;
For friend or foe, to bear them thence,
  They search the night, and search in vain.
In vain—for they must bleed and die:
  No succoring hand may reach them yet;
Both sides had gained the victory,
  And both must save their etiquette!

Still fell the rain on friend and foe,
  On dead and living, through the night,
The wind outhowled the cries below;
  Till broke the morning's sombre light.
The driving rain had swept the plain,
  And washed the pools of blood away;
But nothing recked those "victors" then,
  As cold, and pale, and stiff they lay.

## MY KINSMAN'S FALL.

AT COLD HARBOR, VA.,

MAY 24TH, '62.

LET us rest awhile, my comrade,
  Our stubborn foe has fled,
And left us here the victors,
  Where so much blood was shed.
And I do not wish to look upon
  The pale and mangled dead.

You wonder at my sadness,
  And why I could not feel
The thrilling joy of victory,
  When with such fiery zeal
We charged upon their columns,
  And bathed in blood our steel.

When broken and in terror,
  They left the gory plain,
Where many of their number lay
  Beside our mangled slain—
You wonder that I turned away,
  As if it gave me pain.

I did not falter, did I,
  There by the fence, you know,
Where the fierce fight raged so hotly,
  And so much blood did flow,
And where of our brave comrades
  So many were laid low?

But when that bullet struck me,
  And numbed my arm with pain,
And I saw upon my rifle
  The ruddy crimson stain—
I felt then as I hope I ne'er
  May feel in life again.

I felt that my blood circled in
  The veins of him that sped
The ball that did so nearly
  Lay me among the dead—
I felt he was my kinsman,
  And turned away my head.

And when we charged upon them,
  Like a swift river's flow,
I knew that my own kinsman
  Would meet me there a foe,
And thought that mine might be the sword
  That there should lay him low.

When they fled before us, vanquished,
  And we stumbled o'er the dead,
I saw a face all pale and stark,
  And with its own blood red—
I knew 'twas him, and felt my blood
  Thrill with a nameless dread

I knew he was a traitor,
  But could not hate him—no!—
For my own blood once warmly
  Did in his pulses flow;
And I wished that some hand other
  Than mine had laid him low.

But let us not speak of it,
  For in this evil time,
Such ties should be forgotton;
  To falter would be crime,
When treason's bayonets glitter
  All o'er the land like rain.

Let us go on now, comrade;
  See how the sun's rays gleam
O'er yon long line of corpses—
  How like a fearful dream!
No!—let us go 'round them,
  Down this way by the stream.

F. J. BECK

## DEAR FATHER WHEN YOU ARE FAR AWAY.

AT THE BATTLE OF WILLIAMSBURG, VA.,

MAY 25TH, 1862.

DEAR father, when you're far away;
  Think of your little Lutie;
There's one at home who'll often pray
  You may not shrink from duty.

Think not, when all your sky seems dark,
  Oh, think not of repining;
Remember that the darkest clouds
  Must have a silver lining.

Go forward in the threat'ning strife,
  Remember 'tis for freedom;
No life's too great a sacrifice,
  If our dear country need them

If in this struggle we should fall,
Freedom is lost forever;
For the sun of other lands is set
To rise in future, never.

With wistful eyes to our land they look,
And think that hope is dawning;
Soon will their night be turned to day,
And be as lovely morning.

Thus, when your path seems dark to grow,
And you weary in discharge of duty,
Think what's at stake in the present war,
And the prayers of your child Lutie.

PIERSON.

## ONCE AGAIN YOUR COUNTRY CALLS.

SECOND CALL FOR VOLUNTEERS.,
MAY 25TH, '62.

ONCE again your country calls,
Sons of Freedom's sires arise!
Spread the order o'er the land,
Sound the tocsin through the skies;
Treason stalks with powerful charms—
Freedom's sons to arms, to arms!

Where Virginia's river flows,
There your friends imperiled stand,
Fathers, brother, husbands—all
Ask of you a helping hand;
By the memory of the slain,
Will ye hear their plea in vain!

'Tis no time to falter now,
  Cast aside all party strife;
List your country's wailing cry,
  Struggling for a nation's life.
Is it not enough to know
Your native land entreats you—go?

Go! revenge her grievous wrong,
  Go! sustain her drooping arm,
Go! support her banner bright,
  Keep her bulwarks safe from harm;
Haste, o'ercome her direst foe,
Liberty's adopted—go!

By the grave, where sleeps the brave,
  By the crimson-purpled sod,
By the blood-stained river's stream,
  By the truth-avenging God,
Freemen of the loyal North,
Rouse! and in your strength go forth.

Wake! ye sons of freedom's sires,
  Pledge your lives, your fortunes, all;
Light anew the patriot fires,
  By your country stand or fall;
Live or die what'er may come,
Strike! O strike! for manhood's home.

ANONYMOUS.

## E PLURIBUS UNUM.

BATTLE OF HANOVER COURT HOUSE, VA.,

MAY 27TH, '62.

THE harp of the minstrel with melody sings
When muses have taught him to touch and to tune it,
But tho' it may have a full octave of strings
To both maker and minstrel the harp is a unit;
So the power that creates
Our Republic of States
Into harmony brings them at different dates
And the thirteen or thirty, the union once done
Are *E Pluribus Unum*, of many made one.

The science that weighs in her balance the spheres
And watched them since first the Chaldean began it,
Now and then as she counts and measures their years,
Brings into one system and names a new planet:
But the old and new stars
Venus, Neptune and Mars
As they drive around the sun their invisible cars
Whether faster or slower their races they run
Are *E Pluribus Unum*, of many made one.

Of that system of spheres should but one fly the track,
Or with others conspire for a general dispersion,
By the great central orb they will all be brought back,
And held each to her place by a wholesome *coercion;*
Should one daughter of light
But indulged in flight,
They would all be engulphed in old chaos and night;
So must none of our States be suffered to run,
For *E Pluribus Unum, we all go if one.*

Let the demon of discord our melody mar,
Or treason's red hand rend our Union asunder;
Break one string from our harp or extinguish one star,
The system's ablaze with its lightning and thunder:
Let the discord be hushed,
Let the traitors be crushed,
Though legion their name and with victory flushed;
For aye must our motto stand fronting the sun,
*E Pluribus Unum*, though many, we're one.

JOHN PIERPONT.

---

## OH LORD OF HOSTS.

EVACUATION OF CORINTH, MISS.,

MAY 29TH, '62.

O LORD of Hosts! Almighty King!
Behold the sacrifice we bring!
To every arm thy strength impart,
Thy spirit shed through every heart!
Wake in our breasts the living fires,
The holy faith that warmed our sires;
Thy hand hath made our Nation free;
To die for her is serving Thee.
Be thou a pillared flame to show
The midnight snare, the silent foe;
And when the battle thunders loud,
Still guide us in its moving cloud.
From treason's rent, from murder's stain,
Guard Thou its folds till Peace shall reign,
Till fort and field, till shore and sea
Join our loud anthem, PRAISE TO THEE.!

## MISSING.

AT THE BATTLE OF FAIR OAKS, VA,

MAY 31TH, 1862.

THERE's scarce, within our country's utmost length,
One home where standeth not a vacant chair;
Some son hath bowed down in his manly strength—
Some daughter in her loveliness so fair;
In every cot some picture decks the wall,
To tell of one who answered at Death's call.

Here hath the sire departed in his age;
Here hath the mother drooped beneath her cares;
Brother and sister flitted from the stage;
The wife her husband's clammy couch here shares;
E'en the sweet babe, whose dimpled cheeks we kissed
All have departed from us—all are missed.

'Tis sad to part, to watch the fading cheek,
The eye grow languid and the lip turn pale;
To list the feeble accents as they speak;
To mark the tottering footsteps as they fail;
Yet there is something sweet in that caress—
The last fond imprint of earth's tenderness.

Yet infinitely sorrowful the throe
Which wrings the heart with bitt'rest agony,
When those who from the fond home threshold go,
Are called upon in distant scenes to die;—
No kindly hand to soothe with tender care;
No gentle voice to breathe a parting prayer.

Within a cot upon a river's brink
  Where gathered father, mother, and one son—
The pride of their old age—the brightest link
  That bound them to earth's shores—the only one;
And he had heard of wars, and fain must go
Upon the battle-field to meet the foe.

It was a parting sad to all their hearts,
  Yet hope upheld them in the darkest hour;
They saw the foeman tremble 'neath his arts,
  And low beneath his threat'ning sabre cower;
They saw him victor 'mid war's din and wrack,
Then proudly hailed their valiant hero back.

But mark the contrast. On the wood's outskirt
  A little picket band is widely spread;
Each eye, each ear is eager and alert,
  And soft and careful is each footstep's tread;
The foe are gathered in yon dark, dense wood,
Watching and thirsting for the country's blood.

Mark where our hero leans against yon tree:—
  His eye is languid and his cheek is pale;
Forced marches and scant rations, it may be,
  Upon his frame begin to tell their tale;
Yet all this could he suffer; but the worst—
  His canteen empty—is this *dreadful thirst!*

At break of day the pickets are withdrawn,
  And each tried soldier hies him to his tent,
Hailing with joy the morning's cheerful dawn—
  Proud to have done his duty, and content;
But as the sentry checks the picket list
He pauses in alarm, for one is *missed!*

His comrades sadly at their morning meal
  Discuss his merits, nor forget his faults;
Tell of his valor, of his hasty zeal,
  His bravery amid the foe's assaults;
The sun the western clouds at eve hath kissed—
The guard is stationed—yet he still is missed.

Days, weeks, aye months, roll on and pass away;
  In camp his very name hath been forgot;
Yet still his parents watch, and weep, and pray,
  Within the chamber of that little cot;
Each night, each morning pours its fervent blessing,
In holy prayer for him who still is missing.

One eye, save God's, knows of his resting place,
  Maddened by thirst he sought a river's brink—
Thinking anon his footsteps to retrace—
  And stooped from out the cooling stream to drink;
A coward foeman dogged him to the spot:
Stooping, he fell beneath the trait'rous shot.

Here is his grave:—his feet beyond the bank;
  The treach'rous bullet mark upon his brow;
His cheek pressed to the verdure dark and rank;
  A smile e'en resting on his features now;—
Here, low in death, the cold moist earth caressing,
Lies all that once was him, who now is "MISSING!"

WALTER.

## THE SOLDIER'S FAREWELL.

### BEFORE THE BATTLE OF NEW BRIDGE, VA., JUNE 5TH, '62.

FAREWELL, mother, I must leave thee,
I must leave my childhood's home,
'Tis the love of freedom calls me
From my dearest friends to roam;
And I must leave my aged sire—
Sisters, brothers—leave them all—
I must go—('tis my heart's desire)
Answer to my country's call.

Hark! I hear the drums loud beating;
Now the air is rent with cheers,
'Tis a patriotic greeting
To the gallant volunteers;
I must go, my country's calling;
Hear the cannon loudly roar;
I must pass through scenes appalling,
As our fathers did of yore.

I must draw the glitt'ring sabre
On the gory battle field,
And, perhaps, against a neighbor,
But to traitors ne'er will yield;
Traitor! would I ne'er had heard it—
That the word was never known;
Oh! that I could now discard it—
Hurl it down from mem'ries throne!

Traitors of the Revolution,
But in history display'd—
Traitors to the Constitution,
In our very streets parade;
They have caused this wild commotion,
They have struck our colors bright—
Freedom's sons, on land and ocean,
Now are rising in their might.

Rich and poor, their homes of quiet—
Quitting for the field of blood,
Bound to quell rebellious riot;
Putting all their trust in God,
All seem ready—all *are* willing—
Working on with ardent zeal,
Soon will musketry and shelling
Make our foes before us kneel!

Since the Union is in danger,
And the Stars and Stripes disgraced;
Henceforth I'll become a Ranger,
Till our banner is replaced—
Till it waves o'er fields of cotton—
Southern forts, and cities, too,
Be it, mother, not forgotten,
I will prove a soldier true.

Go, my son, go on to battle,
For thou hast a manly soul,
Fear not sword nor muskets rattle—
Traitors never should control.
Strike our ensign! they will rue it,
And against our country plot,
Seest a man attempt to do it,
Shoot him—"shoot him on the spot."

JOHN H. WEAVER.

## THE CAMP O'ERSPREAD THE PLAIN.

BATTLE OF HARRISONBURG, VA ,
JUNE 6TH, '62.

'TWAS night; the camp o'erspread the plain,
Where blazing cannons' deafening roar
Had yesternoon swept o'er the main,
From mount to mount, from shore to shore.
No tent showed forth a burning light,
To tell the tale of sleepless minds,
No sound disturbed the silent night
Throughout the camp's well guardedlines.

Save blustering winds as swift they fled,
O'er field and hill and lonely dell
The sturdy guards hard measured tread
And changing cry of " All is well."
Within a tent, apart from all,
A soldier lay in tranquil sleep;
Deaf to all sounds, he hears no call,
But in bright dreams his vigils keep.

While smiles light up his manly brow,
His thoughts to other regions roam,
Where reign in bliss the olive bow,
Where stands his happy lovely home
In dreams he knows the war is o'er,
And peace commands where Mars did roam,
Throws down his sword to fight no more
And onward starts to seek his home.

As on he treads day after day,
  Familiar spots of old so dear,
Where years gone by behold his play,
  He sighs and wipes away a tear.
But, oh! what joy! Among the trees
  He sees the curling smoke on high,
That, wafted by the morning breeze,
  Tells him full well his home is nigh.

At last he nears the house, the gate—
  His wife and child stand by the door,
They run to meet—but horrid fate!
  He never met those dear ones more.
He woke to hear the tread of troops,
  The deafening din of human strife,
The cries of chiefs to flying groups,
  The deadly fight for limb and life.

To hear the shrieks of maimed around,
  The thunder of the cannon's roar,
To see dead comrades strew the ground,
  He woke to see and live no more.

WILLIAM J. C. MEIGHAN, S. M.

## THEIR BANNERS FRESH TORN.

### AT THE BATTLE OF CROSS KEYS, VA.,

### JUNE 7TH, '62.

THE battle is over, and grim is the field,
Where cannonry thundered and musketry peal'd,
The bellicose legions in haste have withdrawn,
Their infantry scattered, their banners fresh torn.
Victorious and strong are the National host,
Rebellion is weakened, its prestige all lost.
Bright freedom still reigns amid war's dread array,
And patriots rejoicingly hail its proud sway.

Oh, dark is the spot where the conflict did rage,
O'er-blended with horrors that sorrows prestage,
Wide-strewn with mortality murdered and pale,
While oft and anon rises agony's wail.
As gory and feeble the wounded doth lie
'Till rescued, or mahap to groaningly die,
No flash of artillery lights up the plain,
But the sun sheds its glory o'er heaps of the slain.

Foes slumber enchained in the chill clutch of death,
Foes mingle their cries with life's fast-fainting breath,
Smoke clouds the sad view as crimson streams flow,
And warrior-hearts die or writhe in their woe.
The thickets' green vesture is sullied with blood,
Down the hill-side ravine fall the bright life-flood,
'Mid the quietude lies the ravage of war,
The keen sword usurps, and calm peace flies before!

Dear Honor enshrines every patriot's grave,
And gloom wraps the mound of Treason's base slave;
The Nation's loved standard triumphant yet stands,
And courts Heaven's breezes—the joy of all lands!
Exultant I gaze at each full-flowing fold,
Its colors of beauty—of heavenly mould—
And pray that while earth in rotation doth turn,
The fires of our liberties ever shall burn.

WILLIAM J. M'CLURE.

## THE BAYONET BEFORE RICHMOND.

AFTER THE BATTLE OF WHITE HOUSE, VA.,

JUNE 13TH, '62.

MARSHALED there for home and altar,
  Grimly stand the stalwart free,
Vast and solid as Gibraltar—
  Sinews strong and bended knee.
"Forward!" See the Northmen's onset!
  Robed in flame and girt with steel!
Warrior-breasts by shell are riven—
  Crushed beneath his comrades heel!
"Onward! Scorn the feeble Southron!"
  Then their ranks in terror broke,
When we pierced their vaunted phalanx
  As the lightning rends the oak!
Bay'nets backed by brawny Northmen,
  Are the bulwarks of the Free,
And have shone o'er waves of crimson,
  Talismans of Victory!

CLARENCE F. BUHLER.

## HEAVEN DEFEND THE RIGHT.

### BATTLE ON JAMES ISLAND, S. C., JUNE 14TH '62.

WHERE is my soldier to-night?
Oh, stars in the heavens, do you know
Is he staining his hands in the bloody fight?
Is he dealing death to the traitorous foe?
Out of the South O! fair winds blow!
Where is my soldier to-night?

Is he ill or dying now?
Pitying angels what is the worst?
Is he pleading for love's cool touch on his brow?
Is he calling for water to quench his thirst?
By what strange hand is my hero nursed?
Would I were with him now!

What if he sleeps with the dead?
God! how my brain reels with the thought!
And the bitter waters mine eyes have shed
Roll back on my heart. Friends, if he be shot
For the value of my poor life, dare not
Tell me that he is *dead!*

Peace! I am growing wild;
I must not think of ills that may be
Franky, my darling—our child—his child
Dreams with his bright head upon my knee:
Cherub, smile in your sleep on me,
Let not my thoughts run wild!

A. L. MUZZEY.

## A WOUNDED SOLDIER'S SOLILOQUY.

AT THE BATTLE OF FAIR OAKS, VA.,
JUNE 17TH, '62.

Two DAYS and nights, upon the field I've laid;
A hundred times at least, to God I ve prayed
That to some surgeon I might be conveyed,
 That he might ease my pain.
I cannot wait much longer, and I fear
That I will have to draw my last breath here;
My wife, my family and my home so dear,
 To see no more again.

To leave us thus to suffer, is indeed unkind;
They ne'er should leave the wounded men behind.
But try at least, some shady place to find,
 Where we might wait for aid.
If help don't come to this poor soldier soon,
He'll shortly fall into his long last swoon:
If he's not helped, he'll surely die by noon;
 He'll die but partly by the blade.

Perhaps our comrades do now all they can;
These are but the ravings of a dying man;
Not a soul to talk with, and no one to fan
 The heat from off my brow.
The way we fought the battle, Time can ne'er erase,
And now we're wounded, death stares us in the face.
I feel I'm falling into death's embrace,
 I know I'm dying now.

E. C. BRETON.

## THE LAST LETTER.

BEFORE THE BATTLE CUMBERLAND GAP, TENN,

JUNE 18TH, 1862.

DEAR Rose, to you I send this present writing,
To let you know how this world goes with me;
Our glorious boys have done some glorious fighting,
A left arm lost, alas! has done for me.
We've great successes in our track advancing,
The cruel grape has shaken our poor homes;
We've sacked whole cities, but a spent ball glancing,
Pays me my share of booty in my bones.

From an old hospital this word I'm sending,
To leave it soon at death's call for the grave;
I send an eagle by him who does my mending,
For them I've sold the body he can't save.
I send the pieces, for I'm just now thinking
That if to-night must see me in the earth,
I can't do less for one whom love's been linking
So close to me than give her *all I'm worth.*

My poor old mother when I left her crying,
Was nearly gone and looking close to death;
I've writ a line to tell her I'm dying,
But I do hope she's taken her last breath.
For if the dear old women is still living,
Her heart's so soft that if she hears I'm gone,
She cannot stay, and I shall death be giving
To her who gave me life, now left alone.

My little Rose, there's one old friend I cherish,
  You won't desert—my good old dog I mean;
He mustn't know I'm dead—for sure he'd perish
  If he but thought of me the last he'd seen.
He's looking now to see me home returning,
  At least a Corporal, if not something more;
Then guard him well, and keep the dog from learning
  I died a private on this earthen floor.

It cuts me to the heart to think of dying
  Far from the village, and from you, my Rose;
No chance to say good night to friends, or, sighing,
  To press your hand before my eyelids close.
At home they'd soon my shattered bones be laying
  Hard by the church—a cross above my head,
There my Rose would sometimes come, and praying,
  Ask God to keep him whom she loved though dead.

Then good by, Rose, good by; and don't be weeping
  Farewell, farewell! I'll see you dear, no more;
For in the company I'll soon be keeping,
  They give no furloughs, though you beg them sore.
All's turning round—I feel I'm just departing,
  I've got my orders and must leave you here;
Good night, good night!—One word before starting;
  God bless you, Rose, and don't forget me, dear!

CHARLES LEVER.

## THE TENTED FIELD.

### BATTLE OF OAK GROVE, VA., JUNE 25TH, '62.

GRIM darkness dwells upon the tented field,
Where shadows live, and vapors from the grave,
Unfleshed, impalpable, like clouds sweep o'er
The glorious field of death! All sound reposes!
No deep-toned baying give the dogs of war—
Nor lightning flash, nor sob, nor groan
Break through the misty bulwark of the night!
Death frowns and plants his throne 'mid heaps of slain,
While slowly wand'ring through the crimson dead
An angel shade glides o'er the fest'ring mass,
Attentive marking every mangled corse!
But look! it pauses o'er a monument of dead—
Where hardly quenched, the smould'ring flames of war
Still faintly blaze within some patriot breast.
Above them there, o'ertopping all the slain,
As 'twere to show his soul disdained to fly
Till others less determined had succumbed to death,
Or else, perhaps, some lucky chance had smoothed
The brow of Fate that he a time might live
To rear his monument of ghastly slain—
There lay a youth, stern browed, though young—
Ghastly in death, and firm and terrible!
A very warrior—one whose soul inherits
The fires of Jove direct from heaven's self!
One hand doth clutch the silent air, the other
Still grasps a starry flag, whose glorious folds
Embrace his ragged heart, where bullet torn
It sleeps alone with glory!
Here paused the angel shadow on its way,

And raising from the dust that starry flag,
Whose hues were known in Heaven, it set the seal
Of Heaven once more upon it—and turning,
On the warrior's brow it dropped a tear
That sparkled in the blackness of the night
More brightly than the stars—who from their thrones
Looked down and wept!
Impotent Treason howled in rage afar,
But dared not tread the hallowed spot—
And still the angel dwelt around the corse.
Meanwhile, bright spirits of the long ago
Returning, kissed the banner that they loved,
And with the spirits of the patriot slain,
Fled to their home in Heaven!

EDWIN F. DENYSE.

## TO THE RESCUE!

AFTER THE BATTLE OF MECHANICSVILLE, VA., JUNE 27TH, '62.

AROUSE! Arouse all gallant sons
And to the rescue go,
For many on the battle-field
To-day lie faint and low.
And will you see them one by one,
Like flowers of Summer, fall?
Oh! no, your hearts are better far,
You'll answer to the call.
You'll answer to the call for men
To reinforce the brave,
Who valiant fought and nobly fell
And found a soldier's grave.

M. J. HIGGINS.

## THE REINFORCEMENT.

AT THE BATTLE ON THE CHICKAHOMINY, VA.,

JUNE 28TH, 1862.

DARK, starless night had hushed the busy hum
Of murm'ring voices, and the fife and drum,
And clarion bugle, now no longer swelled
Their startling notes above that fatal field.
Wearily, heavily, our tired soldiers slept
On the dank earth, as silently we crept
To danger's post, and watched the dark array
Of foeman's hosts, till wore the night away;
But ere it passed how long the moments seemed,
As gazed we o'er where countless camp-fires gleamed,
Kindled by vengeful foes. How freighted they
With thought of home and loved ones far away;
With hopes and fears, and thoughts of strife and death,
That ere another night must hush the breath
Of many a noble form aud generous heart,
Who for their country well had borne their part—
Then grasped with firmer hand our fire-locks true,
Whose touch gave courage, strength and life anew—
We watched and waited till the light of day
Should gleam o'er earth, and give us light to slay.
It came anon, and through its misty light
We saw the foeman marshalled in his might,
With gleaming steel and flashing blades, move down
As some dark cloud, that spreads o'er earth its frown

While rolling thunder—vivid flashes tell
Of the dark storm that comes o'er hill and dell.
On, on they come! Guards unsheath each sword
Hearest thou not in that tangled cedar glade
A voice that tells the battle-storm is nigh?
Heard not the deadly shell shriek fiercely by?
Seest not that traitor host pour thick and fast,
Across the fields like waves on ocean vast?
Already there, where lacks a hopeful word,
His blade is seen, his cheering voice is heard,
And at their posts were others, strong and true,
Braving the storm where death-shots thickest flew.
Heroes they fought—like heroes many fell,
And crimsoned with their blood that fatal dell!
'Tis vain! 'tis vain! the heart that never quails,
'Gainst triple arms and equal valor fails!
Ah! yield we must, and leave our comrades slain
To welter there upon the gory plain!
Fly! fly! Is there no hope—no aid? Oh, say,
Must godless traitors win this bloody day?
Must noble men—thus hosts of noble slain,
Fall on this gory field, and die in vain?
No! no! it comes! the wished-for aid is near!
"Relief!—relief!" rings gladly on the ear.
Dire then the fray and fierce the carnage there,
And cannon roar pealed loudly on the air!
They yield! they yield! the Rebel tide is stayed,
Their columns faler, and fall back dismayed!
Saved! saved! the bloody day was saved—not won!
And of our bloody task not half was done!
Days came and went, still raged the battle storm,
O'er gory fields, and many a lifeless form,
Till its wild fury ebbed. The field was won—
The foe had fled—our fearful task was done!

ELSINE MAY.

## OH! HOME OF MY SIRES.

BATTLE OF PEACH ORCHARD, VA.,
JUNE 29TH, '62.

OH! home of my sires,
  Of the brave and the free,
My prayers are ascending
  To Heaven for thee,
That thy armies now marshalled
  In battle array
Shall be, by God's power,
  Thy strength and thy stay.
Then up with thy banner,
  The rifle and sword,
On the Rebels come down
  In the might of the Lord.

God save thee, my country,
  From *traitors* and *knaves!*
May their lives all be blasted,
  Dishonored their graves.
They talk not of pity,
  The mercies they feel
Are as cruel and fierce
  As the death-doing steel;
But thy strength, oh, my country!
  Is in God and the right,
And thy stars, all undimmed,
  Shall emerge from the fight.

Oh! never, my country,
  Shall we leave thee forlorn,
To be crushed by the traitors,
  A mock and a scorn;
Let them come with their legions,
  And banner of "bars,"
We'll on to the contest
  'Neath the stripes and the stars;
Even now they are trembling,
  The hand-writing they see—
They have failed, oh! my country,
  To disunite thee.

FINLEY JOHNSON.

## WHEN STATESMEN FAIL.

BATTLE OF SAVAGE STATION, VA.,
JUNE 29TH, '62.

When statesmen fail to guide the public mind,
And lengthen'd speeches cannot lead the *blind*,
Let poets boldly to the world proclaim
The laws of Justice and the traitor's shame;
Nor spare the vices of disreputive men,
But draw their portraits with impartial pen.
Ye master minds, inspired from on high,
Strike now the strings of love and unity;
The clouds are looming, and the thunder's roar
May yet shake our country from shore to shore;
Pollution reigns and fills the atmosphere,
The wheels of government are out of gear.
May yet some noble mind adjustment make,
Not for himself, but for his country's sake,

JOHN H. WEAVER.

## 'TIS MIDNIGHT O'ER THE BATTLE FIELD.

AFTER THE BATTLE OF MALVERN HILLS, VA.,
JULY 1ST, '62.

'Tis midnight; o'er the battle-field
The chilly wind is sighing;
And moonlight steals thro' deep'ning mist
Upon the dead and dying.
No longer bursts upon the air
The rifle's vivid flashing—
All silent is the place where rung
The sabre's rapid clashing.

Amid the bodies stiff in death
One man, with life, is lying;
Though fast upon his weary heart
His bosom's blood is drying;
But faster down his pallid face
The tears are hotly streaming,
For far away his sad thoughts roam,
To loved ones sweetly dreaming!

As vividly, with magic skill,
The past fond mem'ry traces,
He sees again his happy home,
Dear forms and smiling faces!
His little children clasp his neck—
He smoothes their sunny tresses;
And warm upon his lips and brow
He feels their soft caresses.

Again he hears his wife's low voice
  Her hand his own is pressing;
And fondly, sadly, to his ear
  Still floats her parting blessing!
And now the din of war steals in
  Upon the field of battle—
He fights, though wounded, till he faints
  Amid its deaf'ning rattle.

Now colder to his ghastly brow
  The misty air is creeping;
And from his weakly-throbbing breast
  The blood is faster leaping.
He faintly mourns, "My home, farewell!
  God soothe my poor wife's anguish!
I'd rather die here, on the field,
  Than as a *captive* languish."

He speaks no more! As if in sleep
  His weary eyes are closing;
And soon the moon shines o'er his form,
  In peaceful death reposing.
The morning dawns, and sunlight falls
  O'er bodies cold and gory;
But *he* beholds a brighter dawn—
  The dawn of Heaven's glory!

MATILDA BURTON.

## MOTHER WOULD COMFORT ME.

AFTER THE BATTLE OF PLEASANT HILLS, MISS.,
JULY 11TH, '62.

WOUNDED and sorrowful, far from my home,
Sick among strangers, uncared for, unknown,
Even the birds, that used sweetly to sing,
Are silent, and swiftly have taken the wing
No one but mother can cheer me to-day—
No one for me could so fervently pray;
None to console me, no kind friend is near—
Mother would comfort me if she were here.

If she were with me I soon would forget
My pain and my sorrow, no more would I fret,
One kiss from her lips, or one look from her eye,
Would make me contented and willing to die!
Gently her hand o'er my forehead she'd press,
Trying to free me from pain and distress;
Kindly she'd say to me, "Be of good cheer,
Mother will comfort you, mother is here."

Cheerfully, faithfully, mother would stay,
Always beside me by night and by day—
If I should murmur or wish to complain,
Her gentle voice would calm me again.
Sweetly a mother's love shines like a star,
Brightest in darkness when daylight's afar,
In clouds or in sunshine, pleasures or pain,
Mother's affection is ever the same.

CHARLES CARROLL SAWYER.

## EVER THE SAME.

ENGAGEMENT ON THE YAZOO RIVER, MISS.,

JULY 12TH, '62.

THE glorious band of patriots,
  Who gave the flag its birth,
Have writ with steel in history,
  The record of its worth.
From east to west, from sea to sea,
  From pole to tropic sun,
Will eyes grow bright and hearts throb high
  At the name of Washington.

Ah! proudly should we bear it now,
  And guard this flag of ours,
Borne bravely in its infancy,
  Amid the darker hours;
The brave alone may bear it thus,
  A guardian it shall be
For those who well have won the right
  To boast of liberty.

The meteor flag of Seventy-six,
  Long may it wave in pride,
To tell the world how nobly
  Our patriot fathers died;
When from the shadows of their night,
  Outburst the brilliant sun,
It bathed in light the Stars and Stripes,
  As now in Sixty-one.

ANONYMOUS.

## THE DRUMMER BOY.

AT THE BATTLE OF MURFREESBORO, MISS.,
JULY 13TH, '62.

THE solemn work at last was o'er,
  And then towards the camp,
The weary soldiers went their way
  With slow and heavy tramp;
And as the lanterns' fitful gleams
  Shone o'er the field around,
What was it that sent back the light
  Upon the bloody ground?

There, with his drum beside him laid,
  That should have been a toy,
Was stretched the gory body
  Of a little drummer boy.
Nine summers scarce had blessed him
  Ere his little life went out,
Amid the battle's thunder,
  And the foe's inglorious rout.

His golden hair in clustering curls,
  Lay on his pallid face,
And on his lip a gentle smile
  The soldier's eye could trace.
His sweet blue eye was glassy now,
  His little hand was still,
And his young heart no more, alas!
  With joy and pride would thrill.

Ah! curse the traitor hand that sped
 That bullet swift and sure!
Was there no power to ward it from
 That little bosom pure?
And was not stern death satisfied?
 Could naught complete his joy,
But the widowed mother's only hope,
 That little drummer boy?

A year ago the little one
 Was in his village home,
And often to his childish ear
 The sad war news would come,
This friend was dead, that battle lost,
 Until his swelling heart
Within him burned, to take his drum,
 And bear his little part.

His widowed mother—bless her, Heaven!
 Proudly bade him go,
And bare his little bosom to
 The bullet of the foe,
Nor sigh, nor tear escaped her when
 She gave the parting kiss;
Did ever Spartan mother make
 A sacrifice like this?

And now her heart is desolate,
 Her prayers ascend on high,
That God in tender mercy
 Will allow her but to die;
For if in answer to her prayers
 The asked-for boon be given,
She'll meet the darling of her heart
 And dwell with him in heaven.

But still not one repining word
  Her sorrowed lip will speak,
For her spirit is a noble one
  Although her heart be weak,
And had she yet another son
  She'd freely let him go
Where Willie went to meet his death
  Before his country's foe.

A. M. O

---

## THE MAN OF THE IRON WILL.

BATTLE OF MEMPHIS, MO.,
JULY 18TH, '62.

AYE! toll! toll! toll!
    Toll the funeral bell!
And let its mournful echoes roll
From sphere to sphere, from pole to pole,
O'er the flight of the greatest, kingliest soul
    That ever in battle fell.
Yes! weep! weep! weep!
    Weep for the hero fled!
For Death, the greatest of soldiers, at last
Has over our leader his black pall cast,
And from us his noble form hath passed
    To the home of the mighty dead.
His form has passed away!
    His voice is silent and still!
No more at the head of "the old brigade,"
The daring men who were never dismay'd,
Will he lead them to glory that never can fade,
    The man of the iron will!

ANONYMOUS.

## PICKET SHOOTING.

AT HARRISON LANDING, VA.

AUG. 1ST, 1862.

To AND fro upon the green banks,
'Neath the moonbeams pale and fair,
Paced a picket, silent, lonely,
Thinking of the home afar,
With his gun upon his shoulder,
To and fro he slowly trod,
And his eyes were dim and misty
As they fell upon the sod.

"It was here," he murmured, sadly,
"That poor Charley Stanton fell,
Shot down by some lurking foeman,
Here, within this little dell;
Here it was we found his body,
When the golden morning broke,
With the red blood on his forehead,
From the gory bullet stroke."

Then the soldier looked around him
With a searching, anxious look,
Peered behind each clump of bushes,
Searched each silent, leafy nook,
But no foeman sprang to meet him,
And he murmured wearily,
"There's no rebel lurking near me,
Nothing lies in wait for me."

Scarcely had the words been spoken,
  When there came a blinding flash
From a clump of swaying willows,
  Moaning in the midnight blast;
And the picket with a wild cry
  Fell upon the dew-wet ground,
With the red blood streaming redly
  From a gory, ghastly wound.

## CAVALRY RAID.

### TO BATON ROUGE, LA., AUGUST 5TH, '62.

"To HORSE! to horse!" the trumpet's breath
Is wafted o'er wide fields of death;
A thousand horsemen mount their steed
Like tigers from the jungle freed,
A thousand sabres flash in the air—
A thousand hearts are beating there,
Whilst downward to the Gulf they move
O'er plains and hills and mighty flood.

Again the bugle sounds: and now
A gleam of light breaks on each brow,
As each his sabre freely draws
To vindicate our injured laws;
Each warrior feels that on him rest
A nation's hopes by wrongs oppressed,
And each looks forward to the hour
When victory lights on vale and bower.

No craven voice is heard to cry,
No coward with his downcast eye,
But firm resolve is pictured there,
And Freedom's banner floats in air
Above their heads like spirit bright
That wills to watch the bloody fight;
Proud gonfalon that ever flies!
Like golden cloud in summer skies.

Their tramp is like the ocean's roar
When mighty billows crowd the shore,
Or like the avalanche that glides
From mountain top adown its sides;
A rapid torrent dark and swift
That leaps in scorn the rocky cliff,
Their beating hoofs like aspen make
The earth with fearful echoes shake.

Death leads the van, and then
What piteous beings press the plain;
What horrid shrieks apall the ear,
What startling echoes answer near;
What manly forms are overthrown,
What streams of blood in torrents run;
Traitors beneath their falchions bleed,
Or trod to death by fiery steed.

Some seek by hasty steps to hide
Them from the wasting tide,
And hurry from that fearful doom
That frightens with its horrid gloom;
Whilst others in their mad career
Fight bravely on still scorning fear,
And give and take the deadly thrust
That drags their honors down to dust.

The sabre's edge is clogged with gore,
And yet it drinks and cries for more;
Whilst onward o'er the plains they fly
Like flocks of vultures in the sky,
Shouting and battling in their rage—
Can nought but blood their thirst assuage?
Must brother fall by brother's hands,
And fatten plains of arid sands?

Yes! 'tis the doom of traitors; on
Till darkness veils the blazing sun.
No look of sympathy to mock
With pallid lip this battle shock;
But hoof and steel and death
Breathe as of erst their angel breath,
Till each conspirator's vile form
Is served as banquet for the worm.

The bugle calls from strife; the sky
Is covered o'er with shadows nigh,
And darkness with its sombre form
Comes down and hides them from the storm;
As if to save from trampling feet
The traitors in their quick retreat,
Who fly from slaughter as the hind
In haste avoids the human kind.

How many souls in fear have fled!
How many more sleep with the dead;
How many sons of heroes slain
Lie stretched upon the bloody plain?
How many mothers, sisters mourn,
And wait and watch their safe return;
Alas! a civil war in madness walks
Along our fields, in carnage stalks.

And treason with its hollow eye
Lifts up its guilty head on high,
And threats with fratricidal knife;
To fill our homes with blood and strife;
The 'venging blade our country calls,
Our banners float on the outer walls,
The Stars and Stripes forever wave
To lighten up each patriot's grave.

And sabres flash from many a side
To swell this host of loyal pride,
And many a palace hall is lit
And echoes with its children's feet;
While humble roof and cottage poor
Echo the shout of volunteer!
Seizing with willing hand the knife
That ends at once this bloody strife.

Onward they march; above the rest
Rides the young hero with his waving crest,
With blade that flashes in the sun—
Proud signal that his victory's won!
The spires in distance pierce the blue.
And Baton Rouge breaks on the view;
Eight hundred miles they now look back
Where burning cities mark their track!

OSCAR J. WISNER.

## THE DYING COLOR-BEARER.

AT THE BATTLE OF LONE JACK, MO.,
AUGUST 10TH, '62.

OH! take me home to die, brother;
Oh! Take me home to die—
For I'd look on our native hills
Before I close mine eye—
Would dream again the pleasant dreams
Of happy days of yore—
Of the sweet songs that mother sang,
Which I shall hear no more,

Near where the laughing forest stream,
Leap'd its pebbly bed,
Close by the old, moss-grown churchyard,
Where rest the honor'd dead.
Thus, dying in my country's cause,
I there would long to sleep,
That in the morn, the tear-gem'd flow'rs
May o'er me bow and weep.

'Mid trumpet's call, drum's dreaded roll,
And cannon's fearful roar,
Bright bay'nets glance and sabres flash,
Yet warm with human gore—
Our men, with steady front, charged on
Upon the rebel foe,
Where carnage red looked on dire deeds
Of sickening, mortal woe.

Thus in the battle, I upheld
  The flag of liberty,
And thought how sweet it were to die,
  Oh! father-land, for thee—
Then as traitor's bullet sped
  Toward my trobbing heart,
I cried with joy, midst shriek and groan,
  I, too have done my part!

A. P. AUPER.

## RALLYING ROUND THEIR STANDARD.

MASSACRE AT FORT RIPLEY, MINNESOTA,

AUGUST 20TH, '62.

'TIS heard, 'tis heard, that dreadful sound—
  Stern Battle's vengeful crash;
War's angry thunders echo 'round,
  While lightnings from the columns flash.

Grand woods ring out with trumpet blast,
  And sharp the musketry contends;
Opposing ranks pour thick and fast,
  Their murd'rous fire that horror lends.

Hostile bands in desperate fray,
  Wake the air with clarion shout;
The booming cannon lowly lay,
  And force the weaker to the rout.

Batteries send in bounding notes,
  Their messengers of speedy death;
The tocsin sound with clearness floats,
  The slain they strew the dewy heath.

The dying cries of suffering life,
  Rise piercingly from mossy dale,
As onward peals the bitter strife,
  And onward fly the leaden hail.

Warm, crimson tides flow fast from breasts
  Now rent with ghastly, gaping wounds;
The victims of those wild behests
  With which the will of power abounds.

The soldier falls! aye falls in blood,
  Of comrades shattered, dying, dead;
'Tis on that field where strong he stood,
  He claims a warrior's hard death bed!

How desolate once happy bowers,
  Where naught was known but home delights;
The mighty sword exerts its powers,
  The conflict shows its hideous frights.

Both cot aud mansion 'neath the sway
  Of these demoniac legions fall;
And seething, rise the smokes so gray,
  As ruin mark 'mid forests tall.

Quick rallying 'round their standard high,
  They rush defensive of their cause,
And cease when victory casts its die,
  On either horde—'tis then they pause.

Oh, dearly bought, unholy prize,
  At cost of human creature's doom;
Ye rulers, shun the sacrifice,
  And save the many hearts from gloom!

WILLIAM J. M'CLURE.

## DIRGE OF THE RAPPAHANNOCK.

AFTER THE BATTLE ON THE RAPPAHANNOCK, VA.,
AUGUST 21ST, '62.

OH, there are thoughts that have no form,
  Deep, wide, and strong to bring them forth,
Wild as the pent-up wintry storm
  That lingers in the frozen North,
Till changing skies give their dark whirlwinds birth.

Such, Rappahannock, is thy tale,
  That rushes like thy tide to ocean's deep—
Would that some ocean-bosom might prevail
  To hold the burden which each bound doth leap
  To pour its onward force relentless in its sweep.

Not Israel's seat whose shadowy vale of death
  Spread its unnumbered hosts before his sight,
Hail thy dark horrors steeped in dying breath,
  The ever resting, gloomy mist of night,
  No sun shall ever pierce with ray of cheerful light.

Ye spirits, marshal up your ranks again,
  Ye knew the horrors of that day of gloom,
Gather your serried hosts and let the plain
  Where hangs the drapery of a nation's tomb,
  Echo the tramp that march'd you to your doom!

No more—the thought is idle as a dream,
  Yet Rappahannock's flowing stream must know
The mutter'd curse that hath the raven-scream,
  "On all her banks let deadly nightshade grow,"
  Nor poet's line e'er change that bitter curse of woe.

With timid fear the child shall lave his feet,
 Like Egypt's bloody Nile, where rolls thy wave,
While dismal spectres ever more shall greet
 To drive all joyous life from freedom's grave,
 Where many thousand fell, the bravest of the brave.

Ah! 'tis a tale which shall curdle in the veins
 Of youth and age for centuries to come,
And bloody horsemen tightly grasp the reins,
 Pausing and shivering to list thy spectral drum,
Thy terror, which shall strike the warrior dumb.

And pulpit men, whose mission was of love,
 Yet clamor'd for this fray with vulture beak,
In memory led these gloomy banks shall rove
 Where waken'd conscience her vengeance wreak,
 And tell stern truths the heart alone can speak.

It hath been writ that war was once in heaven,
 Whose starry heights gleam'd with infernal fires,
That dragon-blood hath well its fruitage given,
 And hell's deep hate the human fiend inspires,
That mingles in the heart where pity's voice expires.

Walk o'er these grounds, ye sordid men of gain,
 Thriving as vampires, on politic strife,
On Rappahannock's ripen'd fields of grain
 Feast in your thought your elements of life—
 The food becomes ye well—the harvest day is rife.

The chivalry of peace changes in war,
 To midnight prowl the fierce hyenas make,
Could yet not let the cover'd corpse be where
 It fell in death, but stripped and naked, take
 The clothes it wore, nor ashes o'er it rake.

ANONYMOUS.

## MY CAPTAIN BEND LOW.

AT THE BATTLE OF CENTERVILLE, VA.,

AUGUST 28TH, '62.

My noble commander, thank God you have come;
You know the dear ones who are waiting at home,
And Oh! it were dreadful to die here alone,
No hand on my brow, and my comrades all gone.
I thought I would die many hours ago,
And those who are waiting me never could know
That here, in the faith of its happiest years,
My soul has not wandered one moment from theirs.
The dead are around; but my soul was away
With the roses that bloom 'round my cottage, to-day,
I thought that I sat where the jessamine twines,
And gathered the delicate buds from the vines.
And there—like a bird that had folded its wings,
At home 'mid the smile of all beautiful things,
With sweet words of welcome, and kisses of love—
Was one I will miss in yon heaven above.
By the light that I saw on her radiant brow
She watches, and waits there, and prays for me now.
My captain, bend low; for this poor, wounded side
Is draining my heart of its lost crimson tide.
Some day—when you leave this dark place, and go free
You will meet a fair girl! she will question of me!
She has kissed the bright curl, as it lay on my head;
When it goes back alone, she will know I am dead.
And tell her the soul, when on earth was her own,
Is waiting and weeping in Heaven, alone,

My Mother! God help her! Her grief will be wild
When she hears the mad Rebels murdered her child;
But tell her 'twill be one sweet chime in my knell,
That the flag of the North now waves where I fell!
It is well, it is well, thus to die in my youth,
A martyr to freedom, and Justice, and Truth!
Farewell to earth's hopes, precious dreams of my heart,
My life's going out; but my love shall depart,
On the wings that my soul has unfurled,
Going up, soft and sweet to that beautiful world.

ANONYMOUS.

## A BATTLE DIRGE.

THE SECOND BULL RUN,

AUGUST 29TH, '62.

OH! sad is the dirge of a nation's dismay,
And bitter the tears, and dark is the day;
The Eagle hath flown from her rock-crested nest,
For her foemen have reach'd to the place of her rest.
Hark! her scream on the air raises up in affright
The tigers of war who quailed in the fight,
While an echo prolongs to each valley and dell
The key-note of sorrow—a dismal farewell.

Farewell to the hopes that cluster'd so gay,
The pennons that flaunted the breeze of that day;
Our prestige of honor—oh! who shall regain—
That lies on the field of the three hundred slain!
Oh, mother, look not out of thy window above—
There cometh no footstep thy welcome to prove;
Oh! wife, linger not the postman to hear—
He comes, but his news hath the mark of the bier.

Oh, daughter—oh, sister—oh, brother—oh friend—
Ye never on earth your greetings may blend;
The warm tear of love is dried on the cheek
By a thrill of the sorrow that faileth to speak.
Oh! hearts that are wrung with the tidings of woe,
How lately ye sang in the morning's fresh glow;
'Tis evening now—sad, lonely and dark—
With the howl of the wolf and the eye of the shark.

And dismal the waves that dash on the shore
With the deep groaning sound of the battle's last roar.
Who—who shall achieve one solace—one ray
To flash thro' the gloom a hope for the day?
Nay—nay, let me twine my lay with the wreath—
With asphodel brought from the regions of death;
Let me hide in the dust the Flag of my pride.
And wail to the tempests that mock and deride.

Then muffle the drum to the slow, measured tread—
To the march of the heroes who follow the dead;
Let the bugle that charged for the battle's array
Wail sad as the wind of the Winter's dark day.
Yet the dirge of the corses that sleep in their gore
Shall come as a tempest the storm to outpour—
Shall nourish to life the hopes that were fled,
And Freedom shall rise from the three hundred dead.

RALPH HOYT.

## A BROTHER'S SAD FAREWELL.

AFTER THE SECOND BATTLE OF CENTREVILLE, VA., AUGUST 30TH, '62.

DARK was the night, with not a star
To guide the sentry's feet,
As backward, forward, to and fro,
He trod his weary beat.
His heart was sad—scarce yet a score
Of years had touched his brow,
And he had been a father's pride—
A mother's care 'till now.

He was the youngest of the flock,
Which once had numbered three,
But now, alas! not one was left
Beneath the old roof tree.
The violets were smiling now,
Amid the moss, that o'er
His sister's grave he planted, but
A few short months before.

And the first-born of that fair group,
Two years had been away,
A reckless wanderer, only God
Knew where his feet did stray;
And he, that beardless boy, had felt
His heart beat high and warm,
When on the Ship of State had burst
The tempest and the storm.

"She must not sink," he cried, "or if
We're powerless to save,
I'll sink with her, when she goes down
Beneath the treacherous wave!"
And he had left his home, with tears
And blessings on his brow—
That youthful sentinel, who kept
His starless vigils now.

"I'll sing," he said, "'twill help to pass
These long dark hours away,
And I must keep this weary beat
Until the break of day."
And so, with low, sweet voice, he sung
A song, which years before,
His mother taught her little band.
Before the cottage door.

And olden memories filled his heart,
And his firm cheek was wet;
He seemed to see his mother's faee—
To hear her voice, and yet—
"Halt! give the countersign," he cried,
As softly on his ear.
Fell a low footstep, and his heart
Beat high, but not with fear.

He strained his eyes through the thick gloom,
The intruder's form to see.
"I do not know the countersign,
But I am Henry Lee."
"My brother!" and he wildly clasped
The stranger's form ere long,
"I knew you Charley, when I heard
You sing our mother's song."

Words are inadequate to tell
  Of that long, close embrace,
Or of the tears that fell from each
  Upon the others face;
Or of the story told, when tears
  Had wept their fountains dry,
And those young hearts together watched
  The starless hours go by.

For they who sung the same sweet songs
  Before the cottage door,
Led by a gentle mother's voice,
  In happy years before,
Had met again; each pledged to what
  He thought to be the right—
The pickets of contending foes,
  That lonely, lonely night.

It mattered not, the angels bend,
  Methinks, and lingered long,
To look upon that holy scene,
  Wrought by a mother's song;
And when the shadows of the morn
  Acrost the valley fell,
With sorrowing hearts, the brothers said
  A tender, sad farewell.

MRS. SARAH A. WATSON.

## MARTYRED.

AFTER THE BATTLE AT FAIRFAX COURT HOUSE, VA., SEPTEMBER 2D, '62.

The banners droop above the quiet camp;
  Night felt, though viewless, fills the tranquil air;
  Each swarthy face is flushed with earnest prayer,
That rises mingled with the sentry's tramp.

A fair-haired youth weeps as the solemn scene
  Calls to his mind our country's better days,
  Before its orbs burned pale through bloody haze,
And mildew fell upon its living green.

The briar-rose that blossomed by the church;
  The clover-balm that through its windows stole,
  Like incense rising from the thymy knoll;
The sombre hemlock and the fragrant birch—

Green spots upon the desert sands of thought,
  With waters purling from an unseen fount,
  Seen in the moonlight shed o'er Memory's mount,
Bring light and bloom to hours with darkness fraught.

Soon combat blurs the sunlight with its breath;
  The hostile weapon smites upon a rock,
  For no less fiercely in the angry shock
His war-note hails the harvest home of death.

Like a huge camp-fire in a snowy vale,
  The red moon flames thro' milky clouds, while stars
  Clustering 'round it, gaze through fleecy bars
Where cheeks that never blanched before are pale.

Rest, martyred youth! beyond the pale of death
  There's choicer music than the village psalm,
  A richer incense than the clover-balm,
A sweeter perfume than the roses breath.

CLARENCE F. BUHLER.

---

## PUT NONE BUT MEN ON GUARD TO-NIGHT.

AFTER THE ATTACK ON PLYMOUTH, N. C.,

SEPTEMBER 2ND, '62.

PUT none but *men* on guard to night;
  Put none but men, *true* men on guard;
Put none but *soldiers* in the fight
  To guard our banner striped and starred.
Let every man act well his part—
  Be honest, faithful, earnest, true;
Ho! patriots give both hand and heart—
  O! 'tis your *Country* calls on you.
Fling out our banners!—let them wave,
  And 'neath them stand, or *fighting fall!*
Then, up!— arouse!—your Land to save.
  *To arms!*—ho! rally, patriots all!
Put none but men on guard to-night;
  Put none but men, true men on guard;

JAMES A. C. O'CONNOR.

## OH, LET US MOURN.

INDIAN FIGHT AT THE LOWER AGENCY MINN.,
SEPTEMBER 8TH, '62.

OH, let us mourn—for the warriors fame
From him forever has fled,
And his noble deeds and his glorious name
Let us link them with the dead,
For he shall not die as the warrior dies,
With his frowning brow to the golden skies.

Oh, let us grieve that ambition has
Bade him to treachery bow;
That he who played once a Patriot's part
Is mingling with rebel's now.
Oh, breathe it not to the winds of heaven,
*Let the traitors's name* from the earth be riven.

Oh, let us weep—for his gallant deeds
Are shadowed now with a cloud,
And many a heart for the warrior bleeds
That was once so stern and proud,
And eyes are now weeping to see the brave
Thus sink to a cold and dishonor'd grave,

Aye, let us mourn—for he must fall,
But not as the brave shall die;
For his traitorous deeds have blotted all
That once shone so gloriously.
For he shall not die as the warrior dies,
With his frowning brows to the glorious skies

FINLEY JOHNSON.

## HE WILL NEVER COME AGAIN.

AFTER THE BATTLE OF MUNFORDSVILLE, KY.,
SEPTEMBER 14TH, '62.

THOU art watching, wife, for Willie,
For his quick and safe return
From the bloody field of battle—
And thy fervid heart doth burn
For the echo of his footstep
At the little cottage door;
But, alas, dear wife, 'tis folly,
Willie can return no more.

Thou art waiting, wife, for Willie,
But thy waiting will be long,
And thy heart will fill with sadness,
As you watch the passing throng;
Then the tears will dim thy vision,
And thy cheek grow pale with fear,
When you learn the fall of Willie,
For the cause he held most dear.

Yes, your Willie died a hero
On the fearful battle plain,
And thy love cannot recall him,
Nor thy gentle voice again
Bring responses from his bosom,
For his heart is hush'd and still,
And you'll miss him, sadly miss him,
In the cottage on the hill.

Kiss the children, wife, for Willie,
  Bid them each a long farewell,
And when years shall give them wisdom,
  Teach them how their father fell,
That their eyes may cease to wander
  Down the little narrow lane,
For a form once so familiar,
  That will never come again.

ROBERT M. HART.

## THE SOLDIER'S REQUIEM.

AFTER THE BATTLE AT SOUTH MOUNTAIN, MD.,

SEPT. 14TH, 1862.

SOUTH winds blow soft where the soldier is lying,
  Tread with your lightest step, whisper more low—
Oh, waft to its home this spirit undying—
  Never a mission more pure shall ye know!
Ever let roses, their fragrance distilling,
  Weep o'er the mound of the hallowed dead;
And, while their cups with dew-tears are filling
  Let the daisies and blue-bells wave over his head.
Long be his name, his fame and his glory
  Joined in our hearts, with the land of his birth—
And let his deeds live brightest in story,
  Chaunted and sung by the fairest of earth!
Keep bright the stars that he left to your keeping,
  Soil not the Banner—for aye let it wave
Over the land where the hero is sleeping—
  Never should land be so proud of a grave!

ANONYMOUS.

## THE SWORD OF BUNKER HILL.

AT THE SURRENDER OF MARYLAND HEIGHTS, MD.,
SEPTEMBER 15TH, '62.

HE lay upon his dying bed,
  His eyes were growing dim,
When with a feeble voice he called
  His weeping son to him:
Weep not, my boy, the veteren said,
  I bow to Heaven's high will,
But quickly from yon antlers bring
  The Sword of Bunker Hill.

The sword was brought, the soldier's eye
  Lit with a sudden flame;
And as he grasped the ancient blade,
  He murmured Warren's name;
Then said:—My boy, I leave you gold,
  But what is richer still:
I leave you, mark me, mark me, now,
  The Sword of Bunker Hill.

Oh! keep the Sword—his accents broke—
  A smile, and he was dead—
But his wrinkled hand still grasped the blade,
  Upon that dying bed.
The son remains, the sword remains,
  Its glory growing still,
And twenty millions bless the sire
  And sword of Bunker Hill.

ANONYMOUS.

## "OH! TAKE ME HOME TO DIE."

### AFTER THE BATTLE OF ANTIETAM, MD., SEPT. 17, '62.

THE night was clear, the moon shone bright,
High in the heavens vaulted hall,
While silently a ship of war,
Lay 'neath the frowning fortress wall;
The peace of heaven smiled around,
" All's well," resounded far and near,
While on that vessel's moon-lit deck,
Reclined a wounded volunteer.

He slowly moved his pallid lips,
In dreams, mayhap, of early life,
Perchance he heard again the crash
And discord fierce of mortal strife!
"Lie still, brave one, the morning dawns,"
A kind nurse said, who stood beside;
" The sun will soon shine bright again,
And naught of ill shall thee betide."

" Where are we now?" he falt'ring asked;
" Has not our ship yet left the shore?
Will I soon see my native State—
Receive my mother's kiss once more?
Oh! tell me nurse—alas! I see
That my fond wish is all in vain;
We have not sailed—your look imparts
What your kind heart seeks to retain."

"Well, be it so—I will not grieve,
  Though my desire is thus pass'd by;
I'd suffer willingly each pain,
  *If they'd but take me home to die.*
My country ask'd of me my life,
  And that I'd give my land to save,
For better far 'tis thus to die,
  Than in its ruins find a grave.

"This to my mother—father—all—
  Relate, when of my death you tell;
Say that for them I braved the strife,
  And for my country, fighting, fell!
Would that I could but see them all
  Before mine eyes in death grow dim;
That cannot be—I feel it now:
  Nurse, sing once more your ev'ning hymn."

With tearful eyes, and trembling voice,
  The nurse with tenderness obeyed;
And as the hymn she softly sang,
  The soldier closed his eyes and prayed.
He slept—the nurse still lingered nigh,
  All watchful of his ev'ry need;
And as she gazed, her tear-drops told
  How her kind heart did for him bleed.

A smile of pleasure lit his face,
  As waking from a dream of bliss;
"Ah! nurse," said he, "I have been home:
  Yes—and received my mother's kiss;
My family and friends have been
  Around me here while thus I slept;
They tried to ease my throbbing wound,
  And o'er me kindly bow'd and wept."

Kind nurse, farewell!—and take this cap—
'Twas with me in our last great fight—
That to my mother give and say
I left for her my last 'good night.'
I ask no more—I am content,
And leave for all a fond good bye—
How dark it is—oh, God! I wish
That they would take me home to die.

The nurse received the sacred charge
And laid it on his heaving breast;
While with sad heart and falling tear,
She watched him slowly sink to rest—
To that sweet rest which naught shall break,
Until the last great trump shall sound,
When Loyalty shall bliss receive,
And Treason's groan through hell resound.

* * * * * * * * *

When morning dawned upon the scene,
The ship was ready to unmoor,
But ere that dawn his brave young soul
Had left for e'er life's troubled shore
They laid him in a Southern grave,
Where patriot hearts in future years
Will pay a tribute to his worth,
And consecrate it with their tears!

J. HENRY HAYWARD.

## MY COUNTRY.

BATTLE OF I—U—K—A, MISS.,
SEPTEMBER 20TH, '62.

My country, my country, though humbled and sore,
Though now thou art bleeding at every pore,
There is joy for thee yet—for thy brow is a crown,
And nations shall envy thy future renown.
My country, my country, thou pride of my soul,
Tho' storm-winds have raged, with no hand to control,
Have rocked thee as rock they the ship on the main,
Thy travail in sorrow shall not prove in vain.

Behind darkest clouds shine the brightest of suns—
And deep shadows fall on the streamlet that runs
In the greenest, the loveliest, sunniest dell,
Where summer birds warble, and mortal men dwell.
But the clouds disappear, the earth smiles again,
More fragrant and fresh from the torrents of rain,
And shadows that darkened the streamlet are gone,
And birds' songs are sweet as their matins at dawn.

My country, my country, oh, One reigneth still,
"Whom He loveth He chasten," as He doth will;
And thou, from the furnace, like gold that is tried,
Shall brighter beam forth, from thy dross purified.
Freedom's fires shall again burn in, hall and cot,
As erst they were wont, in thy happier lot,
The people were sovereigns—when by no despot hand
A sceptre had swayed o'er our Heaven-blest land.

My country, my country, thou art loved next to God!
Though man's blood has reddened thy emerald sod
Till faith has been palsied, we'll wake from the spell,
And hope till the watchman shall cry "All is well.
My country, my country, there is joy for thee yet;
Thy sun, with its glory now dimmed, is not set;
And the kingdoms of earth, that rejoice o'er thy woe,
Shall bow at thy feet when their pride is laid low.

CAUCASION.

## ALL OF THEM.

BEFORE THE ATTACK ON AGUSTA, KY.

SEPT. 27, 1862.

With head erect and lips compressed,
He throws his hammer by;
The purpose of his manly breast
Is now to do or die.
He seeks the camp: "Put down my name,
My boys will mind the shop;
If my country wants my heart's blood,
I'll shed it drop for drop.

"And here comes now the oldest boy;
My son what would you do?"
"Father my brother will drive the trade;
I've come to fight with you."
"God bless him! Well, put down his name
I cannot send him home,
But here's the other boy, I see;
My son, what made you come?"

"Father, I could not work alone;
  The shop may go to—grass;
I've come to fight for the good old flag;
  Stand off here—let me pass."
"Yes, put him down—he's a noble boy;
  I've two that are younger still;
They'll drive the plow on Flushing farm,
  And work with a right good will,

"My God! and here comes one of them!
  My son you must not go!"
"Father, when traitors are marching on,
  I cannot plow or sow"
"Well thank God, there is one yet left—
  He will plow and sow what he can;
But he is only a boy, and can never do
  The work of a full grown man"

With a proud heart, the blacksmith turned,
  And walked to the other side;
For he felt a weakness he almost scorned,
  And a tear he fain would hide.
They told him then his youngest boy
  Was putting his name on the roll;
"It must not be," said the brave old man;
  No, no, he's the light of my soul!"

But the lad came up with a beaming face,
  Which bore neither fears nor cares:
"Father, say nothing—my name is down,
  *I've let out the farm on shares.*"
Now they've marched to the tented field,
  And when the wild battle shall come,
They'll strike a blow for the Stars and Stripes,
  For God, and their Country and Home.

ANONYMOUS.

o

## THE SPARTAN MOTHER.

AT THE BATTLE OF CORINTH, MISS.,
OCTOBER 4TH, '62.

THUS once a Spartan mother spoke—
  "My son go forth to war,
And in the battle's deadly shock,
  Be fame thy guiding star;
Disgrace not Sparta's honor'd name,
But death prefer to loss of fame.

"I'd rather see thee, O my son!
  Borne home upon thy shield
After a victory nobly won
  Than think that thou could'st yield,
Or leave thy arms, to aid thy flight,
From foes, however great their might.

"Remember Sparta's martial laws;
  Think of Termopolea
May all the Gods defend thy cause,
  And send thee back to me,
Enriched with spoils, but richer far
In honors gained in glorious war."

Ah! vain attempt to tell the joy
  That filled that mother's breast,
When she beheld her darling boy
  Return among the rest
And heard 'mid shouts of loud acclaim
Her son, their youthful leader's name.

Mothers in every age should be
  Like this brave Spartan dame,
And tell their sons, the same as she,
  The worth of deathless fame,
And yield them at their country's call
To conquer for her, or to fall.

A. F. A., 2D REGT., N.Y.N.G.

## AWAKE, YE BARDS.

BATTLE NEAR PERRYVILLE, KY.,

OOTOBER 9TH, '62.

AWAKE, ye bards, your torches now ignite,
And spread throughout the land a glowing light;
Illume the world around, both far and near,
Sustain the emblem of our country dear;
Hold up the Stars and Stripes, in ev'ry State
Denounce the wicked but uphold the great—
The *truly* great—who, like our Washington,
Would bask in happiness 'neath Freedom's sun,
Or wade through blood our honor to maintain;
Hurl to eternity the servile chain,
The cause of turmoil in our noble States,
And quench the fire of would-be potentates,
Restore to happiness the land we love;
If war it *must* be, why *then* war approve,
And let the eagle proudly soar above.

JOHN H. WEAVER.

## HOW OUR CAPTAIN FELL.

REBEL INVASION OF CHAMBERSBURG PA.,

OCT. 11 '62.

"ON comrades, to the charge!
Boys, do your duty well!"
Thus cheering forward to the fight,
Our brave young captain fell:
We clustered round his prostrate form,
We bore him from the field—
Nerveless the arm that never more,
A patriot's sword might wield.

He fell—that Christian soldier,
In manhood's strength and power;
Bright rose life's vista on his sight,
In that first fearful hour!
He fell—at duty's post no more,
Fresh honors to obtain;
He fell, while fighting manfully,
The cause he loved to gain!

"Art thou resigned (the question came,
As pierced by wounds he lay,)
Thus in the glorious prime of life,
To pass from earth away?'
"Aye I'm resigned, I soon shall gain
My everlasting rest!"
Fear or repining found no place
In that brave soldier's breast!

## CHARLEY WAS NOT THERE.

AFTER THE BATTLE OF POCATALIGO, S. C.,
OCTOBER 22D, '62.

I HAVE seen the hardy veterans,
As they were marching home,
  Calling forth the cheers of multitudes,
  That rang out on the air;
While people crowded 'tween the ranks,
And welcomed each their own,
  But I stood sad and lonely then,
  For Charlie was not there.

And there were fond embraces then,
When loving hearts did meet,
  And tears of joy were streaming
  From two bright eyes everywhere;
But many where the choaking sobs,
While gazing down the street,
  That well'd up from my lonely heart,
  For Charlie was not there

And the tattered, smoke-stained colors,
With bullet-riddled stars,
  Waved o'er the men as proudly then
  As on that day they were
Unfurled amid the carnage fierce;
Now they show their battle-scars,
  And they drooped in sorrow past me,
  For my Charlie was not there.

I knew that he had fallen then
On that bloody field of strife,
  That the ebbing current of his life
  Had damped his auburn hair;
Yet anxiously I gazed upon
The troops; for I, his wife,
  Clung fondly to the regiment
  Though Charlie was not there.

Yes, how proudly we bade farewell,
But two short years ago,
  I looked upon his manly form
  And left him in the care
Of Him who rules our destinies;
And trusting Him, I know
  He is watching o'er the stricken here,
  But Charlie was not there.

The streets are all deserted now;
My beating heart be still,
  For he in dreams will near me be,
  From his spirit-home so fair.
I'll seek my lonely pillow,
And with joy my heart will thrill
  When in dreams of future happiness,
  My Charlie will be there.

HENRY WHITE.

## HOW FARES IT WITH HIS MOTHER.

AFTER THE BATTLE OF WAVERLY, TENN.,

OCT. 23, '62.

How fares it with his mother?
  A shock so rude, so stern—
Where, in her desolate anguish,
  For comfort will she turn?
She may turn to the blameless life, her son,
  Through the grace of God, did lead,
To the noble sacrifice he made,
In his country's hour of need!

She may dwell on the hope to which he clung
  In that last trying hour,
When the closest, fondest ties of earth,
  To comfort, have no power—
When the Saviour's love alone, can shed,
  A joy o'er parting life;
E'en thus sustained, her loved one passed,
  The bounds of earthly strife!

Peaceful as when in infancy,
  Upon her breast he lay,
So sank he in the conq'rer's arms,—
  He slept his life away;
Earth may not rob him of the crown,
  Which God's redeemed ones wear—
Well may that mother's heart rejoice,
  Though her loss be hard to bear!

E.

## SEMPER PARATUS.

THE OBSERVANCE OF THANKSGIVING DAY BY 21 STATES, OCTOBER 27TH, '62.

BIRTH-PLACE of Freedom !—sweet home of glory,
Despots most tremble where thy banners wave;
Millions ot hearts beat high when thy story
Is sung by the voice of the fair and the brave:
Thy sons, ever ready, stand firm in thy cause,
A breastwork, protecting thy fame and thy laws!

Birth-place of Freedom! land of perfection
Garden of plenty, of sunshine and shade;
Thy vernal beauty is but the reflection
Of a smile, descended from God to thy glade;
Thy sons, ever ready, stand firm in thy cause,
A breastwork, protecting thy fame and thy laws!

Birth-place of Freedom !—pride of our sires,
Home of the exile, and hope of the brave;
On every hill-top burns Freedom's bright fires,
To cheer the oppressed—to comfort and save:
Thy sons ever ready, stand firm in thy cause,
A breastwork, protecting thy fame and thy laws!

Birth-place of Freedom !—thy sons adore thee,
And joyously offer their praise at thy shrine;
The world may bow down in worship before thee,
For thou art the handwork of Wisdom Divine:
Thy sons, ever ready, stand firm in thy cause,
A breast-work, protecting thy fame and thy laws!

J. HENRY HAYWARD.

## WHY.

### CAPTURE OF REBEL CAMP NEAR BERRYVILLE, VA., OCTOBER 29TH, '62.

TWENTY millions held at bay!
  Why, Northmen, why?
Less than half maintain the day,
  Why, Northmen, why?
With the sturdy iron will,
With the pluck, the dash, the skill,
With the blood of Bunker Hill,
  Why, Northmen, why?

Standing yet are Sumpter's walls—
  Why, Northmen, why?
Slumber yet the avenging balls—
  Why, Northmen, why?
Charleston left to scoff at ease!
Richmond vaunting as it please!
Traitor taunts on every breeze!
  Why, Northmen, why?

Hear our wounded eagle wail!
  Why, Statesmen, why?
See our spangled banner trail!
  Why, Statesmen, why?
Coward England mocks again!
Courtly Paris shrugs disdain!
Cordial Russia throbs with pain!
  Why, Statesmen, why?

By our past, so bright renowned,
On, Northmen, on!
By our future, starry-crowned,
On, Northmen, on!
By the South, deceived, misled.
By our hundred thousand dead,
Who for North and South have bled,
On, Northmen, on!

N. P. WILLIS.

## LINT AND BANDAGE.

BEFORE THE BATTLE OF SNICKER'S GAP, BLUE RIDGE, NOVEMBER 3D, '62.

Out from our circle of home joys
Nobly and bravely they go,
Husbands, and brothers, and lovers,
Onward to meet the dread foe;
Though the heart throbs with wild anguish,
Bidding them haste to the fight,
Yet we pray God in his mercy
Ever to guide them right.

While 'mid the thick coming dangers,
Now self-denying they roam,
We must not idly await them,
While they now shield each dear home;
Think, when the battle is over,
Wounded and bleeding they lie,
Bandage and lint we must send them,
Or the brave heroes must die.

O'er the old vestment we linger
  Gleaning a balm for the wound,
Breathing a prayer for their safety,
  There 'mid the cannon's deep sound :
Busily ply we the needle.
  Many a garment prepare,
Many a keepsake so useful,
  Send we to lov'd ones still there.

Come with hands ready to aid us,
  Come with a gift for their need,
Send them a warm word of cheering,
  From the heart bid them " God speed;"
Yes ! we must fly to the rescue,
  Aid now the dear fallen brave,
Rescue with care kind and loving,
  Them from a deeply mourned grave.

JOSEPHINE FURMAN.

## ON, ON VALIANT SOLDIERS.

AT THE BATTLE OF NASHVILLE, TENN.,

NOVEMBER 5TH, '62.

ON, ON valiant soldiers ! the tocsin is sounding
  Arouse ye to action, brave men of the North !
From hill, vale and dell war's alarum resounding,
  Bids us rally to arms and for battle go forth ;
Arm, arm for the conflict! equip for the fight !
And battle for country, for home and for right.

On, on valiant soldiers ! win unfading glory,
  And forever our high, holy purpose shall be
To attest the grand truth of the oft cited story,
  That our own hallowed soil is "the land of the *free.*"
Then arm for the conflict, and fearlessly smite,
Ay, battle for country, for home and for right.
On, on valiant soldiers ! and when future ages
  Would know where the mantle of honor should fall,
Lo ! the records inscribed upon history's pages,
  Shall point to Columbia's sons—noblest of all,
Then arm for the conflict ! go forth in God's might,
And battle for country for home and for right.

AMELIA.

## MUSIC ON THE FIELD OF BATTLE.

AT THE BATTLE OF HARTSVILLE, TENN.,

DECEMBER., 7, '62.

Music on the field of battle—
  Martial music ! how it thrills ;
How it fires the noble soldier,
  And his soul with valor fills !
Music on the field of battle,
  When the fight is raging hot ;
When the cannons loudly rattle—
  *When it storms with grape and shot !*
How it makes of cowards—heroes,
  Makes all braves to falter not,
As on we march to death or glory,
  'Mid a hail of grape and shot !

JAMES A. C. O'CONNOR.

## VICTORY!

### BATTLE OF CRAWFORD'S PRAIRIE, ARK., DECEMBER 7TH, '62.

THERE is a sound of triumph in the air
  From battle-fields where blood was poured like wine,
And human lives were quenched with little care,
  And ghastly carnage swept along the line;
A sound of triumph,—Victory is ours!
No more the sullen war cloud darkly lowers.

By hero hands the victory is won;
  A courage, God-like in its strength, has nerved
Each lion heart; redly arose the sun
  In brightness, and in splendor set, nor swerved
That gallant band until the field was gained,
And they with glory crowned, though battle stained.

Honor to all who battled on that field
  To these the living, and to those the dead,
To one the highest honors we may yield,
  But on the other these cannot be shed;
They have a brighter crown than earth can give,
And in our memory their bright deeds live.

The Nation's heart once more beats glad and high,
  On every hand her song of triumph swells;
Her Eagle leaving his own native sky,
  With Victory beside our banner dwells,
Our Father's God! we thank Thee that our ears
Have heard Thy voice, for it hath quelled our fears!

MATTIE WINFIELD.

## TO-MORROW.

SECOND BATTLE OF FREDERICKSBURG,

DECEMBER 13TH '62.

A SUMMER evening, calm and beautiful;
A forest margin and deep solitude;
The pale moon shining 'mid the floating clouds,
Which ever and anon obscures her face;
A sentry pacing 'mid the shadows deep,
His musket gleaming in the flitting rays
Which now and then pierce thro' the leafy boughs.
Here is a scene of quietness and peace.
Which may be broken ere another night
By all the horrors, din and roar of war!
Thro' many a scene of sanguinary strife
Thus far the soldier hath in safety passed;
And as he treads alone his silent beat,
And thinks of those dear ones, far, far away,
In hopeful accent hear him fondly breathe
The simple word—"To-morrow!"

True, the man
Is at his post to watch the wary foe:
But ah! the heart is in that Northern home,
With those he loves far better than all else,
Save the dear land for which he left them all
To give his life, if need be, for the cause
Of Liberty and Truth!

What happy thoughts
And bright anticipations fill his soul!
What are the loved ones doing now at home?
This is the hour when they were wont to pray,
All gathered 'round him in the olden time,
In sweet communion with the One above,
And are they praying thus to-night, for him,
As he has often prayed for them at eve,
When in the silence of his narrow tent,
Amid the hurry of the midnight march,
Or in the lonely hours of picket-guard?
Will they expect the soldier home so soon?
Oh! blessed hope—to meet them all again,
Far from these scenes of war and war's alarms
While musing thus the picket was relieved,
And sought his quarters in the distant camp;
And as the "sweet restorer" closed his eyes,
And calm oblivion o'er his senses stole,
He murmured fondly that sweet word again–
The word—"To-morrow!"

And the morrow came!
Calm, bright and beautiful was all the scene.
It was the calm before the fearful storm—
The awful silence ere the earthquake broke!
Scarce had the sun appeared above the hills
That formed the distant Eastern horizon,
When the fierce shock of battle broke the calm,
And warlike legions met in mortal strife!
Great was the carnage as the conflict raged,
With varied fortunes, 'till the close of day;
When glorious victory at last was ours!
The foe retreated from the gory field,
And Freedom's banner triumphed once again
O'er Treason's hated flag!

And where is he
Who longed so fondly for the morrow's sun,
When the long term of service would expire,
And he could seek once more his peaceful home,
And clasp the loved ones to his heart again?
Go look amid yon pile of Union slain,
Where that fierce charge was made on rebel ranks,
And where our brave boys fell beneath their fire
Like grass before the mower's steady hand!
Well done, thou good and faithful warrior!
Thou art now home indeed—gone home to Heaven!
Those anxious ones, far, in that bright home,
Will hear the battle's heart destroying news,
And watch and wait for him they loved so well,
For many a weary day and sleepless night!
Oh, loving spirits, watch and wait no more,
He is another martyr to the cause
Of Union and of Right!

God help them all!
A sad to-morrow it has proved to them
And many others in our stricken land,
But when this gloomy night of life departs,
Before the dawning of an endless day,
When wars and partings shall be known no more,
They shall be with him in that Happy Land,
Forever and forever.

J. GORDON EMMONS.

## TELL ME DEAREST DO YOU MISS ME.

AFTER THE BATTLE OF GOLDSBOROUGH, N. C.

DEC. 18, '62.

Tell me, dearest, do you miss me
  At the morning's early hour,
When the dewy diamonds sparkle
  In the crown of every flower?
Do you miss me when the sun is
  Straight above our hemisphere,
And the world seems all in motion,
  And seems in the best of cheer.

Tell me dearest do you miss me
  When the stars are coming forth,
And are lighting up their signals
  For the people of the earth?
Do you miss me at the midnight—
  In your slumber does it seem
That my hand is tracing visions,
  Pleasant visions in your dream?

Tell me, dearest, do you miss me?
  No, the answer you may keep,
For I know your thoughts are with me,
  In your wakefulness or sleep.
And it gives me arms of iron,
  Strung to brave whate'er may come,
For I'll but return to honor
  One who misses me at home.

ANONYMOUS.

## THE ISSUE'S MADE.

BEFORE THE BATTLE OF HOLLY SPRINGS, MISS.,
DECEMBER 19TH, '62.

THE issue's made, our Flag displayed,
Let he who dare retard it;
No cowards here grow pale with fear,
For Northern swords now guard it.
The men who won at Lexington
A name and fame in story,
Were patriot sires, who lit the fires
To lead their sons to glory.

Like rushing tide down mountain side,
The Northern hosts are sweeping;
Each freeman's breast to meet the test
With patriot blood is leaping.
Now Southern sneer and bullies' leer
Will find swift vengeance meted;
For never yet since foemen met
Have Northern men retreated.

United now, no more we'll bow,
Or supplicate, or reason ;
'Twill be our shame and lasting blame,
If we consent to treason.
Then in the fight our hearts unite,
One purpose move us ever;
No traitor hand divide our land,
No power our country sever.

JOHN CLANCY.

## GREAT JEHOVAH.

REBEL RETALIATORY PROCLAMATION,

DECEMBER 23D, '62.

GREAT Jehovah! pure and holy,
  Thou who reigneth over all,
Lead us on to deeds of valor,
  At our country's solemn call.

Thou who led our noble sires,
  Through the gloomy days of old;
Oh, forsake us not we pray thee,
  Nor thy gracious power withold.

Be our guide thro' tribulation,
  By the orphan be thou e'er;
Ease the heart where sorrow nestles,
  And, oh! dry the widow's tear.

When this war shall cease its thunders,
  And our blood no longer flow,
May we gather light and wisdom,
  From this fearful shock of woe.

May our hearts be turn'd from anger,
  Love again our bosoms fill;
And the mighty God of battles,
  Lead us onward as He will.

ROBT. M. HART.

## THE SONG OF THE SHELL.

FIVE DAYS BATTLE ON THE YAZOO RIVER,

DECEMBER 27, '62

SULLEN, and strong, and thick, and tall,
Rises the Bastion's moated wall.
The glacis is smooth and the ditch is deep,
And the weary sentry may never sleep;
Over the parapet, heavy and dun,
Peers the mouth of the barbette gun,
While lightnings flash and tempests glow
From the gloomier casemates down below,
Strong is the work and stout the wall,
But before my song they must crumble and fall—
Crumble away to a heap of stones,
Mingled with fragments of dead men's bones,
And red with the blood that flowed as they fell,
Their requiem sung by the howling shell.

Flaunting, and boasting, and brisk, and gay,
The streets of the city shine to-day.
Forts without, and army within,
To think of surrender were deadly sin;
For the foe far over the wave abide,
And no guns can reach o'er the flowing tide.
They can't? Through the air, with a rush and a yell,
Comes the screech and the roar of the howling-shell;
And the populous city is all alive
With the bees that are leaving the ancient hive;

And the market-places are waste and bare,
And the smoke hangs thick in the poisoned air;
And ruins alone shall remain to tell
Where the hymn of destruction was sung by the shell.

Traitorous and bloodthirsty, mad with wrath,
Charleston stands in the nation's path—
Stands and flaunts a bloody rag,
Insulting the stars on the dear old flag.
But Sumter is crumbled and ground away,
And Wagner and Gregg are ours to-day,
And over the water, on furious wings,
The shell from the "Swamp Angel" flies and sings,
It sings of the death of the traitorous town,
It sings of red-handed rebellion crushed down.
Sharp are its cadences, harsh its song,
It shrieks for the right and it crushes the wrong;
And never a blast, shaking nethermost hell,
Cried vengeance and wrath like the song of the shell.

J. WARREN NEWCOMB, JR.

---

## THE SONG OF THE RAIN.

### AFTER THE SECOND BATTLE OF MURFREESBORO, TENN., DECEMBER 31ST, '62.

Lo! the long slender spears, how they quiver and flash,
When the clouds send their cavalry down;
Rank and file by the million, the rain lancers dash
Over mountain, river, and town;
Thick the battle drops fall, but they drip not in blood;
The trophy of war is the green, fresh bud;
Oh, the rain, the plentiful rain!

The pastures lie baked and the furrow is bare;
  The wells, they yawn empty and dry;
But a rushing of waters is heard in the air,
  And a rainbow leaps out in the sky.
Hark! the heavy drop's pelting the sycamore leaves,
Wash the wide pavement and sweep from the eaves,
    Oh, the rain, the plentiful rain!

See the weaver throw wide his one swinging pane,
  The kind drops dance on the floor;
And his wife brings her flowerpots to drink the rain,
  On the step of the half-open door;
All the time on the skylight, far over his head,
Smiles the poor cripple laid on his hospital bed;
    Oh, the rain, the plentiful rain!

And away, far from men, where the mountains tower,
  And the little green mosses rejoice,
And the bud-headed heather nods to the shower,
  And the hill torrents lift up their voice;
And the pools in the hollows mimic the flight
Of the rain, as their thousand points dart up in light;
    Oh, the rain, the plentiful rain!

And deep in the fir-wood below, near the plain
  A single thrush pipes full and sweet;
How days of clear shining will come after rain,
  Waving meadows and thick growing wheat!
So the voice of hope sings in the heart of our fears,
Of the harvest that springs from a nation's tears;
    Oh, the rain, the plentiful rain!

## THE AMERICAN BOY.

### LOSS OF THE FIRST MONITOR, OFF CAPE HATTERAS., JANUARY 1ST, '63.

Loud ring the bells from many a tower—
The year is eighty-three—
A father by the window sits
With a child upon his knee,
And hears the gladsome notes proclaim
The birthday of the Free.

The banner which our fathers loved,
And which their sons shall prize,
With not a single star effaced,
Floats proudly to the skies—
The emblem of a nation's strength
No foeman dare despise.

"Dear father," now with earnest voice
Outspeaks the eager son,
"My teacher told me, yesterday,
What glorious deeds were done
In the war that burst upon the land
In eighteen sixty-one.

"She told me with what patient hearts
Our noble soldiers bore
The toilsome march, the frugal fare,
The hardships of the war;
The greatest—so my teacher says—
That history ever saw.

"I wish I had been living then,
I'd be a soldier, too,
And help defend the noble flag
From all the rebel crew;
I'd be ashamed to stay behind,
Dear father, wouldn't you?"

Upon the listening father's face
A painful flush there came;
The patriot-soldier's meed of praise
He could in nowise claim,
And the question of his little son
Smote him with sudden shame.

## OURS IS A HAPPY LOT.

FIRST BATTLE AT VICKSBURG, TENN.,
JANUARY 3D, '63.

OURS is a happy lot;—we hear the story
Of the bright star, the manger, and the cross,
Of sorrow first, and afterwards of glory,
Of heavenly triumph following earthly loss.

We throng the halls of science and of learning,
We read of noble deeds of other days,
And our young hearts with proud desires are burning
To emulate the heroes that we praise.

We lift our eyes and see our star-strewn banner
Floating its folds above our sheltered homes;
O, noble hero-fathers! in like manner
Would we defend our flag when danger comes.

JULLIA R. M'MASTERS.

## COMRADES! HARK! THE CANNONS RATTLE.

REBEL ATTACK ON SPRINGFIELD MO.,

JANUARY 7, '63.

COMRADES! hark! the cannons rattle,
  Startling night and nature lone;
While shriekingly the god of battle
  Leapeth to his crimson throne!
Slip the demons of your slaughter!
  Havoc deal the hated horde!
Fight for home, wife, sister, daughter—
  Wave the banner, wield the sword!

Comrades! when the hot storm gathers,
  Round shall crowd in unseen show,
Shrieking ghosts of butcher'd fathers
  Guiding the avenging blow!
Death to those who tortures slowly
  Dealt by flame, and rack, and cord!
Onward, for your cause is holy—
  Wave the banner, wield the sword!

Comrades! ye life's chance who give for
  Native land, her peace and fame!
If ye win you've all to live for—
  If ye fall, our tears ye claim!
If you fly your curs'd in story!
  Forward! then with one accord:
Let your cry be freedom! glory!—
  Wave the banner, wield the sword!

JAMES BRUTON.

## THE LITTLE HERO.

CAPTURE OF THE HARRIET LANE AT GALVESTON, TEXAS.

JANUARY 8TH, '63.

A NOBLE youth, scarce ten years old,
He stood amid the storm!
Unmoved and steadfast—truly bold—
All selfish thoughts to scorn;
His little hand was gory red—
He sought the captors wild,
And calmly to the chieftain said,
Slay ye the little child?

He stood beside the cabin door,
Upon the bloody deck;
His heart with faith was running o'er—
He grieved the vessel's wreck;
Yet stood he bravely at his post,
And fired with steady hand;
A hero, patriot, and the boast
Of that devoted band.

His father fell—the child was spared!
He saw his bleeding sire;
His patriotic breast was bared
To meet the Traitors' fire!
And with a firm, unerring aim
He laid the Rebel low;
Though 'round him fell the lurid flame
Of desolating woe.

A. B. ANDERSON.

## THE SOLDIER'S LOVE.

BEFORE THE BATTLE OF RED MOUND, TENN.,
JANUARY 9TH, '63.

"Oh come with me, in my little boat,
Come forth with me my Jane;
For with the dawn I go to the war,
And may never come back again."
She went with him in his little boat,
And they glided down the stream—
'Twas a pity that war, with its bloody front,
Should sadden their love's young dream.
The lover drew close to the lady's side,
And rested his oars awhile,
And the tears were in the lady's eyes,
Though the red lips tried to smile:
"Oh! dry those tears, my own, and give
Thy parting blessing now!"
And tenderly he stooped to press
Her lips, and cheek, and brow.
And stilly glided the graceful boat,
And back to their home they came,
And the boat then landed its loving freight,
That it never might land again.
And the lover went forth with morning dawn,
With many a comrade brave—
They went to conquer on battle-field,
Or rest in a soldier's grave.
The winds one night, tossed the foam wreaths high
From the White Lake's angry breast,
And the storm was fierce, as it swept in wrath
From the hills with their cedar crest:

And faster and faster through the night
  Came the drops of plashing rain,
And wilder and wilder the tempest grew,
  As it beat against the pane.
And the shuddering lady turned away,
  And laid her down to rest,
And her cheek was white as the pillow's white
  Which the sorrowing lady prest;
And was she awaking, or was she asleep,
  Or was it all a dream—
That sad-faced figure dimly shown
  By the night-lamp's waning beam.
And was she awaking, or was she asleep,
  And did she hear her name,
As the outstretched arms were held to her,
  With "Come to me, my Jane!"
And heard she of the battle-field,
  Where the dead and dying lay?
And fainter and fainter grew the light,
  While the wind-gusts rattled the pane
And still the fading figure, said,
  "Oh, come to me, my Jane."
When the Eastern gray had turned to red,
  Then forth the Lady Jane—
Forth from her childhood's home, which she
  Might never enter again.
Away from the hills with their cedar crest,
  Away from each valley and stream,
From the glassy lake when its breast was white,
  'Neath the moonlight's silver sheen.
And she tarried not for food or rest,
  She tarried not for sleep,
Her face was calm, though at her heart
  A grief lay buried deep.

And off to the bloody battle-field
  The lady wended her way,
And searched for her lover, a sorrowful search,
  Where the dead and dying lay.
Brave hearted men, whose hands were red,
  All red with the carnage stain,
Their eyes were wet while they led the way
  For the sorrowing Lady Jane
Where the crimson lay brightest upon the sod,
  They pointed to him there—
And the lady knelt and kissed away
  The death damps from his hair.
And tenderly, lovingly raised the head
  And pillowed it on her breast,
I ween it were a fitting place
  For a soldier's head to rest.
"I fought them well and hard, my love,
  In the hottest and thickest fray,
And many a comrade fell with me,
  And we gallantly won the day.
I thought of you 'mid the crashing shells,
  'Mid the rifles deadly rain—
And I thought of you, longed for you as I fell,
  And you came to me, my Jane."
Then she kissed her soldier's eye-lids down
  Ere the film had gathered there,
And over his face she gathered a pall,
  'Twas her own bright wavy hair.
And they marveled that long and silently,
  She knelt with a drooping head,
And each cheek was blanched when found at last
  That lady Jane was dead.

KATE B. TYSON.

## ON GUARD.

CAPTURE OF ARKANSAS POST, ARK.,
JANUARY 11TH, '63.

LONELY on the border path,
  Lonely by the flashing stream,
Lonely 'mid the wildwood treads
  The man who would his land redeem.
His comrades, 'round the bivouac fires,
  Sleep on their weapons but to rise,
When fierce and vengful foes approach,
  To watch and guard as warriors wise
Proudly on the beaten track,
  He clasps his rifle to his breast,
And thinks of home, of dear ones there—
  His country, with dark strife distressed,
A vow is uttered, as alone
  The sentinel resumes his round:
"My land beloved I'll vindicate,
  Tho' blood shall steep the darksome ground."
His comrades hear the battle-sound,
  And stricter are their vigils now;
In readiness stand every form,
  And Honor lights each manly brow.
The loud command, so sharp and shrill,
  The quietude an echo gives;
"Attention men! To arms! Advance!
  Defeat the foe, and Freedom lives."
Sweet morn in grand effulgence reigns,
  But where are they—the forest band?
Amid the strife, to live or die
  For Freedom, and their native land.

WM. J. M'CLURE

## HE WOULD NOT LEAVE ME ON THE FIELD.

AT THE CAPTURE OF PORT HINDMAN, ARK.,

JANUARY 20TH, '63.

I AM dying, mother! slowly dying,
  Beneath the holly shade;
Upon the hill-side near the river,
  My fainting form is laid.
A wounded comrade's arm is round me
  Soothing me to rest—
Softly pillowed is my fevered head
  Upon his heaving breast.

In the conflict, fierce and wild,
  The Southren ranks to sever—
Foremost struggling in the strife,
  We wounded fell together.
In his arms he gently raised me,
  Nature's strength returning,
While sternly in his eye a vengeful fire
  Was like a meteor burning.

He would not leave me on the field to die
  'Mid the thousand slain;
And he bore me from the storm of battle,
  Weak and tott'ring in his pain.
He is sleeping, mother! sweetly sleeping
  A rest that knows no waking;
And soon shall we, our duty done,
  A heavenward march be making.

S. A. W.

## OUR HEROINES.

GRAND MILITARY REVIEW AT BEAUFORT, S. C.,
JANUARY 29TH, '63.

---

IN BEAUFORT.

Headquarters, Dept. of the South,
HILTON HEAD, S. C., Jan. 25, 1863.

SPECIAL ORDERS,
A. NO. 1.

¶ III. THE Chief Quartermaster of Department
Will give Captain Mary a riding garment—
A long, rich, skirt of comely hue,
Shot silk, with just a suspicion of blue,
A gipsy hat, with an ostrich feather,
A veil to protect her against the wéather,
And delicate gauntlets of pale buff leather;
Her saddle with silver shall all be studded,
And her pony—a sorrel—it shall be blooded:
Its shoes shall be silver, its briddle all ringing
With bells harmonizing well with her singing.
And thus Captain Mary,
Gay, festive, and airy,
Each morning shall ride
At the Adjutant's side
And hold herself ready, on all fit occasions,
To give him of flirting his full army rations.

By Command of, Etc.
CHARLES HALPINE.

## OUR IRISH AMERICAN HEROES.

MOONLIGHT BATTLE NEAR THE BLACKWATER, VA.,

JANUARY 30, '63.

THEN fling out the banner, on high let it wave
  O'er the land of the Exiles affection,
And cursed be the coward, and branded the slave
  Who refuses that flag his protection;
'Tis the emblem of freedom on sea and on land,
  No tyrant shall ever profane it,
By Heaven! it thus shall continue to stand,
  Tho' we spill our heart's blood to maintain it.

Then up with the banner, up, up with the flag,
  While millions of freemen surround it,
Our children whenever we sink in the grave,
  Shall inherit that flag as we found it;
No renegade traitor with dastardly hand,
  Nor foreign assailant shall rend it,
While an Irish-American stands on the soil,
  With a heart and an arm to defend it.

Then fling out the banner, up, up with the flag,
  Before which proud Albion's red ensign
Trailed humbly in dust, an anathemized rag,
  Degraded at Yorktown and Trenton;
Then up with the standard, up, up with the flag,
  Hurrah! 'tis the flag of the world,
We swear before Heaven to fight and to save,
  Or to fall while it still is unfurled.

JAMES TROY.

## THEY COME AGAIN.

REBEL DECLARATION OF THE RAISING OF THE BLOCKADE OF CHARLESTON.

DECEMBER 31ST, '63.

HARK! the tide of war approaches,
  As it came in months agone,
And the traitor fiend encroaches
  On the soil where we were born
Sounds the bugle-call, alarming,
Hosts at rest again are arming,
And 'gainst vile invaders swarming,
  As they did in months agone.
Crush them now, that they hereafter
  May be known as friends that were;
Free us from the scorn and laughter
  Of Britannia's haughty slur,
If our trust has been misplaced,
And our shames yet uneffaced,
Our volunteers have ne'er disgraced
  The holy cause that bids them on!
Children let us be no longer;
  Let us crush them now, or say
That their valor is the stronger—
  That our own has had its day.
Fight to end this red effusion,
Fight to end this cursed delusion,
And break up this dire confusion
  That pervades our land to day.

GEO. G. SMALL.

## "DON'T FEAR DEATH, MEN."

REPULSE OF THE REBELS AT FORT DONELSON, TENN., FEBRUARY 5TH, '63. *

From Donelson's stern, serried hights,
  For our country—God's blessing upon her!—
Brings out our young heroe's brave rallying cry:
  "Don't fear death, men, fear only dishonor!"
Charge bravely for Douglas, to-day,
  Where patriots and traitors are meeting;
Though dead, he shall win the proud field,
  While we shout a victorious greeting,

Remember the land of the West—
  Our homes toward the sun's golden settıng—
That the hearts which have loved us the best
  May have naught for reproach or regretting!
Strike home for our banner to-day;
  For our country—God's blessings upon her!—
For the blood-baptized flag of the free;
  "Don't fear death, men, fear only dishonor!"

Brave words, of a brave, loyal heart,
  Fair sunlight for death's frowning portal;
Embalm them, O, centuries grand,
  In their patriot beauty, immortal!
Ring out that brave rallying cry;
  For our country—God's blessing upon her!—
For the blood-baptized flag of the free;
  "Don't fear death, men, fear only dishonor!"

H. R. M.

## THE WONDERFUL RIVER IS SILENT NOW.

THE RISING OF THE MISSISSIPPI RIVER,

FEBRUARY 20TH, '63.

THE wonderful river is silent now,
  Bolted, and locked, and barred!
Its current is rapid as ever before,
But the navies of peace its bosom once bore,
  Are under suspicion and guard!

Vain are the riches of valley and plain,
  All in that wonderful land;
For the river that wedded the North and the South
Is closed at the middle and closed at the mouth,
  Closed by an iron hand.

On the limitless prairies the corn may grow rank,
  And down in the valleys below,
The cotton and cane may flourish in vain,
'Till God shall see fit to sunder the chain
  That severs the palm from the snow.

The navies that float on the wonderful stream
  Are navies of terror and wrath.
Destruction and death through the valleys they bear;
With sulphurous vapors they burden the air,
  And fury flames up in their path.

The cities are sullen and sorrowful now;
  Their beauty is wasted and worn.
The hamlets and towns are shattered and burned,
The panther, the bear, and the wolf have returned
  To the fields of the cotton and corn.

WM. H. WILLETT.

## IN WAR TIME.

### CELEBRATION OF WASHINGTON'S BIRTH-DAY.

FEBRUARY 22D, '63.

ONCE more, dear friends, you meet beneath
  A clouded sky:
Not yet the sword has found its sheath,
And, on the sweet spring airs the breath
  Of war floats by.
Yet trouble springs not from the ground,
  Nor pain from chance;
Th' Eternal order circles round,
And wave and storm find mete and bound
  In Providence.
Full long our feet the flowery ways
  Of peace have trod,
Content with creed and garb and phrase;
A harder path in earlier days
  Led up to God.
Too cheaply truths, once purchased dear,
  Are made our own;
Too long the world has smiled to hear
Our boast of full corn in the ear
  By others sown.
To see us stir the martyr fires
  Of long ago;
And wrap our satisfied desires
In the singed mantles that our sires
  Have dropped below.

But now the cross our worthies bore
    On us is laid.
Profession's quiet sleep is o'er,
And in the scale of truth once more
    Our faith is weighed.
The cry of innocent blood at last
    Is calling down
An answer in the whirlwind blast,
The thunder and the shadow cast
    From Heaven's dark frown.
The land is red with judgments. Who
    Stands guiltless forth?
Have *we* been faithful as we knew,
To God and to our brother true,
    To Heaven and Earth?
This day the fearful reckoning comes
    To each and all;
We hear amidst our peaceful homes
The summons of the conscript drums,
    The bugle's call.
Our path is plain; the war-net draws
    Round us in vain,
While, faithful to the Higher Cause,
We keep our fealty to the laws
    Through patient pain.
The leveled gun, the battle brand
    We may not take;
But, calmly loyal, we can stand
And suffer with our suffering land
    For conscience sake.

JOHN G. WHITTIER.

## YE SONS AND SIRES OF LIBERTY.

PASSAGE OF THE NATIONAL MILITIA BILL,
FEBRUARY 25TH, '63.

Ye sons and sires of Liberty,
To war's fierce cry awake!
Give up your joys, give up your lives,
For dear-bought Freedom's sake!
Raise ye the Stars and Stripes on high,
And 'neath its shadows swear,—
While life shall last, to keep its folds
In triumph waving there!
Give up your homes, your joys, and all,
For Freedom live!—for Freedom fall!
Ye sons of Liberty.

Ye sons and sires of Liberty,
In marshalled hosts arrayed,
Together called, but to preserve
Dear Freedom's course—betrayed!
Bare ye the steel in this great fight,
Defend your native sod;
Ye war for Freedom and for Right,
For Justice and for God!
Give up your homes, your joys, and all,
For Freedom live!—for Freedom fall!
Ye sons of Liberty.

J. HENRY HAYWARD.

## EXEMPT.

THE GREAT CONSCRIPTION BILL EXCITEMENT, FEBRUARY 27TH, '63.

EXEMPT! from what? a knapsack, and gun,
A blanket and a uniform;
Some weary marches in the sun,
And nights out-doors amid the storm?
That's all:—my boy, I pray you wait
Before you laugh and say, "all right!"
Your papers have not waived your fate,
You have the battle yet to fight!

Exempt! come, have you brains, a tongue,
Within your breast a living heart?
Then stand where you belong, among
The men who fight on Freedom's part!
Stand to your guns! be brave and calm;
Beware the foe with whom you deal,—
His mouth is full of deadly harm,
His lies are worse than cutting steel.

Exempt! there's no such thing, my boy!
You're not exempt while war endures;
Think you your pale face can destroy
Your country's right to you and yours!
Exempt! no more of that poor word—
Or fill it with a better sense;
So shall your country's voice be heard,
In calling you to her defence!

EDWARD EVERETT.

## SPRING AT THE CAPITAL.

PRESIDENT'S LEVEE AT WASHINGTON, D. C., MARCH 4TH, '63.

THE poplar droops beside the way
Its tasseled plumes of silver-gray;
The chestnut pouts its great grown buds,
Impatient for the laggard May.

The honeysuckles lace the wall;
The hyacinths grow fair and tall;
And mellow sun, and pleasant wind,
And odorous bees are over all.

Nor Nature does not recognise
This strife that rends the earth and skies;
No war dreams vex the winter sleep,
Of clover-heads and daisy-eyes.

She holds her even way the same,
Though navies sink or cities flame;
A snow-drop is a snow-drop still,
Despite the nation's joy or shame.

When blood her grassy altars wet,
She sends the pitying violet
To heal the outrage with its bloom,
And cover it with soft regret.

O crocuses with rain-wet eyes,
O tender-lipped anemones,
What do ye know of agony and death
And blood-won victories?

No shudder breaks your sunshine trance,
Tho' near you rolls, with slow advance,
Clouding your shining leaves with dust,
The anguish-laden ambulance.

Yonder a white encampment hums;
The clash of martial music comes;
And now your startled stems are all
A tremble with the jar of drums.

Whether it lessen or increase,
Or whether trumpets shout or cease,
Still deep within your tranquil hearts
The happy bees are murmuring "Peace!"

O flowers! the soul that faints or grieves,
New comfort from your lips receives;
Sweet confidence and patient faith
Are hidden in your healing leaves.

Help us to trust, still on and on,
That this dark night will soon be gone,
And that these battle stains are but
The blood-red trouble of the dawn—

Dawn of a broader, whiter day
That ever blessed us with his ray—
A dawn beneath whose purer light
All guilt and wrong shall fade away.

A. J. ELLARD.

## EAST TENNESSEE.

BATTLE AT SPRINGFIELD, TENN.,

MARCH 5, '63

East Tennessee! East Tennessee!
My soul is glad at thought of thee
Upon thy everlasting hills,
And in the murmuring of thy rills,
Are heard the songs ot Liberty,
Sung by thy sons, East Tennessee.

But with thy songs is heard a wail,
Coming from hill, and plain and dale,
On summer breeze, 'tis borne along,
I hear it now, "great God how long
Before my exiled sons shall see
Once more, their own East Tennessee?"

Not long, not long, for God is just,
And right is strength, prevail it must;
Ten thousand stalwart men declare,
To avenge thy wrongs, to do and dare,
To fight and bleed, and die for thee,
The Patriot's home, East Tennessee!

LIEUT. JOHN H. KINGSTON.

## THE LIEUTENANT-COLONEL.

AT THE CAPTURE OF YAZOO CITY, MISS.,
MARCH 12TH, '62.

You think his parents can never more
 Above his grave see *the country* rise :
Well, it may be so, for often before
 The angels have beamed to blinded eyes!
Let me tell you—not one of their kith or kin
 Has lived so nobly or died so well;
And before another like him they win,
 Every man of the race may meet his knell.

One day in the churchyard—think of this!—
 Twenty graves may lie, twenty tombstone stand;
And around nineteen shall the serpents hiss
 And the weeds outgrow the sexton's hand.
But the twentieth—o'er it a nation weeps,
 While it covers the others with cold neglect,
Unheeding where leech or jurist sleeps
 Or giving, at best, but a chill respect.

" Ah, here," says the patriot, seeking the spot—
 " Here, amid these rubbishy common bones,
There lies one man of a nobler lot,
 Whose name and deeds the country owns.
Here, George, the Lieutenant-Colonel, lies,
 Who fell when the last Union fight was won!
Gone upward—the brave man never dies!
 Heaven prosper his soul when all is done!"

HENRY MORFORD.

## FIFTY YEARS.

AT THE GREAT UNION LEAGUE MEETING, N. Y.

MARCH 14TH, '61.

IN fifty years, the little commonwealth
Our little league of states, that, in its early day,
Skirted the long Atlantic coast, has grown
To a vast empire, filled with populous towns
Beside its midland rivers, and beyond
The snowy peaks that bound its midland plains
To where its rivulets, over sands of gold
Seek the Pacific—'till at length it stood
Great 'mid the greatëst of the Powers of Earth,
And they who sat upon Earth's ancient thrones
Beheld its growth in wonder and in awe.
* * * * * * * Fierce is the strife,
As when of old the sinning angels strove
To whelm, beneath the uprooted hills of heaven,
The warriors of the Lord. Yet now, as then,
God and the Right shall give the victory.
For us, who fifty years ago went forth
Upon the world's great theatre, may we
Yet see the day of triumph, which the hours
On steady wing waft hither from the depths
Of a serener future; may we yet,
Beneath the reign of a new peace, behold
The shaken pillars of our commonwealth
Stand readjusted in their ancient poise.

WILLIAM CULLEN BRYANT.

## THE BLACK REGIMENT.

EXPLOITS OF THE COLORED TROOPS IN FLORIDA, MARCH 16TH. '63.

DARK as the clouds of even,
Ranked in the western heaven,
Waiting the breath that lifts
All the dread mass, and drifts
Tempest and falling brand
Over a ruined land!—
So still and orderly,
Arm to arm, knee to knee,
Waiting the great event,
Stands the black regiment.
Down the long dusky line
Teeth gleam and eyeballs shine;
And the bright bayonet,
Bristling and firmly set,
Flasbed with a purpose grand,
Long ere the sharp command
Of the fierce rolling drum
Told them their time had come,
Told them what work was sent
For the black regiment.
"Now," the flag-sergeant cried,
"Though death and hell betide,
Let the whole nation see
What! we are fit to be
Oh! what a shout there went
From the black regiment!

"Charge!" Trump and drum awoke;
Onward the bondmen broke;
Bayonet and sabre-stroke
Vainly opposed their rush.
Through the wild battle's crush,
With but one thought aflush,
Driving their lords like chaff,
In the guns' mouths they laugh;
Or at the slippery brands
Leaping with open hands,
Down they tear man and horse,
Down in their awful course;
Trampling with bloody heel
Over the crashing steel,
All their eyes forward bent,
Rushed the black regiment.
"Freedom!" their battle-cry—
"Freedom! or leave to die!"
Ah! and they meant the word,
Not as with us 'tis heard,
Not a mere party-shout:
They gave their spirits out;
Trusted the end to God,
And on the gory sod
Rolled in triumphant blood.
Glad to strike one free blow,
Whether for weal or woe;
Glad to breathe one free breath,
Though on the lips of death.
Praying—alas! in vain!—
That they might fall again,
This was what "freedom" lent
To the black regiment.

GEORGE H. BOKER.

## LAY OF AN IMPRISONED UNION OFFICER.

ARRIVAL OF THE RELEASED PRISONERS
AT FORTRESS MONROE,

MARCH 19TH, '63.

YE may mock, ye may torture
  With bar and with chain,
But the soldier of Right
  Laughs at jeering and pain!
Boast on as *ye* please,
  Of your tyranous flag,
*I* will shout for the Banner
  On *Liberty's* crag—
    For the beautiful Banner,
    The sacred bright Banner,
The UNION'S old, Banner of Stars!

I have hope in the day,
  I have hope in the night:
Honor's Angel flings o'er me
  Broad visions of light!
Your *tyranny* sinks,
  But my *Government* shines
With a grand glory gleamed
  From Eternity's shrines
    While I shout for the Banner,
    The sacred bright banner,
The UNION'S old, Banner of Stars!

WILLIAM ROSS WALLACE.

## LAND OF THE FOREST AND THE ROCK.

BATTLE AT MILTON, TENN.,

MARCH 20TH, '63.

LAND of the forest and the rock—
  Of dark-blue lake and mighty river—
Of mountains rear'd aloft to mock
The storm's career, the lightning's shock—
  My own green land forever!
Land of the beautiful and brave—
The Freeman's home—the martyr's grave—
The nursery of giant men,
Whose deeds have link'd with every glen,
And every hill and every stream,
The romance of some warrior-dream!
O! never may a son of thine,
Where'er his wandering steps incline,
Forget the sky which bent above
His childhood like a dream of love,
The stream beneath the green hills flowing,
The broad armed trees above it growing,
The clear breeze through the foliage blowing
Or hear, unmoved, the taunt of scorn
Breathed o'er the brave New England born;
Or mark the stranger's jaguar-hand
  Disturbed the ashes of the dead,
The buried glory of a land
  Whose soil with noble blood is red,
And sanctified in every part,—
  Nor feel resentment, like a brand,
Unsheathing from its fiery heart!

Q JOHN G WHITTIER.

## THE REPULSE.

GUERILLA FIGHT AT M'MINNSVILLE. KY.,
MARCH 21ST, '63.

THE cannon now resounds, the hurrying drum
Loud beats to arms and tells the foemen " Come;"
Quick forms in line and marches our Brigade,
As gay as if they formed for their parade,
Upon their bayonets bright the sunbeams dance,
The skirmishers come out, spread wide, advance.
The leaders on each side exhaust their skill,
But hours wear on and they but skirmished still.
The rebel leader heads his tiger band,
And boldly seeks to meet us hand to hand;
Like beasts of prey o'er th' intervening space,
His frantic followers loudly yelling race.
Quick from our rear impetuous couriers bound,
Their rapid gallop shakes the echoing ground;
Rushing along, " Give way, give way," they cry,
Comes on their heels the horse artillery.
They sweep by, while a cloud of dust conceals
The panting horses and the whirling wheels;
Down the steep hill with headlong haste they go,
Wheel round their guns and point them at the foe.
The rebels come, the word to fire is given,
And gaping earth and quivering man are riven;
A new host rushes o'er the gory plain—
Again the cannon roars, that host is slain.
Once more the desperate charge the bravest led,
Once more the cannon roared, and all lay dead.

DR. LAWRENCE REYNOLDS.

## "COTTON'S KING."

FIRST BOMBARDMENT OF VICKSBURG, MISS., MARCH 24TH, '63.

So THE haughty satraps cried,
Storming in their godless pride;
Honor, mercy never known,
Justice on a shattered throne,
And the only chorus—" Might,
With his red arms makes the Right—
Cotton's King!"
Hark! there is another cry;
How it sweeps, a tempest, by?
See, a Nation fire-eyed stands,
Freedom's Charter in her hands!
See, the satraps storm no more,
While the guns on Vicksburg roar,
"God is King!"
"Wreaths for heroes fighting!" shout;
Fling our flag, a star, storm out;
Honor has not left the clime;
Justice sweeps the Harp of Time,
Shaking all the ransomed shore,
While the guns of Vicksburg roar,
"God is King!"
Nations, join the joyous cry!
Worlds, that shuddered in the sky
As ye looked down on the chain
Clanking over Earth and Main;
Shout, "The tyrant's reign is o'er!"
While the guns on Vicksburg roar,
"God is King!"

WM. ROSS WALLACE.

## THE REFUGEES.

AFTER THE DESTRUCTION OF THE CITY OF JACKSONVILLE, FLORIDA,

MARCH 27TH, '63.

A WOMAN, one with untimely frost
  Creeping along her hair;
And a boy whose sunny locks had lost
Small store of the gold of childhood, tossed
  By a mother's kisses there.

The clouds hung thick on the mountain's brow,
  And the stars were veiled in gloom,
And the gorges around were white with snow,
But below was the prowling, cruel foe,
  And the light of a burning home.

"Mother, the wind is cold to-night,"
  Said the boy in childhood's tone;
"But oh! I hope in the morning light
That the Union lines will come in sight,
  And the storm will soon be gone.

"I am very weary, mother dear,
  With the long, long walk to-day;
But the enemy cannot find us here,
And I shall slumber without a fear
  'Till the night has passed away.

"So tell me now ere I sleep once more
  The message that father gave
To his comrades, for you and me before
The glorious fight on the river's shore,
  That made a soldier's grave.

Then the mother told with tearless eye
  The solemn words again:
"Tell her I shall see her standing by,
When the calm comes on of the time to die,
  And the wounds have lost their pain.

"And teach my boy for ever to hold
  In his heart all things above—
The wealth of all earth's uncounted gold,
Or life with its sweet, sad joys untold—
  The worth of a patriot's love,"

As his blood at the message quicker stirred
  The boy's bright arteries through—
"I will remember every word,"
He said, "And the angels who must have heard,
  They will remember too."

Then clasped as a mother clasps who stands
  Alone between love and death;
Unfelt were the spectral, chilly hands
That softly tighten the soothing bands
  Over the failing breath.

Mother and child as the fire burned low,
  Slept on the earth's cold breast:
The night passed by, and the morning slow
Broke the veil of cloud o'er the fearful show,
  But never their perfect rest,

GEO P. MORRIS.

## ‘ONWARD TO RICHMOND.”

RUMORED EVACUATION OF RICHMOND,
MARCH 29TH, ’63.

In a dingy old room in a Northern State
Sat a mother alone—a woman whose fate
Was to toil with the needle for *men* who will say
“She has *ample* reward in a shilling per day!”
She sat with her head bowed low on her knee,
While the needle had ceased to work for its fee,
And her thoughts had wandered away to a son
As he marched ’mid the “Grand,” to mystic Bull Run.

Slowly the shirt slid down from her clasp,
’Till it hung by the thread still firm in her grasp,
And sleep, that was sweet, had taken its sway
Where the twenty-four hours were always the day.
Her slumber was calm; anon she would start!
The muscles would twitch, and told that the heart
Was stirred to its depths by a vision of one
As he marched ’mid the “Grand,” to mystic Bnll Run.

She saw in her dream that gallant array,
As weary and worn they plodded their way
To the field that was soon to picture a scene
Of horrors and death! and anguish so keen,
That the Nation has grieved in sorrow and gloom,
O’er the worthy and brave, who courting their doom,
Lay wounded and dead in the light of a sun
That shone angry and hot on the banks of Bull Run.

Then saw she the charge and cavalry's dash,
And bowie and sword, and sharp bayonet clash;
The cannon's bright glare and deafening roar
That told of its track in warm crimson gore!
Their rider and horse, o'ertaken by Death
Sank down on the sod vain by gasping for breath!
Ranks melting away not heeding the gun
Which was masked that day at bloody Bull Run!

But see ye her now, as haggard and pale
She starts to her feet with low moaning wail.
And wild staring eyes that piercing the gloom
Has conjured the scene to her own little room!
In the struggle of death, 'midst carnage and strife,
With his eye glazing o'er in fast ebbing life,
Lay that idolized form still clutching his gun,
As he writhed in his gore on the banks of Bull Run!

With a startling shriek she sank to the floor,
For the vision had riven the heart to the core,
And the sad, weary spirit wended its way
To a better reward than a "shilling per day."
Prophetical Death, that singles out some,
Had spoken to her the news that would come;
Of victims by scores as shouted each son—
"Onward to Richmond! *by way of* Bull Run."

G. A. K.

## TO THE KENTUCKY FARMERS.

**BEFORE THE BATTLE OF SOMERSET, KY., MARCH 30TH, '63.**

LEAVE your plowshares in the furrows,
 Tillers of the fruitful soil;
Leave the grass unmown, ungathered,
 Waste the products of your toil;
Think no longer of the reaping
 Of the full and golden grain,
Only think about the harvest
 Waiting on the battle-plain.

Throw aside your hoes and sickles,
 Swing your keen edge scythes no more,
Draw the swords from out the scabbards
 Which your patriot grandsires wore.
Shoulder arms and march united,
 Singing joyous as you go,
To repel the Southern army,
 To destroy the invading foe.

Be your country's bold defenders
 'Till her dreadful day be past,
With your bodies for a rampart
 Guard her, shield her to the last.
Your's is soil by Freedom hallowed,
 Not a land for lords and slaves;
Let them find no dwelling-places,
 Only death and bloody graves.

PARK BENJAMIN.

## THE RETREAT.

### REBEL RETREAT FROM KENTUCKY.

MARCH 31ST, '63.

SAD scene of woe! Disaster and defeat
Brood o'er the plain and hasten the retreat.
Outnumbered and surprised the patriot ranks,
In dire confusion seek the river's banks.
O'erwhelmed, they turn, but still disdained to yield,
As with reluctant steps they quit the field.
Each thundering roar from out yon grove of pines
Sweeps like a tempest thro' their shattered lines;
Now 'neath the shock, the stricken column reels,
O'er dead and dying roll the crushing wheels
Of fierce pursuers. Now the foe outflanks,
And hurls an avalanche upon their ranks.
Again they rally! By the river's side
They strive to stem the furious battle tide,
But all in vain. The havoc thickens round,
With carnage strewing the contested ground.
Behold, alas! their gallant leader fall,
His bosom reddened by the fatal ball!
Mark where, in crimson heaps, the wounded lie—
See how in agony they writhe and die.
Welcome, ye dusky shades of eve, that now
Creep o'r the scene from yonder mountain's brow,
Spread thy concealing clouds, O piteous night,
And shut the dreadful vision from my sight.

J. L. DUJARRIC.

## OH, FAIR VIRGINIA!

GRAND REVIEW OF THE ARMY OF THE POTOMAC,

APRIL 2D., '63

OH, fair Virginia, erring though thou art,
Thou still wilt clasp them closely to thy heart.
Watch o'er their slumbers. To thy stricken breast
Let the lost heroes lovingly be pressed.
Though traitors have lured thee from thy home,
And taught thy feet in wayward paths to roam,
Dimmed thy fair name, despoiled thee of thy charms.
And snatched thee ruthless from our sheltering arms
Still in thy bosom lives some fond regret,
Some flickering flame all unextinguished yet,
Some tender thought thou cans't not from thee cast,
Which in thy misery links thee to the past.
Thou too hast lost thy children, and dost mourn
Thy noble sons in battle from thee torn.
Then drop with us thy sympathising tears,
E'en as thou would'st have done in former years.
Take to thy breast and proudly cherish there
The holy trust committed to thy care—
Give them within thy heart of hearts a place,
And clasp them kindly in thy fond embrace.

W. H. CLARK.

## THE INVESTMENT.

INVESTMENT OF WASHINGTON, N. C.,
APRIL 4TH, '63.

BUT, hark! the battle strife again is raging,
  Fiercer than before,
And louder thunders in my startled ear
  The loud artillery's roar.
Again our squadrons sweep the bloody plain—
  Again, with fierce desire,
From out our cannon's deadly mouths
  Leap forth their tongues of fire!

Onward comes apace a brave and fearless line,
  With bayonets glancing low;
And battle-flags, of purest white and blue,
  Are rushing toward the foe.
Full well we know each flaunting banner there:
  It is the First Brigade—
The never repulsed dauntless hero host—
  The famous First Brigade.

"Hurrah! hurrah!" they shout, and rushing on,
  Like a loose-cast Alpine snow,
They beat the terror-stricken cravens back
  With one terrific blow.
"Hurrah! hurrah!" again our soldiers cried—
  "Hurrah!" the hills replied;
A faint low whispering word my comrade spoke—
  "Hurrah!" he said, and died.

ANONYMOUS.

## "ALL QUIET ON POTOMAC."

THE PRESIDENT'S VISIT TO THE ARMY,

APRIL 5TH, '63

ALL is quiet on Potomac,
  Save a stirring deep as hell,
Like the thought that stirr'd in Satan
  Ere the hour the angels fell—
  Hour that sorrow's pages tell.

Kisses thus the broad Atlantic,
  On the sands that bound her shore,
Hath forgotton, when in frantic
  Waves she leap'd with thunder's roar,
  Navies from their moorings tore.

Sleeps the wind upon the billow,
  Gently rippling in the sun,
Mindless when it howl'd the pillow,
  Gory beds by battle won,
  When the dreadful fight was done.

Beauteous are the tents by moonlight,
  Gaily float the streamers there;
Glimpses of the bayonet bright,
  Marching the pacing sentry's care
  Where the war-fiend makes his lair.

But those tents shall know commotion,
  And that moon shall light a scene
Wilder than the wrecks of ocean
  Where the wintry howl hath been.
  Changed the smiling landscape scene!

RALPH HOYT.

## THE ATTACK.

### ATTACK ON FRANKLIN, KY.,

### APRIL 10TH, '63.

NOT long this bloody conflict was maintained—
  The vanquished foe fell back,
And the bugle's clarion notes proclaimed
  The evening's bivouac;
While the wings of night their shadows pressed
  Upon the gory field,
And war-worn soldiers, in blankets wrapped,
  Line phantoms were revealed.

Up from the river, the dark flowing river,
  The misty vapors rise.
And an angel's bright bark is floating there,
  To bear me to the skies:
The sail is full—from out of the pearly car
  Glimmers a silvery oar,
To guide us along, thro' the weltering gloom,
  To a bright and golden shore.

But he sits not alone in his mystic car:
  Another as pure and white,
Is waiting and beckoning impatient to me
  To join his heavenly flight;
While earthward bending from the upper sky,
  With golden wings outspread,
I see full many an angel form
  From among the battle dead,

WM. H. CLARK.

## OH, SUMTER! HOW FALLEN!

SECOND ATTACK OF FORT SUMTER, ON THE SECOND ANNIVERSARY OF THE FIRST GUN,

APRIL 11TH, '63.

OH, Sumter! how fallen!—thy glory how faded!—
When in the dark past we thy story review;
When first the base hand of wanton rebellion
Struck down the bright folds of the Red White and Blue

How throb'd then the heart of the awe-stricken nation
As each cannon's voice thunder'd out thro' the land
The summons for freemen to haste to the rescue
Of Liberty bleeding, 'neath Treason's vile hand!

While in the bright ether, enshrin'd in his glory,
The spirit of Wasington swept o'er the main,
With fraternal hand o'er thee outstretched, imploring,
And regal brow bent—but, alas! all in vain!

The fierce blow was dealt then that shatter'd the nation,
The monster Rebellion then rear'd its proud head,
And in deep thunder tones—from iron lips spoken—
Declaimed that the Genius of Freedom was dead!

Then—then, oh, proud Sumpter, thy glory was faded—
Thine iron tongue utter'd each morn a base lie,
When as the sun rose, the false flag flut'ring o'er thee,
Declared that the Union dissevered must die!

Since then, low'ring war-clouds hath shadow'd the altar
Which Freedom and Truth had upreared in the West,
Like the incense of old from the Sacrifice raising,
Hath hid thee in gloom and obscured thy proud crest.

The Nation upon thee hath gazed in deep sorrow,
And view'd thee—ah ! not as the sepulchre dark
Where slumbered the ashes of Union dissevered,
But as they of old viewed the Temple and Ark.

So gazed the whole nation upon thy embrasures,
So gazed they upon thee thro' war's deep'ning haze,
Assur'd 'mid the gloom, that the Genius of Freedom
From out thy dark ruins *resurrected* would raise !

They gazed not in vain—nor hoped they mistaken—
The fiat went forth from the mouth of the Lord;
The buckler of Faith girt the loins of the nation,
As they marched to redeem thee, with fire and sword.

Assembled around thee—a host strong and mighty—
With spirits of wrath panting for the affray,
With iron-mail'd hand on thy firm gates they thund'r'd
'Till 'neath their fierce blows thy stout walls gave way.

" Ope'—open to Justice," the iron throats thunder'd,
" Ope'—open to Truth, now !" the musketry roar'd,
" Too long hath the base hand of Treason retain'd thee.
Thou Symbol of Freedom !" said the voice of the Lord.

The Lord's voice spoke from the mouth of the cannon,
And lo ! thy walls crumbled when thus he had said,
Until soon the base flag of wanton Rebellion
Amid the dark ruins of Sumter was laid.

When out of its portals, amid a bright halo,
Which lumin'd the sky East, West, South and North,
The Genius of Freedom then spread its fair pinions,
And 'mid great rejoicing, to light issued forth—

To carry glad tidings to thousands now waiting
To hear that the reign of Treason is o'er,
When with prayer and thanksgiving the nation united
Shall hail *the old Union as it was of yore.*

Oh, Sumter, tho' fallen, with thy glory faded—
Tho' shatter'd thy gates, and in ruins thy wall,
'Twere better to be thus *the tombstone of Treason*
Than a *monument dam'd* of Liberty's fall!

J. HENRY HAYWARD.

---

END OF THE FIRST TWO YEARS.

www.ingramcontent.com/pod-product-compliance
Lightning Source LLC
LaVergne TN
LVHW020109110826
845151LV00001B/110

* 9 7 8 1 4 2 5 5 4 3 9 5 2 *